# 2012

# IN BIBLE PROPHECY

## with
## Shadow Mayan Tradition
## Clearly Cast Behind It

# 2012

## IN BIBLE PROPHECY

### with
### Shadow Mayan Tradition
### Clearly Cast Behind It

## WAYNE REDDEN

Pleasant Word
A Division of WINEPRESS PUBLISHING

Pleasant Word (a division of WinePress Publishing, PO Box 428, Enumclaw, WA 98022) functions only as book publisher. As such, the ultimate design, content, editorial accuracy, and views expressed or implied in this work are those of the author.

Unless otherwise noted, all scriptures are taken from the New King James Version, © 1979, 1980, 1982 by Thomas Nelson, Inc., Publishers. Used by permission.

Verses marked KJV are taken from the King James Version of the Bible.

ISBN 13: 978-1-4141-0136-1
ISBN 10: 1-4141-0136-8
Library of Congress Catalog Card Number: 2004101164

# TABLE OF CONTENTS

# INTRODUCTION

As many are aware, the Holy Bible is the most widely circulated, and as some are not aware, the most important book ever written. With it taking strong positions on issues considered sensitive by modern standards, it has its share of detractors depending upon the particular agenda involved. Nevertheless, it has something to say that strikes to the heart of that which the future holds for every man, woman, and child alive on our planet today! This book purports to be the inspired Word of God, given to His creation for and through His chosen people Israel, for guidance, direction, and warning to all people of the earth. Now, continuing in that vein, it turns out that this generation is a major player in Bible prophecy. We are the subject of much of what is foretold, which it seems, is all of the end time prophecy. Now, this is not necessarily a good thing.

Using the Bible as a benchmark, it appears that we, of this generation, are treading a variety of paths, all leading to the same destination. Like tourists on summer vacation, we spread out all over the map, filling our senses with enticing attributes of the many attractions along the way. But, like homing pigeons that are directionally controlled by instinct, all of us eventually wind up at the same place: home!

Now, when we stop for serious thought, there are really just two eventual homes. One a mansion–the other a hellhole!

Some in this time of uncertainty are reaching dizzying heights in their quest for individual attainment to higher levels of galactic consciousness. This could be seen as reaching for the stars, but not knowing which one to aim for! Generally speaking, this end time generation is searching for answers. The challenge here is to unite the searchers for truth with that book for elevation to a higher level of prophetic awareness. Then too, the challenge expands to aiding truth seekers in attainment to numerical consciousness relating to what some consider a creation to be used by, and for the benefit of mankind; and what others consider as being a terrestrial deity worthy of worship; but nevertheless, is that which we all reside on. It is also that which the book in the dresser drawer wants to warn us of unknown, and impending dangers waiting just ahead!

This work is intended to bring God's end time prophecy into focus as it relates to our time. Whether this effort is successful or not will be up to each individual reader to decide. You are being cautioned now, that while some last days Bible prophecy is good news, much of it is bad news, and some of the bad is very bad!

# CHAPTER ONE

# TWO BOOKS

We just saw reference to biblically inspired numerical consciousness relating to our planet. We will encounter numbers in remarkable applications to the past and future; so look for them–*they are the salt that flavors bible prophecy!*

In this writing, we are about to confront the supernatural power of a literal book, and the natural power of a book expressed through mental imagery. Though the second is an imaginary book, its disastrous effects on mankind are very real.

The first is the *book of truth*, the Holy Bible. This is Christ's book; in fact, He teaches from it, and with it, and we will be enlightened by it in future pages. The other book, the imaginary one, is the *book of human knowledge*. This book, for the most part, denies the truths of the first book. It, however, upon careful inspection, is found to contain half-truths, unintentional misinformation, and a liberal sprinkling of intentional lies. Its main purpose then, can be said to be that of circumventing the effectiveness of the first book. It can therefore be considered to be Antichrist's book, and in its own right can be termed the "antibible."

This second book, the imaginary one, is imaginary only in that it is not a literal book, but rather a collection of conclusions of human origin based upon carnal instinct and mistaken methodology for achieving spiritual and physical gratification. It is extremely dangerous to one's eternal future. Like the first book, this one consists of a series of chapters dedicated to a variety of subjects that contribute their part to the whole.

✗ We shall sample portions of the second book as we progress through this work, which will deal with God's book of truths, and how it relates to man's book of human knowledge. Since God knows the beginning from the end, He has, through His prophets, seen fit to provide this end time generation with written projections of what is about to take place. Following the complex mind of God is not easy, as evidenced by the numerous and varied attempts by a variety of Bible teachers to tell us what God's Word has to say about the end of this age.

It is the hope here, that each person reading this book will check the Scripture references carefully to verify that the context of a Scripture as he sees it, supports the meaning being emphasized in this work. In that way, you will be sure that you are reading truth. Hearing the truth, and being able to recognize it for what it is, buried well within the body of mass confusion that passes for enlightenment today, is imperative. The quality of our eternal lives depends upon each one of us finding it and acting upon it!

This writing is at variance with some of what you may have been told, or may have come to believe. Is it true? Read on, and *you be the judge*!

# CHAPTER TWO

# GLOBAL UNIFICATION—MAN'S ANSWER TO MAN MADE PROBLEMS

It is no longer a total surprise to anyone that a worldwide effort is underway to unify all nations of the world under one governing body. This is a given and seems to be accepted as being inevitable by all. If these same folks who accept this new paradigm as an inevitable fact of life were asked if they would mind living under a Marxist dictatorship, most, if not all would decline the offer in horror at the thought.

Just as the reality of the global government now forming should be no surprise, equally predictable is the organization that will control this near future colossus. It presently exists, and has since the end of World War II. Its main thrust is to make the global government happen and to shape it in its own image. This body, of course, is the United Nations. Its stated purpose has always been world government, and the principal political philosophy of the majority of its representatives leans heavily to Marxist globalism. The governments represented by these people are themselves, for the most part, experimenting with Marxism through the intermediate stage of Socialism. A number, however, are committed to Communism at the present time. Pure Communism is the ultimate objective of these architects of progressive globalism. This utopian state (pure Communism) is a stage so advanced, and the people so indoctrinated into Marxist principles, that they no longer need a leader to lead them. They, as the theory goes, will be fully capable of functioning within the system on their own. This would require considerable professional mind control in order to establish behavioral patterns sufficient to overwhelm the natural nature of man. Mind control is what Communism is about, and; of course, an elite class would still rule!

Pure Communism, as stated, is the final goal. The immediate goal of the globalists is simply to get the thing started; and Socialism, with its toleration of Capitalism with restraints, is the method of choice. For a preview of coming events, all one need do is look at the nations of the world as they exist today. Not many healthy capitalist nations around any more. The Eastern European nations that tried Capitalism in the 80's have been corrupted by organized crime. A number of them have met the European Union's requirements for membership, and so will expand the E.U.'s socialist Grip on Europe. Socialism controls Europe, and has considerable influence on many of the remaining nations of the world. The United States has been holding out, but is slowly capitulating. Islamic dictatorships and Communism control most of the Mideast and the continent of Africa. Asia uses a form of dictatorial democracy and is part communist and part socialist as well, with all systems committed to using Capitalism with restraints as their engine of production.

So here we see a world situation ripe for unification, right down to having its own captive market. And what a market it is. The U.S.A, with its high standard of living built upon its current technological expertise and the residue of its once strong, now faltering manufacturing and weakening agricultural sectors, offers itself free gratis as the supreme market to a world union forming on the basis of free trade. The question becomes: how can the U.S.A open herself up to the world as the market of choice for each and every kind of consumer goods known to man, and still retain a high living standard while at the same time exporting jobs world wide? America, with her seemingly unlimited supply of newly arrived, third world immigrants, and her large number of low pay jobs (by U.S.A standards, but generous by third world criteria), easily absorbs these people, legal and illegal alike, into her growing low-tech work force. Residents of the United States for any length of time have been conditioned to having a reasonably high standard of living—even those on the low end—through a variety of government programs. Many of these are unwilling to risk losing their government subsidized handouts of all varieties and descriptions, for the lure of a low paying and usually low fringe benefit job. In other instances, many of these recipients of government largess, though some are unable, others are unwilling, for one reason or another, to take on a first job in some cases, or second job in others, simply because they do not financially need to; so the low-end jobs go to the newcomers.

America is the answer to a prayer for the third world immigrants coming across her borders and arriving on her shores. The country offers them instant welfare, plenty of jobs, free health care, gratis education for their children, and established support communities of the various ethnic groups already flourishing here to show the newly arrived the ropes and assist them in cashing in. Uncle Sam, good-natured old gentleman that he is, doesn't even ask if they are legal citizens before encouraging them to vote in U.S. elections. This, however, is another story, and so we won't go there. It makes the point nevertheless. Simply put, it is this: these folks never had it so good; and Uncle Sam is glad they are here. He knows they will vote for those who propose to continue and expand giveaway policies. So Uncle Sam absorbs the newcomers, and proceeds to promote his world market operation in which he sops up foreign overproduction, exports jobs, and encourages global union!

We have seen here some of the dynamics of the current situation that the United States is immersed in. As these forces continue to work through our society, they are causing changes that are worth noting. For one thing, with the loss of so many reasonably good paying manufacturing jobs to relocated U.S. manufacturing plants in third world countries, America is growing a large class of underemployed, overqualified, underpaid workers.

The other thing is that the manufacturing sector is no longer the only area of employment relocation; that is, where jobs up and move to third world countries, and where the wages for the job become instantly homogeneous with the local wage structure. White-collar jobs in America, once thought to be rock solid and secure, are floating off our shores like cruise ships in August. Outsourcing is now a phenomenon with prophetic characteristics. What is it? What facilitated it? And what are its consequences? Quite simply, it is the transference of white-collar work by American corporations to third world countries for the benefit of a much lower wage scale. The replacement employee is normally as highly skilled, or more so than the American whose job he/she took over. This job exodus includes such things as accounting, banking functions, engineering, management functions, chip design, auditing, airline ticket reservations, architecture services, reading brain scan images, and on and on! Jobs that were never expected to leave our shores. So why is it happening? We all know the answer to that; to improve the bottom line! America's own highly refined communications technology, applied, tried, and proven, has paved the way for this generosity in spreading around the globe, a portion of her high living standard. This liberal behavior on the part of American corporations is motivated by fear more than greed, fear of an ever increasingly competitive business environment. Fear of stockholders, fear of losing market share, fear of union demands, fear of financial losses, fear of bankruptcy, and on it goes.

With globalization comes compromise for America. Corporations jockey for more wiggle room, and displaced American workers face the cold reality of looking for work in a less than certain economy with increased inflation ahead; while the third world basks in the receding glow of America's economic glory. This does not mean that the U.S.A is going down the tubes—far from it. But globalism has its price, and America is paying it. The truism—when going gets tough, the tough get going—still applies in America. The entrepreneurial spirit is yet strong and will carry the nation through her difficulties, if not at the level of her dot-com and technology stock market bubbles of the nineties, nevertheless, in reasonable fashion, for she has a role to play in Bible prophecy.

Manufacturing overproduction is a glut on world markets, and is lowering prices of manufactured goods everywhere. Third world countries with stagnant to declining economies are trying to manufacture their way to solvency. Western industrialized nations are being whip-lashed by their own technological and entrepreneurial genius, freely given for the best of reasons, as expressed above, and the U.S.A is not an exception. America, however, will work her way through this unsettling time for she has a formula which we will see below. It is now operating and is proving to be successful in spite of the eventual reality that with it, if she maintained the course long enough, she too would become a third world country.

In the realm of globalism, the world is operating on a touch-and-go basis. Not since the Tower of Babel has the world been united, and so there is no proven pattern to follow. It is being accomplished piecemeal, a bit at a time; but it is being accomplished. It seems that the current time of wars, to make the world a safe place for global interaction, was prophesied by Jesus in Matthew 24:6, where He said: "And you will hear of wars and rumors of wars. See that you are not troubled; for all these things must come to pass, but the end is not yet." The world will be made safe for peaceful global interaction for a very short time, and America must remain economically and militarily strong to play her part in making it happen. So then, in effect, the U.S.A.'s operating formula consists of creating a capitalist-based, socialistically enhanced, internationally financed, globally oriented market to the world. A money machine, open twenty-four hours a day, seven days a week; all credit cards accepted.

One fuel source—third world immigrants, can and does survive on the low pay service sector and farm labor wages. The second fuel source includes the high-tech sector, with its high-flying wage scales. This sector, along with a myriad of entrepreneurial enterprises, the retail sector, banking and finance, professional sector, agri-business, construction, the transportation sector, the remainder of the manufacturing sector, communications, and government employment including federal, state and local, supply the bulk of the upper and mid-level employment. The third fuel source is the low cost imported merchandise entering this great self-perpetuating market machine.

With U.S. cost of living steadily trending upward as is now underway, middle and low income levels including the entry-level immigrants, all need a hand up. The burgeoning supply of third world, competitively priced merchandise of every description that is flooding the nation, not only strengthens the retail sector, but just as importantly, it gives a hand up to the financially challenged. It takes some of the dollar pressure off the two lower income levels; the very groups that account for the bulk of the U.S. domestic market's purchasing power.

We can make two points from the above brief diversion into the anatomy of the U.S. market as it presently exists, and as it is destined to continue for a time. We shall see them below.

It is unlikely the U.S.A will be entirely socialized, that is, to the extent that many other nation members of the global union are now. This conclusion is based upon the fact that the world needs the U.S. market. If America maintains a relatively strong capitalistic system, she can continue to function much as she is now. The U.S.A will go on to dabble in Socialism, but for the limited time that we are concerned with, she must remain economically strong in order to fulfill her important part in Bible prophecy; thus Capitalism will continue to be nurtured in America. For a first hand view of Socialism in action, we need go no further than the once great nation of Canada!

Second, the once highly fractured globe is knitting itself together with the yarn of free trade. This is being accomplished by lowering and removing trade barriers of all kinds, with the creative utilization of treaties. The world needs the stability of the U.S. market; and at the present time it needs the stability of the U.S. dollar as well. Dollar value fluctuations, notwithstanding, this financial consideration is sure to continue into the foreseeable future. The planet, as it comes together through the catalyst of free trade, is literally clumping itself together into trading blocs of regionally supportive nations. These regional arrangements not only provide cooperative markets among the members, but also will become more and more necessary for individual nation protection as trade wars erupt between and among the trading blocs. Unrepresented nations will find it very difficult to compete alone, and so will be forced to join, if possible, an existing bloc. In the alternative, they will need to join with other non-aligned nations to form their own trade enhancing collective (reference the now being promoted, October 2004, "Free Trade Area of the Americas", FTAA).

The Bible says that in the last days there will be ten kings (Bloc Chairmen) who will not have kingdoms, but who will receive authority for one hour as kings with the beast (Antichrist), Revelation 17:12–13. This is clear reference to some sort of organization to be controlled by Antichrist. The conclusion drawn here is that these kings will represent ten regional trading blocs of nations that will give their authority to the antichrist. The giving of their authority to Antichrist will subject these trading blocs to the global Marxist tendencies of the United Nations.

Now, continuing toward conclusion of the second point: God's Word tells also that the U.S.A will be hated by these ten kings (possibly a ten-member UN council representing the ten blocs), and that they will destroy her with fire.

19

Carrying on with the second point: if the U.S.A will be destroyed by the very nations that enjoy her market place bonanza, then it seems safe to assume that America will not be an integral part of this cohesive group of ten UN controlled cooperating regions. It can also be assumed that the U.S.A will operate on the fringe of this global union and will, for some reason, be perceived as an enemy to be destroyed. We will confront this unpleasant subject in more detail further on; and will then see the catastrophic cosmic activity that will traumatize the world, announce the Lord's return, and potentially set the stage for the fatal attack on America!

To condense the two points: We know that the one hour of authority to be given to the ten cooperating regions, Revelation 17:12, represents a very short time. Man's grand scheme to create his Marxist world utopia is doomed to failure from the beginning. For those who are becoming troubled about the above indicated destruction of the U.S.A, it should be said here that many, if not most, who study Bible prophecy do not accept, or agree that God's Word is talking about America, in referencing the destruction of the "harlot." That is just one of several valid questions about the immediate future that this writing attempts to answer directly from the pages of God's Holy Word.

As we progress in this work, we will encounter more bad news. The good news, however, is that there is a way out of all of God's prophesied destruction. *His name is Jesus Christ!* Read on, and decide what you will believe and what you will not!

# CHAPTER THREE

# PRELUDE TO A TIME OF TROUBLE

Are we really living in the end times, as is talked about extensively in the Bible, or is the assumption that we are just so much nonsense and unnecessary concern?

Can we connect our present fast-paced travel revolution, and our current technology explosion to any Bible prediction, that would link these things to our modern high-tech society, and that would mark this present time as the time of the end? The answer is: *yes we can!* Daniel, a favored prophet of God, does so in concise and to-the-point language. He tells us that precisely in Daniel 12:4. The verse says this:

> But you Daniel, shut up the words, and seal the book until the time of the end; many shall run to and fro, and knowledge shall increase.

This short verse does two things. First, without doubt, it identifies our time as being the time of the end. Second, it tells us that Daniel's book of prophecy will be shut and locked until that very time, the time of the end. The obvious conclusion has to be that the mysteries of Daniel's book will be revealed and made understandable in the time of the end. As a point of interest, we will encounter several very important revelations further on as we look closely at the book of Daniel. Significant disclosures will then be revealed!

Another prophet, this one much later, said some things about the time of the end and the man who would lead in that final chapter of our current history. This man was the apostle Paul, Saint Paul to some. He refers to one we have come to reference as Antichrist, the highly visible competitor of Jesus Christ in that near future time. He also refers to the coming of Christ, thus establishing his remarks as referencing the last days. The point here is to show that Paul supernaturally knew what the times would be like in this historic time slot. He tells about the return of Jesus and the resurrection of the saints; clearly the end time, in 2 Thessalonians 2:1–2.

Antichrist is labeled the man of sin, the son of perdition, and the lawless one by Paul in verses 3–8. And the apostle points out as well that Jesus will not return until a falling away occurs and the man of sin is revealed. There is discussion about Antichrist's activities; what is presently restraining his appearance, and something about his demise and who will be responsible for it. These are all-important areas of prophecy and will be observed more closely further on. Exciting discoveries and perilous times await in our prophesied future. Some will be ready. Some will not!

We will now look at verses 9 through 12, which describe the way things will be when the antichrist is revealed. The fact is, these verses describe our present time as well as they do the time just ahead. Second Thessalonians 2:9–12 goes on to paint our present time with the same brush as the end time in the following way:

> The coming of the lawless one is according to the working of Satan, with all power, signs, and lying wonders, and with all unrighteous deception among those who perish, because they did not receive the love of the truth, that they might be saved. And for this reason God will send them strong delusion, that they

should believe the lie, that they all may be condemned, who did not believe the truth but had pleasure in unrighteousness.

Here it is plain to see that the portion of the prophecy concerning the presence in the world of "all unrighteous deception among those who perish, because they did not receive the love of the truth, that they might be saved" does, in fact, describe our present time. What about: "the workings of Satan, with all power, signs, and lying wonders," that the Bible says will usher in "the coming of the lawless one"? It just depends upon what one would consider to be a wonder.

*The New Strong's Exhaustive Concordance of the Bible* gives the Greek word for "wonder" as used in the above verse, as being *teras*. It can mean prodigy, omen or wonder. Since a wonder can reasonably be considered an omen in certain instances, we will look at prodigy. *The Readers Digest Great Encyclopedic Dictionary* gives several meanings for prodigy: (A) a person having remarkable qualities or powers, (B) Something that excites wonder and admiration, (C) Something out of the ordinary course of nature; a monstrosity, and (D) a portent.

The same dictionary gives the meaning of portent, among several others as: (A) an indication or sign of what is to happen, especially of something momentous or calamitous, (B) ominous significance.

So now we can begin to look for and recognize satanic power involved in current and future signs and wonders, preparatory to emergence of the lawless one we call Antichrist, into the spotlight of world affairs. Deception and delusion, we are told, will empower and veil this illusionary figure.

The world has been exposed to, and contending with unmistakably clear examples of satanically inspired signs and lying wonders for quite some time now (i.e., extraterrestrials). We will see other instances of this broad based phenomena in a later chapter.

It seems, from the above Scriptures of the prophet Daniel, and the apostle Paul, that our present time lies at the door to the prophesied emergence of the antichrist of the last days. But we don't have to stop here. There is another, very telling prophesied event that was talked about by both of the above-mentioned biblical writers, and which must happen some time shortly after the emergence of Antichrist onto the world scene. In recent world news coverage of the on-again, off-again peace talks involving Israel and the Arabs, this subject has become a serious topic of conversation, a source of great difficulty, and a hot potato in the attempt for a negotiated peace. What is this catalyst, this fly in the ointment spoken of in God's Word, as being a reality in the last days? Like an anchor on the final settlement, it drags down the contentious process and brings it to a grinding halt. When it finally becomes a reality, we can use its existence as assurance from God that His timetable is unfolding as foretold. Its existence has been planned for some time in Israel; details are worked out and are ready. Its future location is presently in the hands of Israel, and has been since the war of June 5–10, 1967. It was in this Islamic-initiated conflict that Israel wrested East Jerusalem and the temple mount away from Jordan.

This contentious issue, of course, is the temple of God, talked of in Daniel 9:27 and 12:11; also by Paul in 2 Thessalonians 2:4 in the context of the last days. Oslo Accord discussions have dealt with control of the temple mount, location of the previous temples of God; both having been destroyed by enemies of Israel, and which is to be the location of the third temple. Even though Israel does now have control of East Jerusalem and the temple mount proper, the mount is presently home to two latter-day mosques, constructed after the destruction of the second Jewish temple. Because of these two Moslem holy sites on the mount, Israel's hands have been tied regarding conducting any activity there. To handle this situation otherwise would mean a certain united Islamic holy war against

Israel, with potentially devastating consequences for both. The time is rapidly approaching when negotiations with Mid-East nations will produce a compromise agreement which will be credited to a man we now call Antichrist. It will give the Palestinians a political presence in East Jerusalem and shared use with Israel of the temple mount.

# CHAPTER FOUR

# THE REVERSE ORDER OF CURRENT DELUSIONAL THOUGHT

There is a truly relevant Bible verse given, not necessarily for this particular time in history, but which does thoroughly apply to our time and that time just ahead, as well as apparently it did to the time in which it was given. It is found in Isaiah 5:20, and says the following: "Woe to those who call evil good, and good evil; who put darkness for light, and light for darkness; who put bitter for sweet and sweet for bitter!"

For example, today it is good to not pray in public schools, and to be able to legally kill babies before birth. It is, on the other hand, bad to damage a public school student's self-esteem by giving him or her a letter grade of D or F for poor academic performance. To prevent embarrassment, creativity is substituted for absolutes. The grade, instead of denoting degrees of success or failure as with letter grades, is given in words of encouragement, such as: Good Work or Try Harder. Mistakes, instead of being corrected, are passed off as creativity!

Then there is Darwinian evolution. This is the belief in a higher authority than God (i.e., time). That is like looking at the new house you just purchased and thinking: "if I had just allowed enough time this house could have built itself."

A significant cause of worldly susceptibility to the multiple delusions that have corrupted it to such a large extent, is that the world has not known God's three-phase plan for mankind's tenure of His planet. It's true, we don't own it, God does. Since it was He who created it, we are His tenants. Despite scientific pronouncements to the contrary, mankind was created by God as well. As distasteful as this fact may seem for some, it nevertheless is shouted from the pages of the Bible, God's Word, the book of truth, and there is much scientific evidence to back it up!

Phase one: man's 6,000 year tenure of God's unique planet is almost complete. The second phase: mankind's 1,000 year Sabbath day of rest on earth, the kingdom of Jesus Christ, will soon begin. After that the third phase—the eternal kingdom, eternity in the New Jerusalem on a changed earth. God's Word is His blueprint for the progression of these three phases. We will keep searching. Proof in abundance awaits!

# CHAPTER FIVE

# THE SEVEN-DAY WEEK

Who is responsible for the seven-day week? Without question, God is! He created the heavens and the earth and all that is—in six days (Genesis 1). Then on the seventh day God rested from all the work that He had done Genesis 2:2. Thus the seven-day week was established. There is no reason to believe that these days of creation were any longer than twenty-four-hour days. We will, however, see where God in certain instances, does attach longer periods of time to days and weeks.

For our purpose here, we can establish that "with the Lord one day is as a thousand years, and a thousand years as one day" (2 Peter 3:8). Now, with this truth in mind, we can see God's logic in providing six, one thousand year days for mankind's free will tenure of His planet. This week, to be complete, will be ended with the one-thousand-year Sabbath day of rest, the seventh day. Our lives are fully integrated into the seven-day week. Saturday and Sunday for synagogue, church, and goofing off. Monday through Friday for work and school, with miscellaneous other requirements, activities, etc. scheduled throughout the week.

We also live by the clock, with our daily activities dictated and controlled by time. We are programmed to understand the preciseness and finality of the passing of time. We do also understand the need to allocate time in the planning process. God, of course, knew these things before we did, and we would expect Him to work within these constraints in dealing with finite segments of infinite time. God has the three phases scheduled that were mentioned earlier, and He affirms it in His Word, the Holy Bible. He gives us the length of the second phase as being one thousand years. He also gives the length of the third phase, eternity, as being forever. He does not, however, precisely pin Himself down to a stated period of time for the first phase, man's six-thousand-year free will tenure of His planet. Rather, what God does do is to make strong hints as to the length of this period. It has become obvious that this length of time, though not proclaimed outright by God, is nevertheless, to be six-thousand years, and as the first phase, it is all but finished. How can we be sure? If we trust God's Word, we will see four reasons given below:

1. First, keep in mind the words of the apostle Peter in 2 Peter 3:8, that "with the Lord one day is as a thousand years, and a thousand years as one day." We can relate a week for mankind with six days for work and the seventh for rest, established by the Creator Himself.

2. We can also see how the prophet Daniel's simple prophecy for the last days fits our time, as though it was given for this specific time in history. Daniel 12:4: "But you Daniel, shut up the words, and seal the book until the time of the end; many shall run to and fro, and knowledge shall increase." The apostle Paul's end time prophecy in 2 Thessalonians 2:9–12, concerning strong delusion and the working of Satan with all power, signs, and lying wonders, points directly to our time and that time just ahead. When will the six thousand years be up? *Very soon!*

3. God said in Ezekiel 37:21–22 that He would bring the children of Israel from among the nations, wherever they

have gone, back into their own land; that He would make them one nation, and one king shall be over them. With the first part of this promise already fulfilled, the tone of the prophecy indicates that the king (Jesus Christ) will not be long in coming. This prophecy, already partially fulfilled, argues strongly for completion in the end time, *Our time!*

4. Revelation 11:1 reveals that the temple will exist in the end time, since the apostle John is told in a vision to measure it. In verse 2, he is told, however, to measure it without the outer court area, because that part has been given to the Gentiles. This speaks of a shared temple mount. And also in verse 2 it continues on to say that the Gentiles (Palestinians) will tread the Holy City underfoot for forty-two months. This refers to a short-lived negotiated peace having been reached with Israel. Are we hearing about these very negotiations now? *Yes we are!* How close are we to the end of the six thousand years? *Very close?*

Both the prophet Daniel and the apostle Paul spoke of the antichrist's involvement with the end time temple. We will later have an opportunity to see these prophecies in greater detail. For our purpose here, their placing Antichrist in the end time temple on the temple mount, shared with Islam, links our present time to the prophesied end time by means of the current, on-again off-again peace talks. How close are we to the end of the six thousand years? *Extremely close!*

This is all quite interesting. But can we discover a more definitive way to establish from the Bible when the six thousand years will be complete without bringing Jesus into the equation. Can we do this without going out on a limb and setting a date for the Lord's return? The answer is *yes* and *no*. God's Word does contain a record of time that accounts for somewhat more than half of the six thousand years. This time period runs from the creation of Adam to the completion of Solomon's temple, and accounts for

3,156 years. In order to complete the total six thousand years, we must find a way to fill out the B.C. years from some point in the 3,156 biblical years up to the beginning of the A.D. years, where our current calendar takes over. Fortunately, there is a way that this can be done by using man's historical record to fill in the gap. So *yes*, it can be done, but *no*, not completely from the Bible. Will it be accurate? We shall see later where we will be forced to bring Jesus into the picture, in a prophecy supported by a historical date that does precisely agree with the work that we are about to undertake here!

# CHAPTER SIX

# ATTEMPTING TO ESTABLISH THE END OF THE FIRST SIX THOUSAND YEARS WITHOUT SETTING A DATE FOR CHRIST'S RETURN

The first part of this effort will involve looking through the Bible record of lifespans for certain individuals and the lifespan of specifically named sons, then adding in the Flood, and the length of time that the children of Israel were in Egypt, up until the Exodus; then adding it all up. We will stop at the Exodus, and so will not use the entire 3,156 years from Adam to the completion of Solomon's temple. God's Word is an entirely accurate book of recorded history. It has never been disproven in the intent of its statements and assertions. It has, of course, been questioned, attacked, and ridiculed by its enemies. Archaeology has always come down on the side of the Bible, supporting it with historical evidence and artifacts.

Pure, truthful science supports creation; it underwrites the Flood; and throws into question and shines the light of day on theories and projections being passed off as fact to an unsuspecting world. With this position statement clearly defined, we can now view the Bible record of years from Adam to the Exodus of the Israelites from bondage in Egypt.

# ATTEMPTING TO ESTABLISH THE END OF THE FIRST SIX THOUSAND YEARS WITHOUT SETTING A DATE FOR CHRIST'S RETURN

God's Word records this period as being 2,669 years. This takes us to the Red Sea crossing in the present Suez region, then known as the Sea of Reeds. See the record of years below:

| | | | | |
|---|---|---|---|---|
| Adam lived 130 years and begot Seth | = | 130 | years | Genesis 5 |
| Seth lived 105 years and begot Enosh | = | 105 | years | Genesis 5 |
| Enosh lived 90 years and begot Cainan | = | 90 | years | Genesis 5 |
| Cainan lived 70 years and begot Mahalaleel | = | 70 | years | Genesis 5 |
| Mahalaleel lived 65 years and begot Jared | = | 65 | years | Genesis 5 |
| Jared lived 162 years and begot Enoch | = | 162 | years | Genesis 5 |
| Enoch lived 65 years and begot Methuselah | = | 65 | years | Genesis 5 |
| Methuselah lived 187 years and begot Lamech | = | 187 | years | Genesis 5 |
| Lamech lived 182 years and begot Noah | = | 182 | years | Genesis 5 |
| Noah lived 600 years to the flood | = | 600 | years | Genesis 7:6 |
| And it came to pass in the six hundred and first year, in the first month, the first day of the month, that the waters were dried up from the earth | = | 1 | year | Genesis 8:13 |
| And Noah was 500 years old, and Noah begot Shem, Ham, and Japheth. | | | | Genesis 5:32 |
| Shem begot Arphaxad 2 years after the flood | = | 2 | years | Genesis 11:10 |
| Arphaxad lived 35 years and begot Salah | = | 35 | years | Genesis 11:10–26 |
| Salah lived 30 years and begot Eber | = | 30 | years | Genesis 11:10–26 |
| Eber lived 34 years and begot Peleg | = | 34 | years | Genesis 11:10–26 |
| Peleg lived 30 years and begot Reu | = | 30 | years | Genesis 11:10–26 |
| Reu lived 32 years and begot Serug | = | 32 | years | Genesis 11:10–26 |
| Serug lived 30 years and begot Nahor | = | 30 | years | Genesis 11:10–26 |
| Nahor lived 29 years and begot Terah | = | 29 | years | Genesis 11:10–26 |
| Terah lived 70 years and begot Abram | = | 70 | years | Genesis 11:10–26 |
| God changed Abram's name to Abraham. | | | | Genesis 17:5 |
| Abraham was 100 years old when Isaac was born | = | 100 | years | Genesis 21:5 |
| Isaac was 60 years old when twin boys Esau and Jacob were born | = | 60 | years | Genesis 25:26 |
| Jacob was 130 years old when he and his family moved to Egypt | = | 130 | years | Genesis 47:8–9 |
| God changed Jacob's name to Israel | | | | Genesis 35:10 |
| The Israelites were in Egypt 430 years | = | 430 | years | Exodus 12:40–41 |

| | | | |
|---|---|---|---|
| Total years, Adam to Exodus | = | 2,669 years | |

33

# CHAPTER SEVEN

# THE PHARAOHS

Why an interest in the kings of Egypt? Because their reigns are recorded in dates B.C. (before the birth of Christ). What we need to do is to connect the name of the Pharaoh in the book of Exodus by the dates of his reign to the Exodus of the Israelites from Egypt. The Bible simply refers to him as Pharaoh. There is, however, one important clue that points to this particular Pharaoh, found in Exodus 14:6–9. He mounted up onto his chariot, and personally led his army in pursuit of the fleeing Israelites. This is an unusual king. Most would have sent their best qualified general out into the field to lead the army in what could become a heated battle with a desperate and numerous adversary.

This king was no ordinary king. He undoubtedly was an experienced military man, possibly having been a general at some earlier time.

We are now challenged to bridge the gap from the Exodus, which was B.C., to the beginning of A.D. years (in the year of our Lord), which begins our current calendar. We can do this by looking at the reigns of Egyptian kings of record. It soon becomes apparent that there is date variation between encyclopedia editions.

With this in mind we can then justify selecting the edition to use, showing reigning dates for the target pharaoh that most effectively bridge the gap.

We will start the examination of a segment of the reigns of Egypt's kings with one we are all familiar with, Tutankhamen. His reign lasted from about 1347 B.C. to his death in 1339 B.C. He is thought to have been about eighteen years old at his death, the cause of which is unknown. Having come to the throne at the early age of about nine, he had an assistant, a vizier (minister of state) by the name of Ay, who aided him in his kingly duties. Tutankhamen, at his death, was succeeded on the throne by his vizier, Ay.

Pharaoh Ay was succeeded in his rule of Egypt by a leading general named Horemheb. Pharaoh Horemheb is our king of interest. Horemheb was followed by Pharaoh Ramses I, who reigned for just one year immediately preceding Pharaoh Seti I, who in turn reigned from about 1318 B.C. to 1303 B.C. With the year 1318 B.C. as the beginning of the reign of Pharaoh Seti I, and the one year reign of Pharaoh Ramses I inserted between Seti I and Horemheb, this would indicate 1319 B.C. as the year in which the reign of Pharaoh Horemheb ended. It appears then that Pharaoh Horemheb, previously General Horemheb, was the Pharaoh with military leadership experience who personally took charge of his army in pursuing the Israelites and was drowned in the Red Sea. We will see that this date of 1319 B.C., in which Pharaoh Horemheb's reign came to an abrupt end with his drowning is crucial in its supportive role of complementing the Bible timeline.[1]

Dates for Pharaoh Seti I's reign, as used here, were stated as being about 1318–1303 B.C. These dates derive from a personally owned 1962 edition World Book Encyclopedia, Vol. 16, p 251. The dates of this reign, however, are at variance with the Encyclopedia Americana, edition 2000, Vol. 10 p 33, which has Seti I's reign as being about 1303–1290 B.C., and with Ramses I and Horemheb preceding him. The Bible timeline rejects the later-reign version, and supports 1318–1303 B.C. Recall, Seti I followed Ramses I, whose one-year reign followed Horemheb. We can then logically place the end of Pharaoh Horemheb's reign in the year 1319 B.C; one year prior to the beginning of Seti I's reign. We will soon see Bible support for this 1319 B.C. date as it relates to Jesus. It comes down to this: said date produces no destructive conflict with the Bible record showing Jesus to be less than twelve years old when Joseph and Mary brought Him back to Israel from Egypt.

In Luke 2:39–42 Jesus, age twelve, is pictured as taken by His parents from Nazareth to Jerusalem for the celebration of the Feast of the Passover. With Pharaoh Horemheb drowning in the year 1319 B.C, one year prior to Seti I's coronation as king (separated by Ramses I's abbreviated one year reign), this works out to Jesus being seven years old on His return from Egypt. Age seven is compatible with Luke 2:39–42.

You may ask: "Where is Jesus' age of seven coming from?" For the answer, we must again go to man's historical record. *The Illustrated Dictionary of the Bible*, page 476, tells us that Herod the Great ruled Judea from 37–4 B.C. The 4 B.C. date is the year of his death. Matthew 2:19–20 makes it clear that when Herod was dead, an angel of the Lord appeared in a dream to Joseph in Egypt (where Joseph and Mary had fled with the baby Jesus to protect Him from Herod, who wanted to kill Him.), and in an urgent tone said to Joseph: "Arise, take the young child and His mother, and go to the land of Israel, for those who sought the young child's life are dead" (Matthew 2:20). There is no mistaking the urgency of the message in this verse. We must, therefore, conclude that Jesus returned to Israel in the year of Herod the Great's death; 4 B.C., according to our current calendar.

We will now add the years—Adam to Jesus—to find the actual number of calendar B.C. years (Before Christ). To do this, we add 2,669 years—Adam to the Red Sea crossing and Pharaoh Horemheb's death by drowning—to the 1,319 years from the

*Pharaoh's drowning—to the actual birth of Jesus* (Beginning of calendar's Christian Era, a.k.a. Common Era, A.D.1):

| | |
|---|---|
| Adam to Pharaoh Horemheb's death | 2,669 years |
| Pharaoh Horemheb's death to birth of Jesus (Begins the Common Era) | 1,319 years |
| Total years, Adam to Jesus (Common Era) | 3,988 years |

When we carry on a bit further and subtract the total years (3,988, Adam to Jesus) from biblical (6,000 free will years for mankind), the result, 2,012, translates to A.D. 2012. (See Table #6)

If we let the biblical year 3,988 be represented by the calendar year that it falls on, that calendar year is 12 B.C. We could say that this calendar date, 12 B.C., represents the final B.C. year prior to Jesus' birth the following year, in 11 B.C. It is made clear as well that year A.D. 2012 ends the biblical 6,000 years. (See Table #6) When we subtract the year of Christ's return from Egypt in 4 B.C. from the year of His birth in 11 B.C., we find that He would have been seven years old when returned!

We now have a coincidence to deal with that involves the early Mayan Indian nation and their calendar.

# CHAPTER EIGHT

# EARLY MAYAN INDIAN CULTURE

The Mayan civilization flourished in what is known to-day as Central America, and is thought to date back to several thousand years B.C. Being highly superstitious, it is said that the Mayan people had a strong affinity for the number nine. It was integrated into their religious convictions and spilled over into the routine of their daily lives. This is not surprising, as we will find later in this writing: an astonishing attribute of this number and an amazing connection of the number nine to some very sensitive end time Bible prophecy; some having enormous implications for America!

The Maya had an advanced form of written communication and worshipped many gods, the sun and moon included. The reason for our interest in them at this point is their advanced calendar. The priests developed a 365-day calendar, which they used within a cycle, a period of time. This cycle lasts for more than 5,000 years and will end—yes, that's right—in our soon to come year A.D. 2012.[2]

Not only does the long cycle *end abruptly* in A.D. 2012, but it is Mayan belief that the end will involve infertility, drought, famine, and *many other unusual and frightening occurrences* at the time; just prior to the new cycle and embarking upon *uncharted waters*. Mayan records are scarce, as missionaries had the Spanish collect and burn all the bark books that could be found. The Catholic Church held that the writings were from and of the devil. The destruction of the heathen writings was, therefore, sure and almost complete.[3]

The church, of course, was correct in this assumption, the Mayan writings were Satan inspired. At that time in history the Maya did not know God, nor did they know Jesus. This people, who indulged in human sacrifice, and whose every decision and action was based on superstition and luck, while not knowing God the Father, nor Jesus the Christ when the priestly writings and the calendar were produced, did, however, know another power. This power, manifested through the worship of their many gods, was that of Satan, the delusive god of this world!

We know Satan as a liar and the father of lies (John 8:44). Satan's fallen angel followers, those we know as demons, are also not constrained by the truth; in fact, their goal is to deceive, mislead and instill fear, doubt, and confusion whenever and wherever possible. Knowing this, should we put much faith in this date, which is not from God, but from the very antithesis of God? The answer to the question is this: even without the Mayan date, the Bible-generated date of A.D. 2012, representing the projected end of the 6,000 years, seems quite accurate based upon all that we have looked at so far. The Mayan date just adds additional support. As stated earlier, in order to follow accepted protocol regarding this sensitive subject, we are leaving Christ's return out of this particular research. The Bible does, however, speak for itself, and later in this work we shall find that God's Word does indeed, support Christ's return at this time. Then criticism notwithstanding, *the truth must be told!*

Jesus said in Matthew 24:36: "But of that day and hour no one knows, no not even the angels of heaven, but My Father only." Jesus said also, in Matthew 24:44: "Therefore, you also be ready, for the Son of Man is coming at an hour when you do not expect Him." Daniel 12:4 indicates that God's prophesied Word will become more clear in the time of the end.

Although we will not know the exact hour of Christ's return, God's Word gives ample information to allow us to know within a very narrow range when He will return, based upon a series of events leading up to the darkening of the sun and the moon. These occurrences will immediately precede His return with power and great glory (Matthew 24:29–30). He will come as a thief only to those who reject Him, to those who do not know Him (Revelation 3:3). His return as a thief implies complete surprise and wrath to those mentioned above (2 Peter 3:10).

Again, Matthew 24:29: "Immediately after the tribulation of those days the sun will be darkened, and the moon will not give its light; the stars will fall from heaven, and the powers of the heavens will be shaken." Matthew 24:30 goes on to say that this is when the sign of the Son of Man will appear in heaven, and He will be seen on the clouds of heaven with power and great glory. (Although this is in the wrath, we will find the loophole through which the saints and the Jewish remnant shall escape.) Matthew 24:31: "And He will send His angels with a great sound of a trumpet, and they will gather together His elect from the four winds, from one end of heaven to the other."

God's Word is not unclear concerning the return of Jesus. What was just read is an easy-to-understand description of the second coming of Jesus Christ. Notice that this account plainly states that Christ's return will occur: "immediately after the tribulation of those days."

Each of these verses: (Matthew 24:43–44); (Mark 13:32–37); (Luke 12:39–40) deal with a parable spoken by Jesus, in which He taught that those of His followers who would tire of waiting for His return and fall away would be like those who did not know Him in the first place. They too, would not be watching (prepared) when the sign of His coming appeared in heaven. Their salvation then, would also be stolen. The parable spoken of in the above verses does not indicate that Christ's return can occur at any time, but rather, that after certain conditions are met, a bit of uncertainty will still exist (i.e., time zones, and possibly more).

# CHAPTER NINE

# ABOUT THE TRIBULATION

In Matthew 24:9, Jesus said this: "Then they will deliver you up to tribulation and kill you, and you will be hated by all nations for My name's sake."

Jesus was talking about His followers, who, in the end time, would feel the heat of disdain, isolation, and then persecution by their worldly brothers; those who fear true Christians because of their unwillingness to compromise their Christian beliefs and their moral positions on controversial issues. Jesus tells how bad it will come to be in John 16:2:

> They will put you out of the synagogues [read that churches as well]; yes, the time is coming that whoever kills you will think that he offers God service.

A united one-world religion is presently in the process of forming. The time is close at hand when the melding of the world's religions and others into one unified, all-inclusive body will be achieved. A united global religious movement that will mutate into a spiritual haven for the lost, the searching, and the confused is in an advanced stage. This is best described as a church of *clay* mingling with, but not adhering to, the *iron* of the teachings of

Christ (Daniel 2:43). Many who call themselves Christians, but who are not born again in Him, will fall away into the morass of this lost cause. We will learn more concerning the united one-world religion in pages ahead; how it will relate to the final world empire, how it fits in the riddle of the seven heads (Revelation 17:7–11), and who will lead it.

What is routinely called the Tribulation in reference to the final seven years of current history is to some extent, overblown. According to custom, these seven years are hinged directly onto the seventieth week of Daniel 9:24 and 9:27. They swing on the seven-year peace accord to be reached by Israel and her Islamic neighbors. In reality, the Bible does not indicate the full seven years as the Tribulation; but does, in fact, provide a number of years in which true Christians will see tribulation. We can see it clearly presented in the book of Daniel. Daniel 7:24 tells about ten kings who will arise from the old Roman Empire, and another (horn) king who will arise after them (instead of "after them" it should read "again, himself". This shall be resolved later) and will be different from them—Antichrist.

The next verse, Daniel 7:25, tells what we are looking for: "He [Antichrist] shall speak pompous words against the Most High, shall persecute the saints of the Most High, and shall intend to change times and law [present himself to be worshiped as God, as in ancient times]. Then the saints shall be given into his hand for a time and times and half a time" [three-and-a-half years].

These three-and-a-half years will begin about three months before Antichrist will enter the temple of God in the middle of the negotiated seven years of peace. (See Table #1)

In Matthew 24:6–8, Jesus tells about the time that will precede the Tribulation:

> And you will hear of wars and rumors of wars. See that you are not troubled; for all these things must come to pass, but the end is not yet. For nation will rise against nation, and kingdom against

kingdom. And there will be famines, pestilences, and earthquakes in various places. All these are the beginning of sorrows.

It seems that the world is contending with these very circumstances at the present time. If we take stock of what is going on around us, it is not difficult to see the beginning of sorrows unfolding on all sides. As the curtain is drawn back, we see the specter of terrorism as a backdrop, hanging over and clouding the future of mankind's attempt to ever attain a peaceful world! Man's solution, of course, is a world of oneness; no rich nations, and no poor nations, just oneness. No national borders, no variations in cultures, and no special privileges. Nations with natural wealth will need to share their bounty with those in need (forests, potable water, minerals, oil, agricultural products, etc.). And then those nations with manufacturing expertise, technological know-how, special talents and abilities, will, of course, share with the have-nots. The engine of this worldwide venture, as we know, is free trade, which, of course, means no trade barriers. Add to that—no borders, and we can begin to see what is happening in the U.S.A, in Europe, and soon the world.

The obstacles to this all-encompassing, cooperative venture stand out clearly when the worldwide political landscape is perceived as a monolithic entity. Tyrannical governments, in pursuit of nuclear, chemical, and bacteriological weaponry, and the delivery systems with which to terrorize the world, are marked for extinction. Free trade must be allowed to work its uniting wonders, unfettered and undisturbed by modern day equivalents to the pirate scourge inflicted on traders of old!

Terrorist nations, and those others that pose a threat to peaceful coexistence (those others: Serbia, Rumania, Bulgaria, Bosnia-Herzegovina, Kosovo, Haiti, Grenada, Nicaragua, Panama, etc.), appear to be subject matter as well, of the wars and rumors of wars, that account for a major portion of the beginning of sorrows. Comment:

when put into perspective, it becomes obvious that this world-tidying-up process has been going on for some time now.

The Bible identifies three time periods that, when taken together, account for all of the last days. With the brief look at the beginning of sorrows and the Tribulation we have had here, that still leaves one more. The shortest, but most intensively destructive period of the last days remains, and requires our attention. Its status, in fact, is important enough in God's eyes that He lends His name to it. In Bible prophecy it is sometimes called the Day of the Lord, and it occupies the larger part of the book of Revelation. We will be deeply involved in this segment of end time mayhem as we progress in this work; but for now, we will have a small taste of what this six-month-long Day of the Lord is all about.

# CHAPTER TEN

# THE DAY OF THE LORD

There is just no gentle way to portray the Day of the Lord as anything other than what it is: the wrath of God inflicted upon the unrepentant. God's holy Jewish remnant will be protected through this extremely difficult time at the end of these 6,000 years. The prophet Daniel, in Daniel 12:1, called this very dangerous time by a different name: "and there shall be a time of trouble, such as never was since there was a nation." Jesus, too, referred to it, still in a different way: "For then there shall be great tribulation, such as has not been since the beginning of the world until this time, no, nor ever shall be." So we will look briefly at it here for a definition of what God's wrath involves. We will first go to 2 Peter 3:10, which clearly describes one particularly undesirable aspect of the time of trouble, or great tribulation to occur as the Day of the Lord. The verse says: "But the day of the Lord will come as a thief in the night, in which the heavens will pass away with a great noise, and the elements will melt with fervent heat; both the earth and the works that are in it will be burned up." We shall come to see how fires will ignite and spread to consume large areas!

The next reference is 1 Thessalonians 5:2–4, which clearly points out that followers of Christ will understand and not be in the dark or dismayed by the natural disaster that will usher in the Day of the Lord. Here we see reassurance that followers of Christ await a heavenly call:

> For you yourselves know perfectly that the day of the Lord so comes as a thief in the night.
>
> For when they say, "Peace and safety!" then sudden destruction comes upon them, as labor pains upon a pregnant woman. And they shall not escape.
>
> But you, brethren, are not in darkness, so that this Day should overtake you as a thief (1 Thessalonians 5:2–4).

Paul continues in verse 9:

> For God did not appoint us to wrath, but to obtain salvation through our Lord Jesus Christ (1 Thessalonians 5:9).

Verse 9 tells that Christ's followers will not be punished by wrath, though Jesus did clarify that these would see tribulation (Matthew 24:9). We shall see also that the Resurrection will occur *shortly after the wrath begins*, with Christ's saints being protected through it until His return. We shall be made aware as well, of a specific natural disaster that will come upon the earth as labor pains upon a pregnant woman, which will be the cause of the darkness that will prevail at our Lord's return. We will come to see how God's two people groups, the Jewish remnant and Christ's saints, will be saved through wrath: the Jewish remnant through all the wrath of the Day of the Lord, while for Jesus' saints, just through the initial effects up to His return. We shall observe, step-by-step, how the nations will come to be in Israel as well!

We can now evaluate the third Scripture reference that clearly defines *wrath*, as the Day of the Lord. This Scripture comes from the mouth of Christ Himself, and shows how His return will be timed to coincide with a certain point shortly after the natural disaster strikes. These Scriptures deal also with a great natural disaster of history and are found in Matthew 24:37–39. They tell us this:

But as the days of Noah were, so also will the coming of the Son of Man be.

For as in the days before the flood, they were eating and drinking, marrying and giving in marriage, until the day that Noah entered the ark,

and did not know until the flood came and took them all away, so also will the coming of the Son of Man be.

Here we see that the ark represents not only the Resurrection, but also the means for some to be kept safe for a short time while wrath rages all around them. Lift-off will occur at the very point at which waters rose sufficiently to float the ark, while at the same time, devastating the earth. God's few were protected from harm until their large lifeboat was floating free of the carnage below! *Christ's return will coincide with the flood's depth at which point it lifted the ark!*

According to the Noah verses, the flood came upon the unsaved as a thief in the night. Not because they had not had ample warning; it took Noah and his sons considerable time to build a structure as massive and as precise in detail as the ark for the work it was intended to do. No, the reason that the lost were unaware, unconcerned, and without any hope of salvation was that they believed Noah didn't have both oars in the water, so to speak. He was, no doubt, ridiculed and pointed out as someone of less than average intelligence. Does this attitude in relation to Christians have a familiar ring? The fact is, as with Noah, we know something they don't know. Not that we are trying to hide it from them; just the opposite is true. Our responsibility is the gospel message of salvation through Christ. Some will listen; some will not. As Christ said in Matthew 24:14: "And this gospel of the kingdom will be preached in all the world as a witness to all nations, and then the end will come." All will hear, but not all will heed!

But we are getting ahead of our story. Yes, Bible prophecy does have a story line. Prophesied events are often clouded and layered one upon another, that is, having shadow, latter-day occurrences keyed to the original prophecy, but applying to a different entity and a later time. Then, too, prophecy is not always in sequence. With this brief background statement in place, we will look closely at a prophecy that has puzzled Bible students down through history. Time trend (the unfolding of current events) is our friend in understanding heretofore veiled Bible prophecy, i.e., Daniel 12:4. His prophecies were sealed until our time (end time).

Many have wondered why, as important a role as the United States of America has played and is presently playing in modern history, why it wasn't mentioned in the Bible. The fact of the matter is that the U.S.A is spoken of in both Old and New Testaments. Different names are attributed to it, none of which is the U.S.A. In these particular references, it is mentioned in connection with its destruction. Then, if it is not named in a manner easily identifiable today, how can we know that which God's Word refers to in the above instances is actually the U.S.A? It is being pointed out here, that one-time Christian America is now predominantly pagan, secular humanist, and atheistic. God knew this would happen, and had several of His prophets of old prophesy against this mighty last-days power, referring to it by names of major pagan city-states of that day. The Bible makes specific statements concerning this last-days colossus, which God considers, in this her latter stage, to be wayward. God, in fact, makes no bones about His feeling for her now, as evidenced by His reference to her as a fallen woman. We will now view a prophetic shadow of an ancient pagan world trader, which falls on and exemplifies in detail last days America!

# CHAPTER ELEVEN

# TYRE/U.S.A.

The ancient city-state of Tyre on the Mediterranean coast, in what is now the country of Lebanon, just north of Israel, was like America today—marketplace to the world (Isaiah 23:3). This chapter gives God's intention to punish pagan Tyre for her harlotry (which we will come to see as a shadow reference to America). Her trading partners agonize at the loss of this market. While in Isaiah 23, we will look at verse 15, which sets the stage for the second meaning of the chapter in its shadowy reference to the U.S.A. Verse 15 says:

> Now it shall come to pass in that day that Tyre will be forgotten seventy years, according to the days of one king. At the end of seventy years it will happen to Tyre as in the song of the harlot.

The key point is this: Tyre/U.S.A will be forgotten, or more to the point, will not present a strong political/spiritual influence in the world for seventy years as she once did. In the case of the U.S.A, she was involved in internal growth and healing of the self-inflicted wounds of her Civil War; and then enmeshed in several protectionist inspired wars completely void of social, spiritual, or political interaction that God calls harlotry. In the case of Tyre, it is difficult from history to see evidence of seventy low profile years with subsequent activity as described in verses 16 and 17, which we shall read here:

> Take a harp, go about the city [UN Headquarters, New York City], you forgotten harlot; make sweet melody, sing many songs, that you may be remembered.

> And it shall be, at the end of seventy years, that the LORD will visit Tyre. She will return to her pay, and commit fornication with all the kingdoms of the world on the face of the earth (Isaiah 23:16–17).

When God uses the terms fornication and harlotry in reference to cities or nations, He means social, political, and spiritual interaction in which sin results. As with ancient Israel, her fornication and harlotry was not brought on by armed conflict with neighboring nations, but rather, involved adopting their pagan religious beliefs and practices while on a peace time basis. With the U.S.A, her fornication and harlotry with other nations is a broader spectrum. For one thing, we see in verse 17 that it applies to all kingdoms of the world on the face of the earth. True, Tyre was a world market and a world trader, but there is one important difference between Tyre and the U.S.A as she came out of her civil war. The United States of America was for the most part a Christian nation, while Tyre had always been pagan. Pagans interacting with pagans is not something that would arouse God's intense anger, since their eternal prospects have always been dismal. With the U.S.A, as with Israel, God's attitude is much different. He does not like losing these two nations to the enemy. This is abundantly clear in His Word, especially concerning Israel—God is a jealous God. This attitude of His applies also to America, once having been a Christian nation; God does not like losing her, either!

Now to focus on the seventy low profile years, i.e., seventy isolationist years of no intentional social, political, spiritual interaction with nations that would result in sin. Examples of this sin will come later, but now a look at the seventy protectionist years.

In Isaiah 23:17 God says in so many words: "After seventy years of concentrating on protective, internal matters, Tyre (U.S.A) would again go back to harlotry with the nations." In the case of the U.S.A, this seventy-year period is clearly seen as extending forward from 1877, the year reconstruction in the south ended in the wake of the Civil War. The freed slaves could now legally vote, and on April 24, 1877, those federal troops remaining in Louisiana, the last in the south, were withdrawn; providing for healing and vigorous national growth. With the nation once more united, and her Christian ethic intact, America resisted foreign alliances in favor of rebuilding unity, while adopting a protectionist world stance. *America minded her own business.* She was forced to exert her military strength in 1898 in a protectionist confrontation with Spain to dislodge that nation's military from Cuba, thus preventing a repeat of European imperialism from again taking root in the Americas. The First World War dragged her into a brief alliance with foreign nations against Germany, but she resisted the globalist scheme of the League of Nations, resulting in its early demise. Soon, protectionist America was again drawn into war in a foreign environment, this time against Japan, Italy, and Germany (This was protectionist inspired, not politically motivated). With victory once more behind her, she was again faced with the temptation of foreign involvement. This was the year—1945 and her membership in the fledgling global United Nations. Then two years of making melody and singing sweet songs, and with the UN up and running, the year was now 1947. This was a momentous year for America, for the children of Israel, and yes, for the entire world!

First, 1947 *ended the seventy years of America's isolationist/protectionist world stance.* Second, it was the last of 1,877 years that Israel was without her homeland (1947 minus A.D. 70 equals 1,877 years). Israel regained her land the following year, in 1948. The year 1947 began America's larger-than-life presence on the world scene. The mechanism for accelerated change and foreign involvement was the *National Security Act of July 26, 1947.* This major legislation enabled the U.S.A to utilize her great wealth, military power, growing technologic advancement, and in addition to these, her steadily growing Marxist-inspired will for global union to "commit fornication with all the kingdoms of the world on the face of the earth." (Isaiah 23:17)

The springboard for this new national direction was America's superpower status coming out of World War II. The National Security Act of 1947 provided the political machinery and the funding for global activity in that it established the American National Security Council. This is headed by the president, with general oversight of the following newly created agencies brought into being by the same act: a secretary of defense, a national military establishment, a Central Intelligence Agency (CIA) and a National Security Resources Board.[4]

With these new additions to her political infrastructure in place, America was in position to accommodate those of her hidden government, that from behind the scenes pull the levers of power and who so passionately desire, diligently plan, and tirelessly strive for global union! It is sufficient to point out here, however, that the Bible records God's foreknowledge of their efforts. It states in no uncertain terms and makes God's intent very clear that although they would have a marked effect in furthering worldwide global union in concert with globalists of other nations, America's much-despised (by American globalists) Constitution and Bill of Rights will prevail in preventing a complete immersion of America into the Marxist uni-world government!

With America's membership in the world government leaning United Nations and tiny Israel a canker sore on the face of the Islamic Mid-East, we see some of the ingredients for global intrigue. Add to that the fact of America's newly acquired agency structuring for global interaction that is the National Security Act of 1947, and it is not difficult to see the U.S.A playing the part of the harlot, as foretold in Isaiah 23:17. (After seventy years of protective self-indulgence.)

As high-tech spectators of world events through TV, radio, newspapers, etc., we have had a ringside seat in observing the harlotry of America in her wheeling and dealing in world affairs. Much, if not all with good intent, but, nevertheless with more and more dire results at home.

The U.S.A's post-World War II trade in goods and technology, her worldwide financial aid with its many strings attached, associated political negotiations and her global military and financial alliances with the UN, NATO, the International Monetary Fund, the Federal Reserve Bank, the World Bank, NAFTA, the WTO, etc., provide a sampling of overt operations. Covert operations take on a life of their own. It is sufficient to say for our purpose that the newly authorized Central Intelligence Agency of the 1947 legislation and its black budget became a force to be reckoned with in its undercover manipulations, deals, and so-on and so-forth. Its legitimate role, of course, was to neutralize the Soviet Union's KGB, which it did with considerable success, and so we are left with the following summary:

America's harlotry with all nations in the world on the face of the earth comes at a high price to her people. This does not reference high taxes paid by Americans to financially bankroll all this global activity, though they are substantial. No, this refers to the moral free fall, the spiritual tailspin and the pornographic fixation that now grip America in and outside her Christian churches. America's sanctuaries (*churches*) have been *defiled* (Ezekiel 28:18).

Instead of falling prey to temptation by singling out and recounting insufficiencies of Christ's church today in its generally mixed emotions, some of which lead toward and into apostasy, we will focus instead on a point of interest passed over in the work above. This refers to an awesome and likely heretofore unrecognized and unknown numerical bond that exists between the modern nation of Israel and the U.S.A. The door was opened to it above in showing the number of years that Israel was without her homeland as promised by God. This was determined by subtracting A.D. 70, the year Rome conquered Israel, destroying Jerusalem and God's holy temple in the process, from the year 1947, which ended the 1,877 years that Jews wandered the globe without their promised homeland. These 1,877 years were Israel's quiet time. It was not, however, a time of stagnation. The Jewish people have more than held their own; in fact, they have excelled in their various fields of endeavor in their adopted countries.

Very well, this is all true, but where is the connection between modern Israel and America? The connection exists in the number 1877. This is the year that America began her seventy years of quiet time according to God's prophecy of Tyre/U.S.A in Isaiah 23:15 and which was found to have ended in 1947! As global spectators of world events on a daily basis, we see America's bold stance in global political maneuvering, fueled by dollars and, superior military and communications technology. This superpower status was birthed in 1945 with victory ending World War II. Other nations of the world were worn down militarily, financially and emotionally, burnt out and used up; America's wartime allies included. America, on the other hand, emerged stronger in all categories than was her condition upon entering the war.

With the National Security Act of 1947 in place, America was a powerhouse. Sporting her newly gained world prestige, her seemingly unlimited quantity of dollars, with foreign policy well planned and with the best of intentions, she was propelled onto the world stage. She sought out the less fortunate and had no trouble finding them. She pitched in with her great resources and built the foundation that the terrible wartime destruction was rebuilt on. So, what went wrong?

There were lots of deals, and dealing involves give and take. By most standards, America was very successful. Using the world's yardstick for measuring progress, the world has much to be grateful to America for. But, alas and alack, the world has a short memory.

America's success in her worldly enterprises has bred some very negative attitudes on the part of many of her global neighbors and recipients of her many favors.

So here we see a thumbnail sketch of what God terms harlotry. But where is the sin? The sin resides in the absence of God and His Son Jesus Christ in the mechanics and the intent of all this purely secular, humanistic undertaking. God warned early Israel not to have dealings with her pagan neighbors. When Israel rejected His warning and indulged in reciprocal relationships, she would become infected with their deadly spiritual, communicable venereal diseases. This was intolerable to God, as He requires a clean, healthy body of believers. When the disease had spread to overwhelm the once-healthy body, God would administer the medicine, which could be equated to something stringent and very distasteful: defeat by an enemy!

When America went to war in the Big One, she had a healthy body of believers. Her military units all had chaplains to administer God's Word to the troops. Even General George S. Patton, said to be a believer in reincarnation himself, relied upon chaplains to administer God's Word to his troops and for prayer to God Almighty through His Son Jesus Christ to provide victory over his enemy. The folks at home were, for the most part, churchgoers, and the Christian ethic was not banned from schools or other public places. People prayed a lot to God through Christ in those days and our nation was rewarded with, not only victory over those who would oppress us, but with the wherewithal and the desire to pick them up, dust them off, and guide them in becoming self-sufficient through democratic principles. America did not, however, emphasize Christ or Christian values in her dealings then or later when she became the queen of the world, and she said: "in her heart, 'I sit as queen, and am no widow, and will not see sorrow'" (Revelation 18:7).

For example: soon after America's victory over Japan and the American occupation was established in that nation, rebuilding its government on democratic principles from the ground up, General Douglas MacArthur, under whose authority the occupation was carried out, is reported to have made a plea. He appealed to America's churches to "send in the missionaries!" The missionaries were not forthcoming and so a great opportunity for America to do God's will was lost. Not only were the people of Japan worse off for this great act of neglect, but the people of America and the world continue to pay a heavy price for the insertion of secular humanism in the place of God's grace through Jesus Christ no matter where it occurs on the planet! It is like a creeping cancer, spreading its diseased cells throughout a body suffering with a weak immune system! The body's defenses not only cannot fight off the invading infection, it cannot even identify it as an enemy! And so it becomes weakened even more to where it now, with inverted vision, sees itself as healthy and anyone with a healthy immune system is seen as sick!

America's churches failed then and too many are failing now, seemingly mesmerized by the spirit of wealth. Much of today's preaching focuses on prosperity over missions, to become ensnared in the trivia of worldly pleasure seeking, while slacking in the first calling, to be a light to the world in sharing the good news of the free gift of eternal salvation through Jesus Christ!

The result of America's good works, while leaving out Jesus Christ, was to cause a large vacuum to exist within the realm of U.S.A's values. Since America was not and is not exporting Christian values in any of her myriad of global arrangements, deals, agreements, treaties, etc., this large, ballooning vacuum is being filled by spiritual seepage from off her shores and from across her borders. It is obvious to anyone that this is true and that it has had and is having a negative effect on her Christian ethic in general, including moral values and the knowledge and belief that Jesus Christ is the second Person of the Godhead.

This growing vacuum is being filled with other things as well, including pornography, growing religious cults that attempt to strip Christ of His deity, and an outright frontal attack by those with atheistic/secular/humanist values through a progressive court system to sanitize this growing secular nation of any vestige of Christian/godly values. This judicial rule from the bench has been increasingly tolerated by a legislative branch seemingly bewitched by the demands of political correctness and mainstream thought.

Jesus said in Matthew 12:30: "He who is not with Me is against Me." This sums up America's current position in God's eyes and why He considers America's perceived good works as harlotry. It is not the good that these works produce that is at fault. It is the good that these works do not produce that is at fault; facilitating the stripping away of Christian and godly values from the public conscience as is happening all around us. This can be compared to removing the steel spines of an umbrella. With the steel framework gone, you no longer have a functional protective covering. You now have, instead, a bag over your head and you face the reality of a life of spiritual blindness and misdirection!

The numerical bond, 1,877 or A.D. 1877 depending on its use, with 1,877 years of quiet time ending for Israel, and A.D. 1877 being the year that America's 70 years of quiet time commenced, is bolstered by yet another numerically common bond. The year, 1947, was the *last* of Israel's 1,877 low-profile years with no homeland, while for America it was the year *In which* her 70 low-profile years ended. Exactly as Isaiah 23:15 prophesied that it would be: "Tyre will be forgotten seventy years, according to the years of one king." With an individual, a king in this case, his age is counted from the year of his birth to the year of his death. With Tyre/U.S.A, the date marking the beginning of her quiet time was April 24, 1877, the end of reconstruction in the south. These seventy years ended (as with the years of one king) on July 26, 1947. The period of time was seventy years and three months or as with a king, he would have been considered to be seventy years of age.

But is this the end of it? Not quite! We find one more numerically common bond between Israel and America. We have been using it throughout this study, the number 70; God's number seven multiplied ten times. Israel having been conquered this final time in A.D. 70 by the Roman Empire, and what remained of her fragile nation scattered to the four winds is part of it. Then God established 70 years for the latter-day nation of Tyre/U.S.A to be generally absent from the world political scene, to then become a driving force; making her presence felt by: "all kingdoms of the world on the face of the earth."

In addition to being aware of these three numerical bonds that bind Israel and America in a God-ordained relationship, we must recognize the foundational cause of their existence. It is no accident and it is not coincidental. As stated above, it is God-ordained, but why? The answer is simple; and it is unpalatable to much of the world today. It is nevertheless true and is proven by God's Word and by pure, unrevised history. *Both these nations were established by the will of God!* All one need do to prove it is to read God's Word and American history! Forces within America are now revising history, and the world is articulating denial of the truth of God's Word! So where do we go from here? As we proceed through this work options will appear, which answer that question and point out the penalty for making the wrong choice. It needs to be made clear, however, that powerful forces are also at work on a daily basis reshaping or attempting to reshape the public's perception of Israel's claim to the land that she now occupies and which God gave to that nation long before the exodus of Israel from bondage in Egypt.

It is important to understand also that America's involvement in the worldly scheme to separate Israel from a portion of God-given land—land that God looks upon as His in conjunction with Israel, is problematic for America, and in combination with other misdeeds, has America in God's Word, labeled as a harlot.

As we have seen, and are well aware, there is currently taking place in America a united and concentrated effort to erase God/Jesus from public view. This movement, which is proceeding with humanistic and spiritualistic approval, is oozing into America's churches. God's absolute Word is being watered down and perverted in some churches. Emphasis is moving from the Trinity to entertainment, with the result that America's churches in numerous cases are being defiled.

> You defiled your sanctuaries by the multitude of your iniquities, by the iniquity of your trading; therefore I brought fire from your midst [The Hebrew word for midst can also mean (pile), as in U.S.A.'s scattered nuclear weapons stockpile presently targeted for potential future missile attack by Russia.]; it devoured you, and I turned you to ashes upon the earth in the sight of all who saw you (Ezekiel 28:18).

Why could this verse not apply to Tyre? It could not apply because *Tyre has always been pagan* by choice. There was a period of time when the Crusaders occupied Tyre, and there was a Christian community there in New Testament times as evidenced by the apostle Paul's short stay there (Acts 21:1–7). The fact of the matter is, that when Christians or godly Jews were there, Tyre's multiple destructions were already history. It has not been a maritime trading force since it was destroyed by Alexander the Great in 332 B.C. Since then, it has lingered on in various stages of disrepair, with its influence on the world scene completely shattered. Jesus, in Matthew 11:21, referred to both Tyre and Sidon as pagan, and which would have repented had His preaching occurred there.[5]

The key to knowing that it is not Tyre referred to in Ezekiel 28:18 is right there at the beginning of the verse: "You defiled your sanctuaries, by your iniquities, by the iniquity of your trading; therefore I brought fire from your midst." Tyre's sanctuaries (temples), had always been centers for corrupt, heathen idol worship *right from the start!* They had always been corrupt. They never had any redeemable value from the beginning. Then, too, destruction by fire from her midst does not fit the historical episodes of her multiple ruins either. Fire is not mentioned in any of the recorded history of Tyre's destructions. In fact, fire by burning of flammable materials would have been minimal, since the city was built on a rocky coastline and constructed mostly of that material. With serious consideration to the above mentioned points, it is difficult to not clearly see that the Tyre of Ezekiel 28:18 and of Isaiah 23:17 is not the old pagan Phoenician trading city-state of ancient times!

But there is another verse that drives the point home even further. Recall, Isaiah 23:17 pointed out that Tyre/U.S.A would, after a lull of seventy years, return to her harlotry "with all the kingdoms of the world on the face of the earth." Now, verse 18 follows with this:

> Her gain and her pay will be set apart for the LORD; it will not be treasured nor laid up, for her gain will be for those who dwell before the LORD, to eat sufficiently, and for fine clothing. [Blessings for God's people; but Tyre had none!]

At the times when there was a Christian presence in Tyre, her grand command of the seas was ancient history and she was a non-event, *unable to engage in harlotry with all nations of the world on the face of the earth!* America, prior to her civil war, was a great seafaring nation of the world. Involved in whaling and trading, her specially designed Yankee clipper ships were the fastest, most functional, and beautiful trading vessels to grace the world's oceans to that time.

Isaiah 23:18 does not apply to the old Phoenician city-state of Tyre, simply because her sanctuaries had always been defiled with paganism and there were no godly people in Tyre when her world trading was in progress and she was being prospered by her trade. There was no one there who dwelt before the Lord. All were pagan Amorites or Canaanites; worshipping as many as seventy gods and goddesses—an abomination to the Lord (*Illustrated Dictionary of the Bible*, 205).

Isaiah 23:18 could apply to America; however, and we shall see below, that it unquestionably does! For clarity, we will read the verse again: "Her [Tyre/U.S.A] gain and her pay will be set apart for the Lord; it will not be treasured nor laid up, for her gain will be for those who dwell before the Lord, to eat sufficiently, and for fine clothing."

God uses America's harlotry to bless His people, with the result that the blessings fall on God's just and the unjust alike. When the just are removed, the blessings being wrung from America's harlotry will cease! (Matthew 5:45).

Ezekiel 28:16 strikes directly to Tyre/U.S.A's slave trade as causing sin:

By the abundance of your trading [slaves] you became filled with violence within [Civil War], and you sinned . . .

Old pagan idol worshipping Tyre was always deep in sin. Early Christian America, with the sin of the slave trade on her hands, became filled with violence within, erupting into civil war.

Ezekiel 28:16 continues:

Therefore I cast you as a profane thing out of the mountain [government] of God; and I destroyed you, O covering [protective] cherub, from the midst of the fiery stones.

(Reference here to the spirit of America as the protective, sheltering safe harbor for Christians, known by God in the Garden of Eden wherein she was spiritually covered with fiery gemstones.) (Ezekiel 28:13).

As many know, God established America as a Christian nation. The reference above to her being cast "as a profane thing out of the mountain of God" points to her slave trade harlotry leading to civil war and her harlot status. As prophesied, this harlot status extended through a dormant period which lasted 70 years from the year 1877, the year reconstruction ended in the south, to 1947. Then, to break out anew, in harlotry with: "all the kingdoms of the world on the face of the earth."

Now, we will see another Bible reference to a harlot. This one called The Great Harlot, is given another name as well. The other name: Mystery Babylon the Great, The Mother of Harlots and of the Abominations of the Earth. Strong words, causing disagreement as to who or what this great harlot is. The case is here being made that this Great Harlot is in reality the U.S.A! Will you agree? Read on and see!

# CHAPTER TWELVE

# MYSTERY, BABYLON THE GREAT, THE MOTHER OF HARLOTS, AND OF THE ABOMINATIONS OF THE EARTH

It is difficult for some to come to grips with the thought of America being biblically referred to in this way. We have seen compelling evidence from God's Word in combination with secular history, which suggests that certain Bible references to Tyre are, in fact, referring to the U.S.A. The ancient pagan shadow seemingly falling on America continues to expand here. Revelation 18 is fully devoted to destruction of *mystery Babylon the great*, which exhibits numerous similarities to America. With the U.S.A destined for her major role in the last years of these first 6,000, and not coming on stage until late in the final act, God chose to refer to her by the names of pagan city-states that shared some common characteristics with her. We are then left to match this major last days world force, America, with her appropriate predecessors for a preview of coming events straight from the mouth of God! To this end, we shall proceed with Revelation 18:2 setting the stage with an angel saying: "Babylon the great is fallen, is fallen." Verse 3 continues: "For all the nations have drunk of the wine of the wrath of her fornication, the kings of the earth have committed fornication with her, and the merchants of the earth have become rich through the abundance of her luxury." Verse 4 provides a warning: "And I heard another voice from heaven saying, 'come out of her, my people, lest you share in her sins, and lest you receive of her plagues.'"

Regarding verse 4: God does not mean for His people to leave the country. He means rather, come out of her abominable ways; have no part in her sinful practices. What is this loathsome behavior to be avoided? Some examples follow: on a personal basis, we can list such things as abortion, pornography, lies, hedonism, worshipping things, stealing, selfishness, pridefulness, adultery, etc. In a second category, there are those corporate sins that the nation as a whole is involved in. These include attempting to force Israel to give up God-given land to her enemies, marketing aborted baby body parts, removing God from the public arena, U.S.A involvement in advancing a godless Marxist global government, funding and promoting pornographic so-called art, legalizing and funding abortion, promoting the evolution lie, gene splicing, fetal stem cell research and cloning.

Then there is spiritual sin in America. Paganism and religious cults, false gods; humanism, man himself as god; new age, meaningless spirituality with demonic overtones; atheism, no God; witchcraft, demonic magic dabbling; and straight-out Satan worship. God says, "have no part in any of it." The harlot represents the world, and will ensnare the unwary! Romans 12:2 says: "And do not be conformed to this world, but be transformed by the renewing of your mind." John 15:19 says, "If you were of the world, the world would love its own. Yet because you are not of the world, but I chose you out of the world, therefore the world hates you." Now, to carry on with Revelation 18:6–7. These tell of the great harlot being deserving of punishment. Verses 8–11 follow:

> Therefore her plagues will come in one day; death and mourning and famine. And she will be utterly burned with fire, for strong is the Lord God who judges her.

> The kings of the earth who committed fornication and lived luxuriously with her will weep and lament for her, when they see the smoke of her burning,

standing at a distance for fear of her torment, [nuclear fallout] saying, 'Alas, alas, that great city Babylon, that mighty city! For in one hour your judgment has come.'

And the merchants of the earth will weep and mourn over her, for no one buys their merchandise anymore.

Verses 12 and 13 tell of luxury items in terms of two thousand years ago, that this great market will no longer be importing after its destruction:

merchandise of gold and silver, precious stones and pearls, fine linen and purple, silk and scarlet, every kind of citron wood, every kind of object of ivory, every kind of object of most precious wood, bronze, iron, and marble [manufactured goods];

and cinnamon and incense, fragrant oil and frankincense, wine and oil, fine flour and wheat, cattle and sheep, horses and chariots, and bodies and souls of men (Revelation 18:12–13).

The only item above needing possible clarification is the bodies and souls of men. The conclusion of choice here is that this is a reference to a U.S.A open immigration policy, which is well established at this time with no sign of impending reversal in sight.

Verse 14 deals with the reality of the great harlot's loss of the fruit (or good results) that she, in her heart longed for from her perceived good works, much of which, in God's eyes, was harlotry. It deals as well with the finality of her loss of all that was rich and splendid. Verses 15 through 18 tell of how sad the merchants of the world will be at losing this great market for their products. Verse 19 pictures the despair of the world's merchants with the following lament:

They threw dust on their heads and cried out, weeping and wailing, and saying, "Alas, alas, that great city, in which all who had ships on the sea became rich by her wealth! For in one hour she is made desolate" (Revelation 18:19).

Verses 20 through 23 discuss certain aspects of the harlot's demise, and a number of specific things that will no longer be seen, heard, or found there.

This brings us to verse 24, the last in Revelation 18. On the surface, this verse is difficult to relate to the U.S.A. We will now read it, and then find the connection to America:

> And in her was found the blood of prophets and saints, and of all who were slain on the earth (Revelation 18:24).

So, how does America fit this description? It all has to do with the U.S.A as a nation turning away from Jesus Christ, as now is the case. Consider carefully, that when America ceased being predominantly Christian, she became predominantly a pagan, atheistic, secular, humanist nation. The important outcome of being a *repentant* Christian, whether it be a person or a nation, is that sin is forgiven by God. The U.S.A, being the world's melting pot, is populated by people who have arrived in America from other nations and by those whose ancestry can be traced to foreign lands as well. Since America ceased being predominantly Christian, the bloody acts of her citizens, as well as the blood shed by their ancestors including those in primitive, pagan, and atheistic societies, accrue to America and become her inheritance. "The blood of the prophets and saints, and of all who were slain on the earth" *is now on her hands!*

The point here being: that God has this unrepentant harlot (Tyre/Mystery Babylon the Great/U.S.A) marked for destruction. Timing, however, is crucial. With the magnitude of severity, this punishment will most certainly be reserved for the Day of the Lord, to become a portion of God's wrath upon unrepentant mankind. As 1 Thessalonians 5:9 clearly points out:

> For God did not appoint us to wrath, but to obtain salvation through our Lord Jesus Christ.

We will see that America's fatal wound shall occur sometime after Jesus will return in the early wrath and remove His people from the scene. Yes, *after* God's wrath shall begin to fall on the unrepentant. Evidence will be seen later that points to Jesus' return a specified number of days into the Day of the Lord. Saints, not being appointed to wrath, and the Jewish remnant with God's seal, will be protected. Fully detailed proof awaits on ahead.

Revelation 17 is about a mystery. It presents the facts, and even though part of the answer is revealed, the meaningful part of the solution is left to the reader's power of discernment to provide total perception. The mystery concerns the great harlot, Mystery Babylon the Great and a scarlet beast.

# CHAPTER THIRTEEN

# THE HARLOT AND THE BEAST

The vision is an allegory, using fictional characters to reveal Bible prophecy. The chapter starts out with the apostle John, the observer and writer of Revelation, being caught up in the Spirit and carried into the wilderness. Here he is shown a revealing scene. There he saw a woman sitting on a scarlet beast labeled with blasphemous names, having seven heads and ten horns. The woman, adorned with gold, precious stones, and pearls, had a golden cup in her hand full of abominations and the filthiness of her fornication. On her forehead was written "Mystery Babylon the Great, the Mother of Harlots and of the Abominations of the Earth."

John saw that she was drunk with the blood of the saints and with the blood of the martyrs of Jesus. Since John expressed amazement at the sight he had seen, the angel with him provided a perplexing explanation. Revelation 17:8 tells what he said:

> The beast that you saw was, and is not, and will ascend out of the bottomless pit and go to perdition. And those who dwell on the earth will marvel, whose names are not written in the Book of Life from the foundation of the world, when they see the beast that was, and is not, and yet is.

So, here in the vision, we see America (the woman) figuratively being carried by a beast that represents a man. This man had once lived, but in John's day, was no longer alive. He was, however, destined to ascend out of the bottomless pit (hell) in the latter days, where, at the time of John's writing, he was being held. Then, he would play his predetermined part in world affairs and proceed to eternal damnation.

Verses 9 through 11 present a riddle for those with wisdom to unravel. The verses are given here which contain some of the important details for identification of the beast:

> Here is the mind which has wisdom: The seven heads are seven mountains on which the woman sits.

> There are also seven kings. Five have fallen, one is, and the other has not yet come. And when he comes, he must continue a short time.

> And the beast that was, and is not, is himself also the eighth, and is of the seven, and is going to perdition (Revelation 17:9–11).

We will start by identifying the key words and phrases in the above verses in order to make sense of it all.

The seven mountains are not actual mountains or hills. They are seven empires. These empires are represented by seven kings or primary leaders. The first five of these empires and their representative kings were history at the time John saw this vision. These were Egypt, Assyria, Babylon, Medo-Persia, and Greece. The sixth, Rome, was in existence at the time of John's vision. The seventh, which has not as yet come, is mentioned in Daniel 2:41. It is presented there as a divided kingdom in the form of the two feet of a giant statue/image in King Nebuchadnezzar's dream, which the king had Daniel, with the help of the Holy Spirit of God, explain to him. The two feet of the statue were made of a mixture of two ingredients; iron and clay, which although mingled together, will not adhere one to the other (Daniel 2:43). The mingling of the clay with the iron will produce an empire that will be partly strong and partly fragile (Daniel 2:42). So then, this soon to appear, divided kingdom/empire, being the seventh on the list of seven, will be divided in two parts, and will have both the strength of iron and the weakness of clay.

Since Revelation 13 tells of two beasts (leaders) that will exercise great control over the then-existing global government, we can presume that they will be the two which head that divided world empire. The one called the false prophet, we can determine, will head the religious portion of the union. That portion is silently and surely morphing into one giant worldwide religious organization, by removing barriers to an alliance, whereby all can worship the same god. It seems likely that with the office of the pope being the symbol of authority and power that it is, that a pope will assume the part of false prophet and will lead this apostate religious empire. Born-again Christians shall not take part, nor will they be welcome to do so.

So now, we can name the false prophet and his apostate religious empire as being the seventh empire (the seventh head of the beast which carries the harlot). But there is another half of this partly iron and partly clay final world union. It is the *political/economic half*. This is the special domain of the beast that carries the great harlot. This beast, commonly called Antichrist, is the eighth king/leader referred to in Revelation 17:11, which reads:

> And the beast that was, and is not, is himself also the eighth, and is of the seven, and is going to perdition.

There are actually two ways that this beast is of the seven, as presented above. First, he leads the other half of the divided global empire; that is, the political/economic half, which combined with the apostate religious half, completes the seventh and final empire. This makes him part of the seventh. Of this divided empire, the clay represents the apostate religious entity, and the iron accounts for the political/economic entity, which will control the military might of the empire, thus the iron strength.

Second, this beast "was"; that is, he had lived before. We will see later that he was a king of the fifth empire, who after having died, went to hell where he was held for a rebirth in the latter days. Having been given back to the world, which he once terrorized, we can expect much of the same from him in his soon-to-be reappearance on the world scene.

His coming debut does not mean that he is not already among us. He is and has been for some time. He is a well-known political figure and has had a significant influence in bringing America closer in her connection with the global union!

A point to remember: this symbolic beast has seven heads and ten horns. Another is that he has literally lived before, has spent time in hell, and according to Revelation 13:4, in his second life, is indwelt by Satan. The significance of the seven heads/empires is that this beast and his empire carry hereditary traits of the previous six empires. As detailed in Daniel 2:45, Jesus, at His second coming, will destroy this paganized final global empire, the feet of clay and iron. And in so doing, will also destroy the hereditary traits of the six pagan empires that preceded it! The last five of all seven are seen in the statue of King Nebuchadnezzar's dream. They are: the head of gold (Babylon), the chest and arms of silver (Medo-Persia), the belly and thighs of bronze (Greece), legs of iron (Rome), and the feet of iron and clay (seventh divided global empire).

Daniel 2:34–35 gives Daniel's words to King Nebuchadnezzar as he told the king exactly what it was that the king had seen in his vision. This description bears repeating here:

You watched while a stone [Jesus] was cut out without hands, which struck the image [statue] on its feet of iron and clay, and broke them in pieces.

Then the iron, the clay, the bronze, the silver, and the gold were crushed together, and became like chaff from the summer threshing floors; the wind carried them away so that no trace of them was found. And the stone that struck the image became a great mountain [kingdom] and filled the whole earth.

So there we have it; evidence that the beast with seven heads and ten horns (Antichrist), being representative of man's final divided global empire, does in fact, along with this final empire, carry hereditary traits of the previous empires of the great image of King Nebuchadnezzar's dream. We see here the fate in store for this last divided world empire; to be crushed by the stone cut out without hands. This stone (Jesus Christ), in crushing the final divided empire, will grind to dust the pagan influence passed down through the centuries to it from its idol-worshipping predecessors.

The point here is this: That previous idol-worshipping empires had added to one another in passing down to the final divided empire, their pagan heritage. This idolatrous heritage will be destroyed by Jesus Christ at His second advent, to be replaced by His one thousand year Kingdom of God!

There is one more common aspect that applies to both multiple empire references that we have been dealing with; that being the inclusion of ten entities in each of the two scriptural multi-empire mysteries. The Revelation 17:3 beast, as well as having seven heads, had *ten horns*. These ten horns have considerable meaning in relation to the final divided global empire.

The other mystery, the great image of Daniel 2, depicts this multinational statue standing on two feet of a mixture of iron and clay. We are told that though the two substances mingle together, they do not adhere one to the other; thus resulting in a weakened final global empire. As we are well aware, two feet, as a natural state of affairs, have ten toes right there on the ends of them. Daniel 2:42 mentions the toes specifically, indicating that they play a special part in the final divided global empire. The verse reads this way:

And as the toes of the feet were partly of iron and partly of clay, so the kingdom shall be partly strong and partly fragile (Daniel 2:42).

Here, we are made aware that the ten toes are an integral part of the divided final global union. But what are they in this world government, and what part will they play? Answers to these questions are found in Revelation 17. We can be quite sure that the ten toes of the image, and the ten horns of the beast with seven heads represent the same entities. Daniel 2:34 expressed the destruction of the final divided empire by relating how the stone (Jesus) struck the feet, and in so doing, pulverized godless hereditary traits of prior pagan empires, as well as man's grand attempt at global Marxism!

Now, for answers to the questions; we read Revelation 17, beginning with verses 12, 13 and 14:

The ten horns which you saw are ten kings who have received no kingdom as yet, but they receive authority for one hour as kings with the beast.

These are of one mind, and they will give their power and authority to the beast.

These will make war with the Lamb [Jesus], and the Lamb will overcome them, for He is Lord of lords and King of kings; and those who are with Him are called, chosen, and faithful.

Verses 16 and 17 follow:

And the ten horns which you saw on the beast, these will hate the harlot, make her desolate and naked, eat her flesh and burn her with fire [Recipients of the harlot's favors].

For God has put it into their hearts to fulfill His purpose, to be of one mind, and to give their kingdom to the beast, until the words of God are fulfilled.

73

Being able to associate the toes and the horns as representing the same ten entities requires that we learn just what it is that they are. We know that they are ten individual entities that are all of one mind, and willingly place themselves under the authority of the beast (Antichrist). World trade has been a visible subject of interest up to now, that is, trade is seen to be the magnet pulling the nations together. It will also serve as the glue that will bind them in a cooperative trade sensitive final global empire.

With nations of the world presently forming trading blocs, the prophetic point here is that the ten toes of Daniel 2:42, and the ten horns of Revelation 17:12–14, foretell the formation of ten trading blocs of nations. These UN members, being of one mind, will give their power and authority to the beast for a short-term final global empire. This empire will be built around world trade and will be partly weak, due to the inclusion of the apostate world religion which will be prominently represented in its foundational tenets and in its operation as suggested by Revelation 13:11–17.

This empire will also possess the iron effect, partly strong due to progressive control of its member's military capability. Revelation 17:16 foretells that these like-minded, politically and economically motivated trading blocs "will hate the harlot, make her desolate and naked, eat her flesh and burn her with fire." (Could a trigger turn out to be Mid-East oil?)

So here we complete the examination of the beast with seven heads and ten horns, upon whose back rides the great harlot. This man has lived before, and has had an influence in globalizing the U.S.A and moving the nation toward a relationship with the global community (final global empire). He will become world-renowned, a phenomenon and a power to be reckoned with. Revelation 13:1–8 says that the symbolic beast that represents him, having seven heads and ten horns, has physical features of three early empires besides its pagan spiritual heritage. Revelation 13:2 paints this picture:

Now the beast which I saw was like a leopard, his feet were like the feet of a bear, and his mouth like the mouth of a lion. The dragon [Satan] gave him his power, his throne, and great authority.

We see that the physical features from three previous pagan empires differ from his paganized spiritual heritage. His most prominent likeness, that being like a leopard, directly relates him to his previous life as a king of a Greek dynasty. His being reborn from a previous life in the second century B.C., to a second life in our time, *does not* constitute reincarnation (rebirth of a soul in successive bodies, or transmigration of a soul) as some would believe. Christians know that it is appointed for men to die once, but after this the judgment (Hebrews 9:27).

This man, the beast (Antichrist), will experience physical death *only once*. Revelation 19:20 explains that he will not die at the end of his second physical life, but rather, will be "cast alive into the lake of fire burning with brimstone." This place is a representation of eternal damnation.

# CHAPTER FOURTEEN

# ABOUT THE MAN CALLED ANTICHRIST

Although it cannot be said with absolute certainty at this time who will have the dubious distinction of being identified as Antichrist in his second life, it is certain who he was in his first life. There is not the slightest doubt that he was Antiochus IV Epiphanes, a ruler of the ancient Seleucid dynasty. This ancient Syrian state, along with several others, became heirs to Alexander the Great's vast Greek empire. After Alexander's untimely death, his empire was divided into a number of individual states. Four of his generals asserted their rights of succession, with each acquiring control of a particular area. Seleucus I Nicator acquired the Greek state of Phrygia, known in the Bible as Aram. Later under the Romans it became known as Syria. Seleucus founded the city of Antioch there, which he and later his successors, used as headquarters of their Seleucid dynasty. These generals and their successors fought among themselves to enlarge their areas of influence. As a result, the Seleucids eventually gained control of Judea.[6]

A number of Seleucid heirs to the throne had the name Antiochus in honor of the city of Antioch. Thus, Antiochus IV, youngest son of Antiochus III the Great, acquired his given name. He was surnamed Epiphanes (*God manifest*) as well, and so the name

Antiochus IV Epiphanes was established. This is a name that has lived in infamy down through the centuries.[7]

A. In 170 B.C., Antiochus attacked Jerusalem, causing destruction to the city wall, massacred Jews loyal to God and plundered the temple, removing everything of value (Daniel 8:9–14 and *Smith's Bible Dictionary*, 40).

B. Two years later, at the close of his fourth campaign against Egypt, he occupied Jerusalem with a force of men, after having been interrupted in his conquest of Egypt by the Romans. Daniel states in Daniel 11:30 that "he shall be grieved, and return in rage against the holy covenant, and do damage." Damage against the holy covenant is just what he did. He desecrated the temple by placing a statue of Zeus, the Greek god, above the altar and then sacrificed a pig on the altar. (*Smith's Bible Dictionary*, 40)

C. Summary of years:

| | | | |
|---|---|---|---|
| From 170 B.C. to 168 B.C., control of Jerusalem | = | 2 | years |
| Jerusalem occupied and temple desecrated on 25th Chislev, 167 B.C. | = | 1+ | years |
| Temple cleansed on 25th Chislev, 164 B.C. (*Illustrated Dictionary of the Bible*, 664–665) | = | 3 | years |
| Total | = | 6+ | years |

Here we see the historical record supporting the 2,300 days (6+ years) prophesied in Daniel 8:9–14, as being the period of time in which attempted forced Hellenization would be inflicted upon Israel until the temple would be cleansed.

The historical record makes it clear that this desecrator of God's holy temple was none other than Antiochus IV Epiphanes.

Daniel 11:31 tells of a second temple desecration that will take place. The first temple sacrilege by Antiochus IV, verse 30, is shown in item "B" above and also is given here as biblically prophesied. This provides a basis to proceed to the second temple desecration described in verse 31. Daniel 11:30 tells us this:

> For ships from Cyprus [Romans] shall come against him; therefore he shall be grieved, and return in rage against the holy covenant, and do damage. So he shall return and show regard for those who forsake the holy covenant.

The second sentence tells, however, that he will return to Jerusalem in his second life as Antichrist (a subtle transference from an early to a much later time) to relate politically with those uninterested in the worship of God. These are likely the secular, politically powerful elite, who will exercise control over the government, and have little or no concern for the religious community.

The second desecration of God's holy temple (to occur after the subtle time transference) is then seen in Daniel 11:31. Antiochus will do it again; this time in his second life:

> And forces shall be mustered by him [Antichrist], and they shall defile the sanctuary fortress; then they shall take away the daily sacrifices, and place there the abomination of desolation.

When Jesus talked about the abomination of desolation in Matthew 24:15 as being a future occurrence of the last days, Antiochus IV had been dead for almost 200 years. Jesus' remarks skip over the Roman temple destruction of A.D. 70, going directly to the temple desecration of Daniel 11:31, the last days sacrilege to be carried out by *Antichrist*! This is the abomination spoken of by the apostle Paul in 2 Thessalonians 2:4; where, in end time context, he said of Antichrist:

who opposes and exalts himself above all that is called God or that is worshiped, so that he sits as God in the temple of God, showing himself that he is God [Third temple, not yet built].

The sacrilege committed by Antiochus IV Epiphanes upon the temple of God was not and is not to this day a small thing. As we saw in item "C" above, the temple was cleansed exactly three years to the day after its desecration. The cleansing brought about by Judas Maccabeus and his followers, who routed Antiochus IV from Jerusalem by military force, is the basis for the Jewish Festival of Lights, celebrated down through the years and known as Hanukkah.[8]

In Daniel 11:30, we saw a subtle transition from one time period to another. Daniel provides another example as well. Daniel 9:26 and 27 together, form the other example of veiled transference from an early to a later time period. With two desecrations prophesied, verse 26 has been fulfilled, while verse 27 has not. We can tell however, from other fulfilled Bible prophecy and the flow of current events as they fulfill still more prophecy, that the realization of verse 27 is near at hand.

To see the subtle transition from the earlier temple desecration by Antiochus described again in verse 26, we need only to look carefully at the two verses.

We begin in the body of verse 26: "And the people of the prince who is to come shall destroy the city and the sanctuary. The end of it shall be with a flood, and till the end of the war desolations are determined." The fact is, that the six plus years that Antiochus was involved in his effort to force Hellenization on the Jews, he destroyed the city wall, plundered the temple, massacred a large number of Jews including priests who resisted his efforts, and then desecrated the temple with the statue of a Greek god over the altar and offered swine on the altar to Zeus. We also know that there was a war carried on by the Jews; where they finally drove Antiochus out, and cleansed and rededicated the temple to God. It is obvious that verse 26 is describing the attempted Hellenization of the Jews by Antiochus IV Epiphanes, ruler of ancient Syria.

Verse 27 reads as follows: "Then [Almost twenty-two hundred years later] he shall confirm a covenant with many for one week; but in the middle of the week he shall bring an end to sacrifice and offering. And on the wing of abominations shall be one who makes desolate, even until the consummation, which is determined, is poured out on the desolate." (Antiochus IV, as Antichrist, defiling God's temple all over again!)

The common thought is that both Daniel 9:26 and 27 refer to the antichrist. The strong evidence that we have observed, however, shows that verse 26 concerns Antiochus IV Epiphanes and his depredations against the Jews and the temple of God. Verse 27 clearly shows his future return as Antichrist, as does the second sentence of Daniel 11:30; then to be expanded upon in Daniel 11:31 and by both Jesus and the apostle Paul as well. There is no mention of it in the historical record as having occurred. The fact is, this third temple of God does not as yet exist!

This prophecy in Daniel 9:27 actually breaks down into two parts: "Then he shall confirm a covenant with many for one week; but in the middle of the week he shall bring an end to sacrifice and offering." Antichrist will confirm (strengthen) an already existing peace agreement, covenant, that has established the last seven years. This agreement was commenced by America's Secretary of State, Condoleezza Rice, on June 19, 2005, between Israel and the Palestinian Authority regarding Israeli settlers leaving Gaza. This begins the seventieth week of Daniel 9:27. The Hebrew word for confirm (gabar) means to strengthen or exceed. When Antichrist later enters the picture, he will be seen as confirming, that is, strengthening/expanding this peace to include many, i.e., Israel's neighbors and their allies. This agreement may have provision for review and renegotiation. Antichrist will assert his authority about three years and four months into the treaty in a negative way. Daniel

9:27 says: "He shall bring an end to sacrifice and offering. And on the wing of abominations shall be one who makes desolate, even until the consummation, which is determined, is poured out on the desolate." (Part 1 = treaty signed—Part 2 = treaty confirmed and later broken.)

This verse, Daniel 9:27 sheds light on the sensitive politics that will be in play in that fast approaching end time. One thing we see is that the Jews will have struck a deal with Islamic nations to allow them to rebuild the temple in order to make sacrifices to God. This very difficult concession on the part of Islamic countries will be met by equally difficult concessions by Israel, all duly noted and contained within the expanding treaty. Israel's military might will be her ace in the hole when push comes to shove in the final dealings to produce a working agreement. He who officiates as chairman of later negotiations will reap recognition and great glory!

We see that the situation will be very much then as it is now. That is, with Israel having sufficient military power to stave off an attack by the avowed enemy, her Islamic neighbors. We know that the peace accord will involve a number of these nations, since verse 27 states that he shall confirm a covenant with many. Antichrist, with the prestige of a new global empire forming behind him, will referee those negotiations and will place his personal seal upon the final document. *Oh glory—he will have brought peace at last to the region!*

Three years and four months after the American Secretary of State's June 19, 2005 success in the peace process, Antichrist will forcibly bring an end to Jews making sacrifice and offering to God in the temple (Daniel 9:27).

Daniel 11:31 says it this way: "And forces shall be mustered by him, and they shall defile the sanctuary fortress; then they shall take away the daily sacrifices, and place there the abomination of desolation." As we know, this abomination was the statue of the

Greek god Zeus when Antiochus first defiled the temple. This time it will be the image of Antichrist that the false prophet will require the followers of the new multicultural world religion to make (Revelation 13:14). This image will be empowered by the false prophet to both speak and cause as many as will not worship the image to be killed (Revelation 13:15). There are a number of ideas in circulation as to just what this image will be—virtual reality, moving picture, television or . . . ? It might be one, or involve a combination of two or more of these, or possibly a yet undeveloped technology.

Television itself, in fact, would meet the requirements of the prophecy. With Antichrist calling himself God, he will require that he be worshipped worldwide. Daniel 11:37 makes this statement: "He shall regard neither the God of his fathers nor the desire of women [pagan goddesses], nor regard any god; for he shall magnify himself above them all."

The apostle Paul, in 2 Thessalonians 2:3–4 has this to say on the subject: "Let no one deceive you by any means; for that day will not come [Christ's return] unless the falling away comes first, and the man of sin is revealed, the son of perdition, who opposes and exalts himself above all that is called God or that is worshipped, so that he sits as God in the temple of God, showing himself that he is God." (TV studio . . . ?)

This would fulfill the apostle John's prophecy in Revelation 13:15 concerning the image being given breath, and the ability to speak. This would also fulfill Daniel's prophecies referring to the abomination of desolation (Daniel 11:31) and in Daniel 9:27: "And on the wing of abominations shall be one who makes desolate, even until the consummation, which is determined, is poured out on the desolate." The consummation, which is determined, being poured out on the desolate, is God's wrath (Day of the Lord), which is determined and will be poured out on the antichrist and his followers, the desolate.

Daniel 12:11 sheds some additional light on this situation by revealing that: "From the time that the daily sacrifice is taken away, and the abomination of desolation is set up, there shall be one thousand two hundred and ninety days." This is approximately three-and-a-half years of broadcasting, or whatever it turns out to be, from the temple. One thing is certain; it will define a period of severe persecution of devout believers in a god, or in God/Jesus; those who will not worship the speaking image!

Then Daniel 12:12 says: "Blessed is he who waits, and comes to the one thousand three hundred and thirty-five days." This prophecy is specific to the Jewish remnant being brought through the Armageddon holocaust and into the millennial rest to be with their Messiah, Jesus, whom they will then worship. In Daniel 12:7 prophetic reference is made to Israeli defense forces being weakened, used up, and completely without power, by the bloody end of conflict with all the military forces that will invade God's glorious land. The verse says it this way:

> Then I heard the man clothed in linen, who was above the waters of the river, when he held up his right hand and his left hand to heaven, and swore by Him who lives forever, that it shall be for a time, times, and half a time; and when the power of the holy people [Israel] has been completely shattered, all these things shall be finished.

After Jesus returns, He, by confusing the invaders to cause them to engage in friendly fire upon their own forces, by bringing cooperating armies to attack one another, and by using Israel as His bow and arrow, His double-edged sword, and His battle-ax, will defeat the nations gathered there in Israel. Zechariah 14:3 explains it this way:

> Then the LORD will go forth And fight against those nations, as He fights in the day of battle.

In the Old Testament, when God gave enemies of the Israelites into their hand, this terminology was used in conjunction with God

2012 IN BIBLE PROPHECY

going forth to fight as in the day of battle— the enemy was always given into the Israelites' hand.

To digress for a moment. Some may be curious as to how the three years and four months were arrived at in reference to the length of time, from the signing of the peace treaty until Antichrist will expel the Jews from the temple and move himself in as a representation of God Almighty. Then, too, in the same vein, this will leave three years and eight months as the approximate length of time, measuring backwards, from the end of the 6,000 years to Antichrist's accomplishment of the same travesty.

The seven years expressed in days, not considering leap years, are equal to 2,555 days.

Daniel 12:11–12 says this:

And from the time that the daily sacrifice is taken away, and the abomination of desolation is set up, there shall be one thousand two hundred and ninety days.

Blessed is he who waits, and comes to the one thousand three hundred and thirty-five days.

We can closely approximate the point in the middle of the seven-year treaty, at which time Antichrist will intercede to prevent Jews from sacrificing to God in the temple.

The 1,335 days include the 1,290 that Antichrist will be in the temple. Then 45 more days dedicated to World War III are added, which also emphasize the remainder of the duration of heavenly intervention extended to the Jewish remnant in isolating them for 1,260 days from tribulation and wrath, including the horrors of this final 45 day phase of the Day of the Lord. These 1,335 days will bring the world right up against the doorknob on the door to the kingdom of God.

Mayan tradition, in expectation of a calamitous time at the end of the 6,000 years seems correct, as the Bible verifies it in great detail!

To measure time from beginning of the peace treaty to Antichrist's cessation of daily sacrificing, subtract the 1,335 days from the total days in seven years. Seven years = 2,555 days–1,335 days = 1,220 days remaining. Three 365-day years (3 x 365)=1,095 days subtracted from 1,220 = 125 days. Then convert the 125 days to months by dividing them by the average number of days in a month. This number is 30.4 days, which averages all months of a calendar year. It is found by dividing the 365 days of a year by 12 months, which equals 30.4 days per month. Divide the 125 days by the average number of days in a month, 30.4, which equals 4.11 months added to the 3 years, equals approximately 3 years and 4 months.

We have here roughly calculated the length of time from signing of the treaty between Israel and her enemies to when Antichrist will expel the Jews from their temple and move himself in to become God in his own sight; but in God's sight, the abomination of desolation.

We shall now measure this treachery from his takeover of the temple until the end of the Third World War, which by definition pinpoints the end of the seven-year treaty, the end of Daniel's seventieth week and the end of the 6,000 years as well! To do it, we subtract the days in 3 years (3 x 365 = 1,095 days) from the 1,335 days that Daniel 12:12 tells us will transpire from the act of Antichrist's treachery until the end of the war, which leaves 240 days. When we divide these remaining 240 days by the average number of days in a month, 30.4, this equals 7.89 months or approximately 8 months. So, here we have the 3 years and 8 months mentioned above. Now, one more step—if we add as below, we will prove our work! (Disclosure: Leap year days in 2008 and 2012 not considered, having no effect on the rough result in months).

> 3 years and 4.11 months = treaty to ending sacrifice and
> offering
> + 3 years and 7.89 months = ending sacrifice and offering
> to end of the 6,000 years

6 years and 12.00 months = last 7 years of current 6,000

Daniel 9:27 says of Antichrist:

> Then he shall confirm a covenant with many for one week; but in
> the middle of the week He shall bring an end to sacrifice and of-
> fering. And on the wing of abominations shall be one who makes
> desolate, even until the consummation, which is determined, is
> poured out on the desolate.

The two periods of time reviewed above place violation of the treaty well within the middle part of the seven-year week as in the Scripture above. Since the prophecy did not specify at midpoint, then being two months off dead center in either direction still places the act of treachery well within the specified middle section of the week.

Looked at another way, the treachery will take place on Wednesday; the middle day (year) of the week. The prophecy does not say, "at 12:00 noon on Wednesday"; it says the middle of the week—that is Wednesday! Two months off center still places the treachery of Antichrist in the middle day/year of the week!

A caveat: Should the accord be continuous, or with a renegotiation point set for longer than seven years, or none at all, the end of the seventieth week, God's stated ending point will overrule man's intent!

# CHAPTER FIFTEEN

# TOUCHING ON
# WORLD WAR III

When Jesus returns, He will collect His own, the saints, and together with all of these, go to Israel. Zechariah says:

> And in that day His feet will stand on the Mount of Olives, which faces Jerusalem on the east. And the Mount of Olives shall be split in two, from east to west, making a very large valley; half of the mountain shall move toward the north and half of it toward the south.

> Then you [Jewish remnant] shall flee through My mountain valley, for the mountain valley shall reach to Azal. Yes, you shall flee as you fled from the earthquake in the days of Uzziah King of Judah. Thus the LORD my God will come, and all the saints with you.

> It shall come to pass in that day that there will be no light; the lights will diminish. [Source of the darkness will be identified] (Zechariah 14:4–6). Here is reference to Jesus' return in the Day of the Lord; a day of reduced light.

So here we see that Jesus will return, gather up the saints, and all will go to the Mount of Olives, which shall be split in two the same hour by a great earthquake. The valley to result from this jolt will provide a means of escape for the Jewish remnant into Jordan. To be brought through God's wrath upon the nations that will fight there in Israel, and to be sustained in Jordan until the end of the war. Then to reenter Israel and embark upon the first 1,000-year leg of their eternal journey with Jesus, their Messiah! The Zechariah verses above present the opportunity to clarify the meaning of Mathew 24:15–16, which in verse 15 states:

> "Therefore when you see the 'abomination of desolation,' spoken of by Daniel the prophet, standing [continuing] in the holy place" (whoever reads, let him understand), (NKJV).

The Greek word for standing, or stand, used in the (KJV) as rendered by Strong's Concordance is "histemi". This word has several meanings other than stand, or standing. One of these is "continue" or "continuing", which is, it seems, the correct way to interpret it in the verse above.

Keeping in mind, (Antichrist continuing in the holy place of the temple after a great earthquake) Matthew 24:16 says:

> "then let those who are in Judea flee to the mountains. (NKJV).

The (KJV) uses "flee into the mountains", as in entering into the mountains. The Greek word for both to and into is "eis". We will see this word again in another critical circumstance later in this writing. It indicates the point reached or entered of place or time. It can also mean (unto, throughout).

Now, in Revelation 11:7-13, the two witnesses who we will see in detail later, but whom, for our purpose here, we shall look at only briefly, relative to the end of their 1,260 days of ministry to show the following:

Verse 7 tells that at the end of their ministry they will be killed by the forces of Antichrist.

Verses 8 and 9 tell that their dead bodies will be left lying in a street of Jerusalem for three-and-a-half days and not be put into graves.

Verses 10, 11, and 12 describe how, after the three-and-a-half days, the breath of life from God entered them and they stood on their feet. They heard a loud voice from heaven saying to them, "Come up here." and they ascended to heaven in a cloud, and their enemies saw them. (This is a microcosm, and a part of the Resurrection at Christ's return).

Verse 13 says that in the same hour there was a great earthquake, and a tenth of Jerusalem fell with the loss of seven thousand lives.

Revelation 16:18-19 tell about an earthquake, which we perceve to be this earthquake, as being the greatest to ever strike since men have been on the earth. Jerusalem will be raised up and divided into three parts later by God as He establishes boundries of His millennial holy district on the newly created mountain top (See Table #4).

Now, back to Zechariah 14:10 where it tells about what we will come to see as being this great earthquake:

All the land shall be turned into a plain from Geba [north] to Rimmon south of Jerusalem. Jerusalem shall be raised up and inhabited in her place from Benjamin's Gate to the place of the First Gate and the Corner Gate, and from the Tower of Hananeel to the king's winepresses.

This area is the temple mount. So at Jesus' return and in the same hour, a great earthquake will strike Jerusalem, splitting the Mount of Olives into two parts as the city is raised up. The temple mount being in one of the later to be designated three parts of the mountain top will carry up with it as it is elevated, the newly constructed temple of God, having been taken over by Antichrist. But could the temple survive such an upheaval? Precast, steel reinforced concrete tilt-up construction is very strong. The precast panels can be constructed elsewhere, hauled by truck to the building site, and installed very quickly on a previously prepared concrete footing. With the modest size that space constraints dictate that this temple would need to be restricted to, it could be very strong and resilient to external stress.

If this is the way it will be, it is apparent then, that Antichrist will have survived the experience, and will be seen continuing in the holy place of the elevated temple.
Matthew 24:16 says:

Then let those who are in Judea [God's Jewish remnant] flee to [into, through] the mountains.

The case is here being made, that these mountains are the two mounts that the Mount of Olives will be divided into by the great earthquake. The valley to result will lead them to safety in Jordan; there, to be watched over by the archangel Michael until after God's wrath is complete, that is: "For then there will be great tribulation, such as has not been since the beginning of the world until this time, no, nor shall ever be (Matthew 24:21). And which will be finished with the terrible battle of Armageddon!

Going back to Daniel 12:1 once more: "And at that time [wrath of God] your people [remnant] shall be delivered, every one who is found written in the book [God knows each one!].

The book of Zechariah has some interesting things to say about Israel defending herself at the time of Armageddon. Zechariah 9:13 lays the groundwork for the destruction of the armies of the nations arrayed against Israel in that end time: "For I have bent Judah, My bow, fitted the bow with Ephraim, and raised up your sons, O Zion, against your sons, O Greece, and made you like the sword of a mighty man."

Here is clear reference to Antichrist and all forces in the Armageddon destruction; with God clearly stating that He will raise up His people, the House of Judah, and the House of Israel (Ephraim) that together make up Zion. He will make them like the sword of a mighty man against the sons of Greece. These, the invading armies, are all represented by Antichrist and called "sons of Greece" due to the Antiochus IV Epiphanes connection. All are puppets of the spirit that indwells Antichrist, and which can be seen manifested as hate. Hate, not only for Israel, but which on the battlefield, will become a blinding force used creatively by God in confusing the armies; to mistake friend for foe, thus a setup for the sons of Zion! Zechariah continues in his prophecy of Armageddon in 12:6:

> In that day [Day of the Lord] I will make the governors [Israeli army officers] of Judah like a firepan in the woodpile, and like a fiery torch in the sheaves; they shall devour all the surrounding peoples on the right hand and on the left, but Jerusalem shall be inhabited again in her own place; Jerusalem.

Zechariah 12:8 continues:

> In that day the LORD will defend the inhabitants of Jerusalem; the one who is feeble among them in that day shall be like David, and the house of David shall be like God, like the Angel of the LORD before them.

So here we find Jesus, the Angel of the LORD, going before Israel to give the enemy into her hand. He will strike her enemies with confusion. Zechariah 12:4: "'In that day,' says the Lord, 'I will strike every horse with confusion, and its rider with madness; I will open My eyes on the House of Judah, and will strike every horse of the peoples with blindness.'"

God's Word goes on to say in Zechariah 14:13–14: "It shall come to pass in that day that a great panic from the Lord will be among them. Everyone will seize the hand of his neighbor, and raise his hand against his neighbor's hand; Judah also will fight at

Jerusalem. And the wealth of all the surrounding nations shall be gathered together: gold, silver, and apparel in great abundance."

The prophet Ezekiel has much to say about this end time Battle of Armageddon, and the aftermath as it relates to Israel. Ezekiel 37:25 foretells concerning the remnant dwelling in the Promised Land after being brought safely through the battle:

> Then they shall dwell in the land that I have given to Jacob My servant, where your fathers dwelt; and they shall dwell there, they, their children, and their children's children, forever; and My servant David shall be their prince forever. [Reference to Jesus being descended from David.]

The nations that wish to take this land from Israel, either by negotiation or force, whichever method works, have not the slightest possibility of permanent success. For as we well know, God evicted the early settlers for having other gods before Him. He gave the land to Israel (Jacob's descendants) forever, to be under the rule of a descendant of David, Jesus Christ, Son of God. The ongoing effort to wrest control of this land away from Israel, as we surely now know, is doomed to failure. But yet much worse, the destruction of all those who try is signed, sealed, and assured by God that it will happen!

It is now appropriate to view several aspects of the war or battle we call Armageddon. This name comes from the ancient walled city of Megiddo, about fifty-five miles north of Jerusalem and situated on what was the main trade route between Egypt and Syria. This is the area that Revelation 16:16 refers to when it says: "And they gathered them together to the place called in Hebrew, Armageddon." The word *Armageddon* means Mountain of Megiddo. Zechariah 12:11 has this to say about this area: "In that day [Immediately after the annihilation of the armies that will attack Israel], there shall be a great mourning in Jerusalem, like the mourning at Hadad Rimmon in the plain of Megiddo" [Area now known as plain of Jezreel].[9]

There shall be a great mourning, not only by the remnant of Israel, for all those who will be lost in the fighting and the attack on Jerusalem, but also by survivors of those of the military forces that will invade Israel and die on the Plain of Jezreel. The surviving nations will mourn their dead, also.

Revelation 19:19–21 describes the scene this way:

And I saw the beast, the kings of the earth, and their armies, gathered together to make war against Him who sat on the horse [Jesus] and against His army [Israeli army].

Then the beast was captured, and with him the false prophet who worked signs in his presence, by which he deceived those who received the mark of the beast and those who worshiped his image. These two were cast alive into the lake of fire burning with brimstone.

And the rest were killed with the sword which proceeded from the mouth of Him who sat on the horse. And all the birds were filled with their flesh.

Here then is a symbolic description of that great coming battle. The apostle John, in Revelation, centers more around Jesus actively taking part, mounted on a horse and smiting the nations with the sword that proceeds from His mouth—speaking the defeat of the nations into effect, while empowering Israel to serve as the sword of destruction. Zechariah, we will recall, in 14:3, said much the same thing:

Then the LORD will go forth And fight against those nations, as He fights in the day of battle.

Zechariah then, however, described how the Lord's army, Israel, would be made up of both houses, Judah and Ephraim—the Lord's bow, Judah, fitted with the Lord's arrow, Ephraim. This army would be elevated to a position of total dominance over its enemies. As Zechariah 12:8 describes it:

> In that day the LORD will defend the inhabitants of Jerusalem; the one who is feeble among them in that day shall be like David, and the House of David [Israel] shall be like God, like the Angel of the LORD before them.

By looking at both Revelation and Zechariah we see the unmistakable picture of Israel, strengthened by Jesus, the Son of God, who will cause a strong spirit of confusion to descend upon the forces of the nations. This will bring them to attack one another, thus setting themselves up for total destruction by Israel.

This great congregation of armies is well documented in Bible prophecy. Revelation, true to its symbolic nature, in 16:12–14, tells of the way made clear for armies from the east to enter the Mid-East, intent upon protecting their vital interest in the then more precious than ever black gold of the Arabian Peninsula; a priceless treasure of national survival!

# CHAPTER SIXTEEN

# GOD'S JUDGMENT—PAST AND FUTURE

Satan, greed, and hate make a volatile mixture in these last days. Greed and hate are propagated by Satan and delivered to the nations by demons. World conditions are now developing that will shake this volatile mixture into a frothy and dangerous brew, which will blow up in a gigantic explosion, leveling the laboratory; thereby destroying the experimenters in the process.

We must read Revelation 16:12–14 (the vision) to see what it was that John saw:

> Then the sixth angel poured out his bowl on the great river Euphrates, and its water was dried up, so that the way of the kings from the east might be prepared.

> And I saw three unclean spirits like frogs coming out of the mouth of the dragon, out of the mouth of the beast, and out of the mouth of the false prophet.

> For they are spirits of demons, performing signs, which go out to the kings of the earth and of the whole world, to gather them to the battle of that great day of God Almighty.

This makes clear who and what will be behind the gathering together of this large number of armed men from all over the world. How large will the gathering be? For this answer we must read Revelation 9:13–16, in which John tells of the sixth trumpet judgment. This is another view of the sixth bowl judgment, which we just read in Revelation 16 above:

> Then the sixth angel sounded: And I heard a voice from the four horns of the golden altar which is before God
>
> saying to the sixth angel who had the trumpet, "Release the four angels who are bound at the great river Euphrates."
>
> So the four angels, who had been prepared for the hour and day and month and year, were released to kill a third of mankind.
>
> Now the number of the army of the horsemen was two hundred million; and I heard the number of them.

The two hundred million seems to more likely approximate the total number of fighting men of all armies that will be gathered there in Israel rather than just those from the east. Another consideration: the number of casualties in this terrible war comprising the balance of the prophesied sacrificial one third of world population above the two hundred million on the battlefield is what is today called collateral damage. (Too many WMD's not yet found!)

Earlier, the identity of Mystery Babylon the Great, the mighty market to the world, was biblically seen to be the U.S.A. We will recall also what Revelation 17:16 had to say: "And the ten horns which you saw on the beast, these will hate the harlot, make her desolate and naked, eat her flesh and burn her with fire." This prophecy, written almost two thousand years ago for our time, is a completely realistic depiction of a nuclear attack! (How much hate would it take?)

We will see later from the Bible that this attack on America will take place in the Day of the Lord, within the six months of God's

96

wrath, but before the war of Armageddon. The entire chapter of Revelation 18 is devoted to graphic details of Mystery Babylon the Great's destruction. Verse 8, however, boils it down to this: "Therefore her plagues will come in one day—death and mourning and famine. And she will be utterly burned with fire, for strong is the Lord God who judges her."

The historical fact is well evident—throughout the Old Testament—where time and time again God destroyed nations that turned their backs on Him as America is now doing. Think of how He used Israel to destroy the nations in and around the land of Canaan. God gave Israel their land and gave them into Israel's hand because they had turned their backs on Him and did detestable things in His sight. Even though Israel was and still is His chosen people, He used other nations to severely chastise her when she turned her back on Him and engaged in detestable practices. This happened time after time. As we know, God used one nation or empire to destroy another. For example: Assyria to destroy Israel (Samaria, the northern kingdom), and Babylon to destroy, or almost so, Judah (the southern kingdom). One empire set against another in a series of chastisements, with God using one pagan empire after another as His rod of iron to subjugate these wayward pagan powers because they refused to worship Him, their Creator!

More recently we will recall Germany under the Kaiser and then under Hitler, Italy and Japan—all severely dealt with by God, using other nations including the U.S.A.

Is America any different? Can she negotiate a settlement with God? Will she even try? America can sidestep God's judgment, bring glory to God, and at the same time salvage her soul and escape sudden destruction. How? *Repentance*; that is true repentance, that which will bring about a reversal in national direction. America is sick. The blood of fifty million dead babies sacrificed on the altar of convenience. *A lot of blood on her hands!* And, the pitiful results of teaching young minds in her tax-supported public schools *That mankind evolved from slime, and the creator God is not allowed on the premises!*

In Israel's long history, she more than once received a reprieve from God's planned destruction by repenting and following His ways. But sooner or later God's chosen nation would fall and destruction would take a heavy toll.

Does the Bible tell of any instance in which God called off judgment of a Gentile state because the people repented and turned to God? Yes, you probably remember Jonah. God had asked him to go to Nineveh, the capital city of the Assyrian Empire that was prominent in Jonah's day. Nineveh had been founded by Nimrod, builder of the Tower of Babel, and was by this time in deep trouble with God for the common sin of the day: pagan idol worship and all the associated detestable practices that went along with this abomination.

Jonah was chosen by God to carry His message of sure destruction of the city if the people did not repent and turn to God. Jonah was not real excited about this assignment, and tried to run rather than carry out this task, which was not without risk. You may remember that he came to be on a ship in a severe storm, and was thrown overboard by the crew in an attempt to appease God; because Jonah had told them that it was because of him that God had brought on the storm.

God had not given up on Jonah and worked out his rescue by bringing a whale along at just the right time to swallow him, preserve his life while in its stomach, and eventually, after three days and three nights, spew Jonah onto a beach.

Jonah then agreed to carry God's warning message to the city of Nineveh. He did so and told them that in forty days they would be overthrown. The king and all the people feared God, and the king proclaimed a fast and repentance:

But let man and beast be covered with sackcloth, and cry mightily to God; yes, let every one turn from his evil way and from the violence that is in his hands (Jonah 3:8).

Verse 10 shows the result of their crying to God, and their true repentance in turning from their evil ways:

Then God saw their works, that they turned from their evil way; and God relented from the disaster that He had said He would bring upon them, and He did not do it (Jonah 3:10).

It is desirable to believe that God will relent in His prophesied destruction of Mystery Babylon, because the nation will repent, cease from her evil ways, turn back to God, and ask God for forgiveness. With the Bible, God's Word, devoting the entirety of Revelation 18 to detailing the aspects of this swift and sure punishment of the great harlot, this makes it quite clear that national repentance will not be forthcoming!

God, however, has not turned His back on the people of the country. Individually, each and every resident of this judged nation has it within his or her power to be miraculously saved from this coming judgment. Here is what God says to us, those living here and elsewhere, concerning transgressions and the wrath that she faces:

And I heard another voice from heaven saying, "Come out of her, my people, lest you share in her sins, and lest you receive of her plagues" (Revelation 18:4).

Fortunately for us, we have something available to us today that the people of Nineveh did not have. Their situation was that they had to all win together or they must all lose together. Had they not all repented, turned from doing evil, and worshipped God rather than idols, they would all have been receivers of God's punishment for the unrepentant sin.

Since then, God sent His Son Jesus into the world to establish His church, give His life as redemption for the sins of others and, thus create a new covenant with mankind to replace the penalty of the law with *grace*. This new covenant then, is contained in and sustained by *the grace of God*. The new covenant is made available to all who are called by the gospel of Jesus Christ. All that is necessary is:

A.  Repent of sin—that is, simply be sincerely sorry or repentant and desire to stop sinning. What exactly is sin? We are all born with a sin nature, which we cannot shed like a snake sheds its skin. We are stuck with it even after we make the conscious decision to stop sinning—breaking God's law. We are, however, no longer alone in our sins if we:

B.  Accept Jesus Christ as Lord and Savior. God then sends His Holy Spirit to dwell within us. The Holy Spirit, if we allow Him, will lead us in changing the way we live our lives so that we will please the Lord. He will lead us through God's Word, the Bible, so that we will begin to learn God's ways and know what it is that He expects of us.

This is what God is telling all people everywhere, in Revelation 18:4: "Come out of her, my people, lest you share in her sins, and lest you receive of her plagues."

God knows who will come to Him, and here calls them: His people. These are the ones who will listen to Him. So when He says "come out of her" He is telling His people everywhere to be careful, very careful, not to partake of the harlot's sins; to avoid sharing in the wrath to fall on those oblivious of the Word of God, who believe Satan's lies, and who are on the wide and smooth highway to destruction.

Anyone who hears the gospel of Jesus Christ can come to Him and be saved from the wrath of God which will soon fall on

America and the entire world. So hiding from it is out of the question. Accepting Jesus Christ as our personal savior provides us with a compound benefit. First, if it is from the heart, sincere and true, God's grace provides eternal salvation from our sins. Without *God's grace*, available only by accepting Jesus' cleansing act on the cross, sin amounts to a death sentence to the soul. Second, the other realized benefit lies in the Resurrection at Jesus' return: *we shall avoid the wrath!*

# CHAPTER SEVENTEEN

# BIBLE PROPHECY—RARE TRUTH FOR OUR TIME

We could borrow a line from a popular 1940's song: "It's a Barnum and Bailey world, just as phony as it can be." This clearly defines the scene of today! Much of what we hear and read now is phony, contrived, misrepresented, and dead wrong. In other words, we are being lied to, misled, lured, and manipulated for the predetermined gain of others. On top of that, we are subjected to a sustained barrage of unintentional misinformation coming from all quarters by well-meaning people.

Is it any wonder that some today find it difficult to believe in Jesus Christ, and simply can't bring themselves to believe what they read or hear read from the Bible? God's Word is difficult to understand, was written a long time ago with language and sentence structure sometimes different from that in use today. This inspired Word of God is also a casualty of the misinformation express running rampant among us. Those who choose to be anti-Christian will, however, at times, cherry pick Bible verses that lend support to a favored point of view, while rejecting the Bible in general as a God–given lifeline to mankind.

Those misguided, deluded, and truthfully challenged are caught up in the worldly web of demonic deception. This web is spun by exponents of various modern day equivalents of what God calls paganism. They work hard to spread their versions of commercially energized spiritual enlightenment, weighted heavily to reincarnation and self-realization. These dangerous perceptions are enthusiastically endorsed by the godless entertainment industry that preaches its various themes of violence, sex, and perversion. Those being influenced by these worldly distortions are being programmed to lose, and lose they will, unless they seek God's truth, find it in Christ, and take appropriate action.

Everyone wants to know the truth today, but few actually seek it out at its source. There are many nowadays who wish to find relevant truth which has something meaningful to offer them. And there are many who claim to have a corner on the truth. Some offer their spiritual solutions; while others promote their contradictions to biblical truth; and still others misinform millions, not by outright contradictions, but by misinterpreting Bible meaning in specific areas, while purporting to be adhering to the contextual intent of God's Word.

Why are so many people of all categories—the highly educated, the less educated, and the uneducated, the fortunate, the less fortunate, and the unfortunate—why are so many allowing themselves to be deceived by the practitioners of deception? The answer is evident. *People are turned off by the Bible!* Not everyone, of course, but too many. Why? For the reasons mentioned above; in a nutshell, *the Bible is hard to understand!* It was in part, purposely written that way. Remember Daniel 12:4? Daniel's end time prophecy was shut and sealed until that very time, our time. Will we see the seals unloosed and removed? If so, by whom? As we will see when we come to the seal judgments, there is only one who is worthy to open the scroll (book) and loose its seals. He is seen in Revelation 5, and is shown to us there as "a Lamb as though it had been slain." Only He is worthy to enlighten, which prompts the comment: but all are worthy to receive these truths! Some will seem troubling, but as you come to know and trust the Lamb, you will experience perfect peace, knowing that *the end justifies the means!*

Now to proceed. For those who are looking, it is not difficult to detect signs of end time activities being positioned for fulfillment of specific prophetic events. As a matter of fact, we can clearly see the accomplishment of several end time Bible prophecies relating to God's people, the Jews, and Israel as a nation. Only God's Word provides knowledge of future events with pinpoint accuracy, as noted with Tyre/U.S.A's seventy isolationist/protectionist years with minimal foreign involvement as she minded her own business. Fighting two major wars to protect her national sovereignty is protectionism; not harlotry! Her renewed harlotry, starting in 1947, resulted in her gain not being laid up for herself, but rather, flowing to and benefiting those who dwell before the Lord. God's rain falling on the just and the unjust alike. America's perceived good works have brought nothing but condemnation, ridicule, and in some cases, naked hate and loathing. Her pay, however, enumerated in her high-tech achievements bought a high living standard, which benefits those who dwell before the Lord. Prophecy fulfilled, just as presented in Isaiah 23:15–18.

It was said earlier that God punished Israel when He could stand her abominations with false gods no longer. He sent prophets to give her warning, which she mostly ignored, and so, at last her punishment would come.

Here we will look at prophetic fulfillments, several concerning the children of Israel, as relates to both the northern kingdom of Israel and the southern kingdom of Judah. In so doing, we shall see the precision of the fulfillment process. Having been made several thousand years ago especially for this end time in which we now live, these prophecies have been fulfilled in minute detail.

Biblical Last Days Prophetic Fulfillment.

Example One:

Did God, through His prophets, tell us in the pages of the Bible, after both houses of His chosen people had been carried away as captives and were scattered around the world, that He would bring them back into their promised land? Yes He did!

God said, speaking of Israel's restoration, in Isaiah 43:5–6: "Fear not, for I am with you; I will bring your descendants from the east, and gather you from the west; I will say to the north, 'Give them up!' And to the south, 'Do not keep them back!' Bring My sons from afar, and My daughters from the ends of the earth . . .'"

Everyone knows that God's people, the Jews, were brought back to what was known as Palestine. This land to which they returned is a part of their original land area and is located west of the Jordan River between the Jordan and the Mediterranean Sea. The original land of the Israelites included some of what is now the country of Jordan east of the Jordan River. This land was included in a mandate given to Great Britian by the League of Nations in 1920. Twenty-eight years later, in 1948, Britain gave up the area just described west of the Jordan River, but including only the west portion of Jerusalem for the Jews to establish— or more accurately—reestablish their homeland. A new nation of Israel was born, fulfilling God's prophecy in Isaiah 43:5–6 to bring back His sons from afar, and His daughters from the ends of the earth, the descendants of His people from the east, west, north, and south.

How did they come to be scattered around the world in the first place? We need only to look at Jeremiah 9:15–16 for the answer:

Therefore thus says the LORD of hosts, the God of Israel: "Behold, I will feed them, this people, with wormwood, and give them water of gall to drink.

"I will scatter them also among the Gentiles, whom neither they nor their fathers have known. And I will send a sword after them until I have consumed them." [The holocaust would qualify!]

Why was God so angry with His people? The reason is simple; yet, very serious. God's chosen people turned their backs on Him and worshipped idols. They deserted Him after all He had done for them; the miracles He had performed for them, and all the times He had delivered them out of the hands of their enemies. These things were not remembered, and they fell victim to the perverted, sexual, idol-worship practices of their pagan Gentile neighbors. God put it this way in Jeremiah 9:13–14:

> And the LORD said, "Because they have forsaken My law which I set before them, and have not obeyed My voice, nor walked according to it, but they have walked according to the dictates of their own hearts and after the Baals, which their fathers taught them."

God gave His people a good deal of time to straighten out, get right, to repent of their wicked ways, and turn back to Him. Those of the generation involved here were taught to worship idols by their fathers, so it had been going on for quite some time. God gave them numerous warnings through His prophets, but to no avail. He even pleaded with them, saying in Jeremiah 6:16:

> Thus says the LORD: "Stand in the ways and see, and ask for the old paths, where the good way is, and walk in it; then you will find rest for your souls." But they said, "We will not walk in it."

Does any of this sound familiar? No question about it; it does! It is clear that America is making the same mistake made by ancient Israel, that of rejecting God. The rejection of God by America is quite similar to that of ancient Israel; because both nations were brought into being by the will and ingenuity of almighty God. American secular humanists, atheists, and the like do not enjoy hearing that America was founded as a Christian nation. It is, nevertheless, true! America was settled and founded by Christians looking for freedom to worship God according to their Christian beliefs. The country thrived under Christian leadership and nurturing, and became the great nation that it was in the first half of the Twentieth Century.

It was shortly after World War II that the Marxist, atheist inspired humanism with global overtones, so generously sown in the 1920's and 1930's by numerous Communist front organizations, began to gain control of government, public education, the entertainment industry, the advertising industry, and the news industry.

Much maligned Senator Joseph McCarthy and his Senate Committee on Un-American Activities in the fifties, uncovered hundreds of Communists who had infiltrated the U.S. government and were quietly working toward socialist secular globalism. He was hounded by the leftist press, the leftist liberal establishment, and leftist members of Congress for conducting a witch hunt. Very little came of his efforts. It is now generally known that Joseph McCarthy was absolutely correct; the U.S. government was riddled with Communists. We now confront the fruit of their labor in the symptoms of moral rot, decay in public education, depravity of salacious hardcore pornography available to any interested person, and the steady movement by America *toward, but not into* a Marxist, One World Government. The 9/11/01 Trade Center attack has become the trigger to unleash America in a determined campaign *to make the world safe for global government.* (Tinhorn, despotic dictators—beware!) To act while the iron is hot, so to speak, seems to describe America's war on obstacles to global union. This early stage of international housecleaning to root out global irritants, has Afghanistan first to fall under the onslaught of a tenuous, but nevertheless, unified globally acceptable pest control program. Iraq is now being brought into the family of global nations, and it seems that Syria, Iran, Pakistan, North Korea, Libya, and Cuba may be seeing the handwriting on the wall!

Now at a crossroads without a strong leader, the UN is becoming seen as being less and less relevant in a more and more constricting global family having greatly divergent national interests. A leadership vacuum exists, which is presently being inappreciatively filled by the United States in her attempt to unilaterally, if necessary, smooth out the bumps in the road to global harmony. Observation: the United Nations and the world seem ripe for a steady hand to take charge in bringing unity in the sea of divergent national currents. The UN needs a strong, politically astute, morally unrestrained leader, someone to take charge and direct the world's engines of production all in the same direction. Will someone with these qualifications soon be forthcoming? The Bible, with all the power of the Lord's omniscience says, "Yes!" It appears that the reported massive fraud coming to light in the UN controlled Iraq oil for food program, and then Secretary General's reported involvement in the unethical scheme to divert dollars from Iraq's needy into UN coffers and other questionable areas, may turn out to be a prophetic omen of coming events.

The previous Secretary General's term of office expired 12/31/2006. In mid-October, 2006 the UN Security Council nominated South Korean Foreign Minister, Ban Ki-moon to succeed the prior UN Secretary General, to be effective on January 1, 2007. The UN general assembly then confirmed the appointment leading to the second Asian to head this world body. Not since U Thant of Burma, over thirty years ago, has the UN had an Asian leader. Being Asian is said to have been a major criterion with a broad consensus within the UN for this selection. All 192 members of the general assembly, including the Vatican supported the nomination (BBC NEWS [Americas] 10/13/2006).

Since we are deeply involved in Bible prophecy here, we must go back to the Bible for an explanation of what may be involved. This writing makes the contention that a Secretary General of the United Nations will turn out to be the forthcoming biblically prophesied antichrist and that the one approved for the position mentioned above is not him. So, what is going on? The Bible, in 2 Thessalonians says that the coming of the lawless one is according to the working of Satan, with all power, signs, and lying wonders.

And with all unrighteous human deception. Need we go further? Most of the world will be fooled by the goings-on yet to unfold, but not all. When will the biblically described antichrist make his move to leadership of the world? See Table #1 for as accurate a timeline as presently possible.

America's current sickness emphasizes the result of godless Marxism. The removal of the influence of God and His Son Jesus from public view encourages the blooming of the *isms*. Humanism, atheism, and secularism, all nurtured and encouraged by Marxism. And then, in the glory of their *isms*, foment another *ism* as well; that being materialism. Marxism has no real quarrel with paganism either and, in fact, is partial to it for its smoke screen effect in blocking out the true light of Jesus Christ and God's saving grace. America's current *ism*-induced moral lapse has fostered many of her non-virtuous acts, some of which have been brought forward in this writing as excellent examples of evil being good and good being evil!

This generally describes end time America—flirting with Marxist globalism, and attempting to divest herself of true fundamental Christianity to make way for the new global religion. This new religious recreation, noting its regressive direction, exemplifies Darwinian evolution. Never mind the reality that mankind is not evolving upward, but rather, downward! The truth is, man's status in time is much different than what is generally taught; that man is and has, over millions of years, been moving upward from a humble beginning as a single cell life form to eventuate as the magnificent creature that he is today! A fairy tale; just the opposite is true!

# CHAPTER EIGHTEEN

# EVOLUTION, OR INVOLUTION AND EXPONENTIALISM?

The process affecting mankind is not as explained by Darwin's theory of macro-evolution as mentioned, but rather just the reverse. The process is more accurately called involution. Biologically, involution is a reversal of development, a degeneration of something, not mankind's improvement as Darwinian evolution's confused theory proclaims as fact. The truth is, that what is being passed off as evolving upward, is in reality involving downward!

Involution explains the process that has been at work for the past six thousand years! Man was made a perfect creation, in control of a perfect environment. When sin entered into this once-perfect laboratory, involution began its painful journey into and throughout all three of man's once-faultless faculties. Physically, mentally, and spiritually, he began to degenerate!

Man is a physical, spiritual being. Sin is like a virulent, lethal bacterium that is out there being expelled *en masse* from the source of all sin, a spiritually ill spirit. Satan, masquerading as the angel of light, actually functions as a terminally ill host to a deadly and contagious disease. He mingles freely with mankind, coughing and sneezing profusely, effectively ejecting his contagious pathogens as a fog of highly infectious bacteria in the paths of unsuspecting human beings. All people on the face of the earth become terminally ill. Fortunately, there is a new cure; a strong, natural antibiotic that replaces the earlier method of animal sacrifice, which can reasonably be equated with use of mechanically pulverized colloidal silver; a less efficient antibiotic formulation without the spectacular strength of its new replacement.

Jesus Christ, effectively relating as the modern electrically generated colloidal silver, a powerful natural antibiotic (denigration of this modern miracle by the ill-informed, notwithstanding), if directions are followed, will knock out the infection. This miracle cure will not only improve one's quality of life while continuing on an outpatient basis; receiving periodic doses, but the prognosis for a superior quality of life extending into and throughout eternity is excellent!

In the beginning man was smarter, healthier, and physically stronger than today. Early on, in the post-creation years, before sin's destructive influence was transmitted sufficiently down through the generations for its debilitating consequences to have taken a very big toll on his longevity potential, his perfection quotient outwardly, was largely intact. Inwardly, however, sin at that time was concentrating its destructive influence primarily in man's spiritual realm; and he was progressively losing favor with God. Nevertheless, at that early stage of man's six thousand year history, he was still inherently healthier, physically stronger, and intellectually smarter than we. He was bright enough to build the Tower of Babel, with its top in the heavens; no small task. And if it had not reached very high, with the potential for greater height, and for the fostering of problematic, unrestrained unity among men God would not have been concerned with it. The fact is, Genesis 11:1–9 tells how man, being one (of one mind), with one language, and in so many words, tells, "That under these circumstances, man's potential to get into trouble is greatly enhanced. And that he does not have the self-control to restrain himself from anything—from being captivated by the imaginations of his own heart." With Satan's influence in the world for man to contend with, this was a dangerous combination! Not dissimilar to man's current love affair with oneness, emphasized by his all-out attempt to slam dunk the world into a one world, Marxist utopia, and with Satan's influence spurring him on!

God's reasoning in confusing man's universal language was to slow down his descent into one gigantic cesspool. Comment: it did slow the process, however, it did not stop it. God's upcoming intervention, according to Bible prophecy, will this time, stop it in its tracks!

Noah's mental and physical abilities were great also. He was smart and strong enough, at the ripe old age of somewhere between five hundred and six hundred years, without the benefit of a chain saw, a circular saw, or tractor with power takeoff to run a lumber milling saw, or anything else that we have at our disposal, to build a gigantic ocean going freighter!

You may say: "Well that's fine, but where is the proof?" Well then, this person would say to that person: "What about the Egyptian pyramids?" No, it was not galactic aliens who gave the Egyptians the information to perform these remarkable feats of construction. Feats that we today are unable to figure out how they did the work, let alone being able to do it without modern heavy equipment using computer-enhanced engineering and architectural calculations and drawings! "Ah," you might say, "I've got you now! We couldn't have accomplished all the technological, medical, manufacturing, communications, transportation, etc., breakthroughs and advancements we have today unless we were smarter than the ancients!"

The answer to that can be summed up with one word: exponential! Despite the fact that the sin sown in the beginning, like a little yeast, working its way through the entire batch, is degenerating mankind in all categories, mankind has yet one thing going for it. The power of exponentialism. It has taken man six thousand years to reach the peak of technological perfection, at which point, he now proudly proclaims himself to be god-like. Even with the benefit of having one invention to build another upon, over, and over, and over, down through the years, man has, little by little, been losing his intellectual acumen. Not that he is becoming stupid; he has been mentally keen enough to figure out how to have artificial intelligence do the heavy work for him! So the adverse effect of sin has been counterbalanced by the simple fact of exponential increase in man's accomplishments; including his ability to develop more and better cures for maintaining his physical health.

We now find ourselves in a period of runaway exponentialism. The first 5,800 years, to Franklin's experiments with electricity, have established the foundation that the remaining 200 years of rapid technological expansion are built upon. It will be temporarily halted at the end of the 6,000 years, to no doubt, be up and running again sometime later in a sin-free environment! It seems techno-advancement may then go ballistic!

The point of it boiled down is that modern man did not, over millions of years, gradually, through accidental change, after change, after change, magically knit himself together from a single-cell life form into mankind as it exists today. The fact is, some things are impossible, and this hypothesis, theory, better known as an assumption, falls into that category. It is impossible! For example: You place a ball of yarn on the ground; then you sit back and wait. How many years will you have to wait, while the yarn experiences all the many changes and effects of a temperamental environment, for it to knit itself into a sweater? Probably not a thousand. How about a million? Well, if not a million, surely a billion years. We can go on, but what for? That ball of yarn ain't never going to knit itself into a sweater! You might say: "Yes, but the single-cell life form was life, while the yarn is not alive." Answer: The complexity of the human body, the earth, and the universe completely preclude any feasibility, whatsoever, that these magnificently designed creations were accidently created by periods of nonthinking time, no matter how long in combination with a nonthinking environment. That is like throwing paint against the wall expecting to produce the Mona Lisa.

It could be compared also, to early Israel's pagan neighbors. God kept warning the Israelites that the Gentiles' idols, in so many words, could not think to be able to talk, or walk, or do anything else!

Long periods of time by some today are given credit for being able to think, and so, it seems, fit neatly into the idol category.

If something is not alive, only God can infuse it with life. Time cannot do it! The magic formula for evolutionists is totally contained in time. Since their macro theory cannot be proven or observed, they take refuge in long periods of time; so they say anything they want, and there are no rebuttal witnesses except the fossil record.

When the fossil record is correctly read, the Bible's very clear description of a worldwide flood is upheld. For example: fish fossils on mountaintops and fossilized tree trunks, called polystrate fossils (many strata), are found all over the world. Why are these upright, buried tree trunks important? Since they extend up through multiple rock layers (strata) creationists see this as evidence of a global flood; with the waters having laid down layer upon layer of sediment in a very short time. The tree trunks were not disturbed; and so, can be seen in excavations to this day, still standing where they stood when suddenly they became submerged and preserved. If millions of years-long ages had transpired from layer to layer, the tree trunks would have been worn down. In fact, the tree trunks would have become dust within the first one or two hundred years; the trunks would not be there.[10]

Not just one, but two bodies of evidence exist. Which are we to believe? Darwin's evolution is reliant upon billions of years to get earth, the universe, and man up to the point that they are today. And in man's case, evolutionists cannot yet explain where that live one-cell life form came from. In the case of the universe and earth, they haven't told us either, where all that matter came from that was supposed to be around somewhere when the big bang occurred. There is a bumper sticker out there that says it best: "God said 'BANG' and it happened!" (bumper sticker from Answers in Genesis ministry update bulletin).

Just giving it serious thought tells us that the theory of long periods of time making things better has a big hole in it. What have you seen that gets better with age other than steak, wine, and cheese? And, of course, our taste buds prefer the age-caused breakdown of sugars, proteins, etc. in the decomposition process. This is not evolution; this is involution! And then the ultimate end that we have all seen, or know to be true, mold, decay, and rot!

Another thought: for every argument that Darwinian evolution raises to back its defunct theory, creation has a clear, straightforward rebuttal. So, you might ask, "Why is evolution taught in public schools as fact, without any mention of creation as an alternative?" It all has to do with humanism. The humanist individual, not wishing to subject himself/herself to a higher moral authority, is grasping at straws and gladly accepts the theory of evolution as a foundational means of proving that God does not exist.

If a reasonable sounding hypothesis can be put forward and presented as fact, and people accept it as fact, what difference does it make if it is fact or not? This is the humanist doctrine. If there is no God (higher moral authority), then the humanist can live according to the imaginations of his own heart. He is very protective of this new foundational premise, and will go to any length to advance it and protect it from being challenged and quite likely disproven. That, in all reality, is why creation is not being taught in public schools today! Humanists are deathly afraid of what they fear might prove to be the truth, and they want you to have no exposure to it. Science museums also fall into this category, and make no attempt to show an alternative answer to the very serious two-part question of how did life come to be on our planet and how did the planet come to be here in the first place?

If we don't want a certain thing to be true, we don't present it as a competitive alternative to our pet view! This sums up the rationale which effectively prevents creation from being taught in the classroom or even brought to the public's attention elsewhere. The same mentality explains why safe sex is promoted in public schools, and abstinence is not mentioned, except in a few locations where parents went to the wall against the school boards and made a difference.

One very telling field of evolutionary conjecture is seen in the mysteriously missing, "missing link" controversy. If, as the Darwinian evolution, macro theory states, "that all living things evolved from a common ancestor", where is the fossil evidence? Where are all the different and various fossils of transitional kinds that, if this were true, would of necessity, need to be plentifully dispersed around the world? Where are the tree people fossils, the bird people fossils, the fish people fossils? Not even one little mermaid fossil can they produce to support their theory!

They say then, that man is supposed to have evolved from apes. Then where are the tree ape fossils, the bird ape fossils, the fish ape fossils? It seems that their theory is akin to the bigfoot mystery; none of his fossils have ever been found either!

The evolutionists have a lot of trouble in this area; however there are some fine artists, with creative minds within their ranks. From a single tooth, a subhuman, apelike creature and its mate were drawn and named, and then presented to the world as proof of man's evolutionary ascendancy from apes. It was considerably later that the tooth was finally discovered to be that of a pig. However, during the time of its exploitation, many people were taught that the human race evolved from apes.

An example of this creative ability also was produced in picture form from as little as a skullcap and the fragment of a jawbone with teeth. This fossil evidence was used as well, to produce a picture of a subhuman, apelike creature, and widely presented to the world as proof of man's evolutionary relationship to apes. The skullcap was later found to be that of a human, and the jawbone was found to be that of a female orangutan.

In summary, we can come away with these distinctions: Darwinian evolutionist's theory of macro evolution (the origin of major kinds), says that all living things evolved over billions of years from a common ancestor. This requires that people and trees have a common mother. It requires also that life entered something and it became alive. How did it happen? According to the theory—by billions of years. Then billions of years is their god and they teach religion in public schools!

Another questionable area of evolutionary transparency resides in the inexact science of using index fossils to date rocks and rock strata. First of all, sedimentary rocks, which contain the fossils, cannot be dated with the radioisotope method. Since the evolution theory holds that life forms become more complex with the passing of time (millions of years), they expect to find the simplest life forms at the bottom of a sedimentary dig. They select certain fossils as index fossils, which progressively show more complexity in their composition, as they are found ever closer to the surface. Then, the layered fossils are each given a subjective number of years that establishes the age of the rock stratum in which each is found, with the simplest at the bottom, progressively becoming younger and more complex as they are found nearer to the surface. So, with these subjective dates, each rock stratum is dated by the index fossil found within it.

This is questionable at the least. Did anyone stop to think that the more complexly developed and adaptable an organism is, the longer it could hold out against the raging currents of the seething, boiling, roiling flood waters as they swept everything that wasn't nailed down (like trees) before them. The most complex creatures would be the last to succumb to the raging soil-filled waters as the heavily silted currents sucked down the simplest first, and then engulfed the next least able to survive, on up the chain to the very most able.[11]

There are many interesting sidelights in the checkered past of the Darwinian theory of evolution as it has progressed down through the years. For those who are interested, and wish to more fully differentiate between truth and fiction, there is a great body of evidence supporting creation. Do yourself a favor and become more scientifically knowledgeable in preparation to win in this life and death struggle with the forces of darkness. They have brought the battle to you. They intend for you to believe as they do.

Strengthened understanding of creation as presented in Genesis, the first book of the Bible can be achieved by even minimal exposure to scientific evidence supporting the creation approach to how and why we are here. This provides the means to enable us to remove, brick by brick, the wall erected by the mistaken between the reality of God's truth and their version, which elevates fiction to a position of dominance over fact.

Many believe by faith and do not need to see the scientific evidence. If you do not yet fit into this category, compelling evidence is out there. *Go for it!*

# CHAPTER NINETEEN

# BACK TO FULFILLED PROPHECY IN OUR TIME

So then, this end time human condition that permeates all societies of the world, with special emphasis on that of America, we will see, was prophesied for this specific time in history almost two thousand years ago by Paul, the apostle to the Gentiles.

Biblical Last Days Prophetic Fulfillment.
Example Number Two:
Paul, in 2 Timothy 3:1–5 describes the end time morality, and the humanist-propagated mentality that now grips the world. We read Paul's words:

But know this, that in the last days perilous times will come:

For men will be lovers of themselves, lovers of money, boasters, proud, blasphemers, disobedient to parents, unthankful, unholy,

unloving, unforgiving, slanderers, without self-control, brutal, despisers of good,

traitors, headstrong, haughty, lovers of pleasure rather than lovers of God,

having a form of godliness but denying its power. And from such people turn away!

Hollywood considers these deviant behaviors to be realism, typical of modern mankind and worthy of exploiting at every opportunity. The entertainment industry is unknowingly advancing fulfillment of Paul's prophecy! Result: prophecy fulfilled. A key point made by Paul above for our purpose here is: "having a form of godliness but denying its power."

This shortcoming describes perfectly the One World Religion, wherein God is worshipped by all major religions that worship a god, but which relegates Jesus down to the status of a wise teacher and a prophet. God's Word teaches that Jesus is the Son of God, and as such is part of the Trinity; that being God in three persons; God the Father, God the Son, and God the Holy Spirit!

Jesus then becomes a stumbling block to the new, tolerant, big tent, global religion being patched together. This combining and joining activity of breaking down doctrinal barriers and establishing rapport and common ground among the world's religions is moving forward rapidly. No one is considered *persona non grata* except fundamental Christians—*those who believe the Bible says what it means and means what it says!*

The global religion features the same god for all people. As the story goes, "all religions worship the same god anyway; just by different names (how convenient)." Absolutely nothing could be further from the truth! The Trinity Godhead has no connection to any of the countless Hindu gods; the millions of Shinto gods, or to the god of any other religion, or to the god of any cult. Heretofore, rigid, intolerant differences in beliefs are being greatly softened, to bring this once-factional group together into one body, under one generally accepted supreme leader—very likely a pope. Revelation 13:11 refers to this religious leader as "the beast coming up out of the earth." He is also called the false prophet in Revelation 19:20. His appearance on the world scene seemingly can not be far off!

Biblical Prophetic Fulfillment.
Example Number Three:

The apostle Peter, in 1 Peter 2:6, referring to Isaiah 28:16, said this:

"Behold, I lay in Zion a chief cornerstone, elect, precious, and he who believes on Him will by no means be put to shame."

Peter continued talking about this stone (Jesus):

Therefore, to you who believe, He is precious; but to those who are disobedient, "The stone which the builders rejected Has become the chief cornerstone,"

and "A stone of stumbling and a rock of offense." They stumble, being disobedient to the word, to which they also were appointed (1 Peter 2:7–8).

Peter is quoting Psalm 118:22 and Isaiah 8:14. Both the writer of the psalm and Isaiah were addressing the houses of Israel and Judah in these prophetic statements concerning their future rejection of the Messiah. This, we know, came to pass at His first coming—prophecy fulfilled!

Biblical Last Days Prophetic Fulfillment.
Example Number Four:
The prophecy (Isaiah 8:14) which says that Jesus will become a stone of stumbling, which we call a stumbling block today, is again being fulfilled in our time regarding His rejection by the new world religion. So then, this prophecy is seeing fulfillment a second time—in our time.

A fifth prophecy, from the pages of the Bible, having meaning for our time and which is now being fulfilled, pertains to the rejection of Jesus Christ as the Creator and Destroyer by flood, of His own creation. Then, too, as the power behind a prophesied, yet to come, cleansing destruction of the same creation. Second Peter 3:3–4, speaking to Christians about the last days says:

knowing this first: that scoffers will come in the last days, walking according to their own lusts

and saying, "Where is the promise of His coming? For since the fathers fell asleep, all things continue as they were from the beginning of creation [evolution]."

The Greek word for creation *ktisis*, can also mean formation, and ordinance. A dictionary meaning of *ordinance* is a system of arrangement. A dictionary meaning of *arrange* is to put in *a proper order*. So it seems that without the word evolution, Peter used the Greek term for what we call evolution today, but which could just as well mean creation. (Since time can't think, it can not put in proper order, but is, nevertheless, given credit for doing so by Darwinian evolutionists; natural selection and mutation occurs only within kinds; think about it!)

Peter continues:

For this they willfully forget: that by the word of God the heavens were of old, and the earth standing out of water and in the water,

by which the world that then existed perished, being flooded with water.

But the heavens and the earth which now exist are kept in store by the same word, reserved for fire until the day of judgment and perdition of ungodly men (2 Peter 3:5–7).

Peter knew what was to come in the last days: the truth of the Genesis account of creation and the flood would be denied by unbelieving man, who would not give any credence to a biblically prophesied impending second destruction of the same creation. (God giveth, and God taketh away!)

In regard to this second destruction, which in terms of millennial clock time is only minutes away, Peter went on to say that "The heavens [universe] and the earth are kept in store [in place] by the same word that created them [God's Word]; and they are reserved for fire until the day of judgment" [Day of the Lord—God's wrath]. We will encounter this Judgment Day of the Lord further on when we come upon the seal, trumpet, and bowl judgments. For anyone wanting to know precisely what to expect in those days just ahead, read on, for God's Word leaves little to the imagination. Comment: There is only one way to achieve God's intended meaning from His prophetic Word. That way is to let God Himself, through His Holy Spirit, *do the work!* Will you see God's fingerprints on any of these projections? Read on and see.

Now we approach the next step in proving that Bible prophecy regarding the end time has relevance for today and the time just ahead. A good number of these prophecies are positioned for fulfillment now. In other words, they are like a loaded gun, cocked and ready to fire. All that is holding them back is that the time has not come for God to pull the trigger. We shall see several of these; but before we do, we will view a late arriving road sign along the way to fulfillment of last days Bible prophecy. It is another example of man's contribution to God's precisely timed and executed events, motivated in the minds of men independent of God's Word, yet which is like the artist's paintbrush. The brush thinks that it painted the masterpiece all by itself! This road sign of end time prophecy fulfillment, we will call example number 1: "The Road Map To Peace," sponsored and backed by an international coalition of nations led by America. So, what is outstanding about it? It provides for establishment of an independent Palestinian state (to be cut out of Israel), and requires a peace accord in the year, 2005.

Keeping this road sign in mind, we will continue to see the hand of God clearly exposed in the pages just ahead.

Example number 2: Revelation 16 views advanced wrath on mankind, poured from bowls held by angels. We shall learn that Christians, not being appointed to wrath, will be protected through the initial wrath, and will be removed before the more advanced stage (1 Thessalonians 5:9). Later, we will see how Christians and the Jewish remnant will pass through a loophole in the immediate effects of early wrath. Christians, are destined for resurrection and translation at Christ's return, while the Jewish remnant will be protected through the fury and death of all wrath.

Revelation 16:12 says:

Then the sixth angel poured out his bowl on the great river Euphrates, and its water was dried up, so that the way of the kings from the east might be prepared.

It is well known that this refers to the Armageddon disaster. An eastern army crosses the natural barrier formed by the Euphrates River on its way into the Mid-East and then on to Israel and its date with destiny. John the apostle completes the picture in Revelation 9:14–16 with this:

saying to the sixth angel who had the trumpet, "Release the four angels who are bound at the great river Euphrates."

So the four angels, who had been prepared for the hour and day and month and year, were released to kill a third of mankind.

Now the number of the army of the horsemen was two hundred million; I heard the number of them.

A gun, loaded and cocked, waiting for the exact hour, day, month, and year. But is this prophecy relevant for today? (2005 + 7 = 2012! See Table#1.)

John, in Revelation 9:17, explains what the horses looked like from what he saw in this vision of the distant future. He could only relate the strange visional objects to what he was familiar with, and so he described a variety of military vehicles as horses wearing armor. We know that they carried modern armament, because he explains that the horses' heads were like the heads of lions; and out of their mouths came fire, smoke and brimstone. This was John's way of describing, almost 2,000 years into the future, what could only be modern tanks, mobile rocket launchers, armored cars, and a host of other military vehicles.

He continues: "for their tails are like serpents, having heads; and with them they do harm." This is an attempt to describe something he had never seen or heard of before, agents of modern mechanized warfare mounted on these vehicles.

Verse 18 continues with this: "By these three plagues a third of mankind was killed—by the fire and the smoke and the brimstone which came out of their mouths." A third of mankind is a huge number of people, even though population will be reduced by the Resurrection and by a cosmic encounter with earth that will precede the Armageddon holocaust. The fire, smoke, and brimstone will undoubtedly include some nuclear and chemical/bacterial tipped missiles in order to have the devastating effect of reducing world population by one-third.

In Matthew 6:19–21, Jesus gave us some sound advice as to where to place our emphasis in establishing priorities for living. We see it here:

Do not lay up for yourselves treasures on earth, where moth and rust destroy and where thieves break in and steal;

but lay up for yourselves treasures in heaven, where neither moth nor rust destroys and where thieves do not break in and steal.

For where your treasure is, there your heart will be also.

Now, back to Revelation 16:12, where the Euphrates River will be dried up to allow the kings of the east and their army to make an easy crossing of this very formidable natural barrier. What about a large dam and reservoir?

The Ataturk Dam in Turkey, built on the Euphrates River, now has that capability; that is, it can dry up this great river for a period of time, which varies depending upon the time of year. So here is a prophecy that for almost 2,000 years appeared to require an act of God to reach fulfillment. God uses and will use man for much of the fulfillment of His prophesy. Take, for example, prophecies that we have looked at earlier concerning Jesus returning to defeat this collection of gentile armies representing all nations of the world with the double-edged sword that proceeds from His mouth. According to Zechariah 12:4–9, Jesus will cause confusion and madness among the armies of the attacking nations. He will then use the armed forces of Israel to deliver the *coup de grace* to this diverse hoard, and will accomplish it by speaking it into reality just as He created the universe.

Israel has one of the most advanced high-tech armed forces in the world today, and with God's help, has the capability to accomplish this feat. So then, not only is the river Euphrates even now fully prepared for its role in the coming war, but Israel as well is prepared and ready for her part, written almost two thousand years ago for this very time.

While we are on this subject, it is timely and relevant to keep in mind that world events have been culminating into the immediate foreshadowing of the prophesied seventieth week of Daniel 9:27. We will look deeper into this important prophecy of the last seven years of current history as we progress. For now, it is sufficient to note that current Mid-East events have moved this prophecy to the place where the world is now positioned well within the last *seven years to Armageddon!*

The biblical starting point—a regional peace accord, seemingly set for the year 2005. Bickering, terrorism, and random acts of violence have kept tensions high; a constant reminder to the world that peace must be secured in the short-term to prevent a wide regional or even worldwide escalation in the long-term.

"Regarding this world recognized need for a peaceful solution to Mid-East tensions: We will here, in early 2006, list several factors that seem to have moved, or are moving into position to play their parts in the Bible prophesied seventieth week of Daniel 9:27, the last seven years of the current six thousand.

A. November 11, 2004: Yasser Arafat passed from the world scene, thus opening the way for more progressive Palestinian leadership in settling the long standing peace process impasse.

B. The current Mid-East peace plan (Road Map to Peace) is on the table, with world approval and no serious opposition.

C. June 19, 2005: Condoleezza Rice, U.S.A. Secretary of State, was credited with bringing Israel and the Palestinian Authority together on agreements resolving the divisive issues of eliminating violence, and in full cooperation regarding demolition and disposal of 1,600 Israeli settler homes in Gaza by the expected target date, August 16, 2005. (New York Times, 6/19/05 article by Steven Wiseman and Greg Myre, titled "Rice Says Both Sides Commit to Cooperation on Gaza Pullout"). This, the first major breakthrough in the (road map to peace) signals the start of the seventieth week of Daniel 9:27, the last seven years of the first six thousand. This beginning will be strengthened (confirmed) later by Antichrist in bringing other nations into peace arrangements with Israel.

D. Syria is now expressing a desire for peace with Israel.

E. The United Nations has a politically wounded Secretary General resulting from alleged large scale fraud and corruption within the organization and under his watch.

F. A recent past president of the United States has been actively seeking the potentially powerful and prestigious office of Secretary General of this world body. This position seems to be the ideal vehicle for one aspiring to an orderly transition from one world power office to the only one remaining and of all things, becoming available precisely in the Bible's last days timeline. How will the details play out? It appears that the higher powers involved, both spiritual and human, will not be long in showing their hands.

G. There is a prominent biblical prophetic condition attached to the one who will close this land for peace deal. The person mentioned above has already met it. We will see the amazing details concerning this special circumstance later.

H. The Universal Church, now with a new pope and a clearly defined, expanding world friendly position on every contentious issue from no longer defending "Merry Christmas" against its secular antagonist "Happy Holidays" to asserting that creation science is not a science and shouldn't be taught in schools alongside Darwin's (where are the transitional kind fossils?) theory of macro-evolution!

Reflecting upon the above: Is an unseen hand reaching down into the affairs of men and arranging the stage for the final act according to a script written many years in advance?

As can be imagined, the final few years will be unlike any other. The embryonic, humanistic, divided world empire, bent to the will of one man, shall have challenges for everyone. All major events of these last seven years will lead unerringly to the explosive climax of human emotions that will escalate and erupt in Israel.

Israel has neutron weapons, which she will use in this coming major conflict. These destroy flesh, but do not damage buildings, machinery, weaponry or land. Zechariah 14:12 tells us:

And this shall be the plague with which the LORD will strike all the people who fought against Jerusalem: their flesh shall dissolve while they stand on their feet, their eyes shall dissolve in their sockets, and their tongues shall dissolve in their mouths.

We have just seen the means to prophecy fulfillment in place and ready for the fateful Day of the Lord, when each will play its special part in the final episode of one-world madness.

Example number 3 involves the Mark of the Beast; the one we call the antichrist. Reference to this mark and how it will be used is found in Revelation 13:16–17:

> He causes all, both small and great, rich and poor, free and slave, to receive a mark on their right hand or on their foreheads, and that no one may buy or sell except one who has the mark or the name of the beast, or the number of his name.

Verse 18 continues:

> Here is wisdom. Let him who has understanding calculate the number of the beast, for it is the number of a man: his number is 666 (Revelation 13:18).

Being created on the sixth day, man's number is six. The three sixes (666) each represent a period of time that will, or has impacted mankind in its own individual way. The first, six thousand years is ending, the last six months is coming, and the six days will be very selective in whom and how they shall be affected! More on this to come later.

It is commonly thought at this time that the mark will be a bar code similar to that used in stores of all kinds today. In the case of the innocuous use by stores, which we are all familiar with, the code featuring heavy bars interspersed among thinner bars, is read by computers. These bars are programmed to carry information on the particular item of merchandise involved. They will be used the same way with humans.

These codes, invented and used by man for the benefit of man, therefore, reference man's biblical number six. We are then, in fact, familiar with the code that will be required of all populations; that will become a systematized component of the physical human body to be forced upon mankind by the second beast of Revelation 13, the false prophet. How will a code with reference to all of our pertinent information keyed on it and placed on the right hand, or forehead, be secured to withstand the many and varied activities engaged in by the bearer in normal daily living? The technology is in use today.

This portion of the prophecy as well has been solved by man for man's benefit. It is no secret that human beings love their pets, and go to great lengths to care for and protect them. The implantation of a tiny radio-sending device about the size of a grain of rice, which emits a constant radio signal, is now being implanted in some pets by veterinarians for the benefit of the pet and the owner alike. If the pet becomes lost or stolen, the radio signal beamed from the tiny device under the skin can be received by a special receiver; the pet found and presumably recovered. Recent news reports declare that this technology is now being tested on humans as well. It is being reported also, that these devices will be reduced in size to that of a grain of sand.

Now, what about the rest of the question—how will the information referenced by the implant affect us as individuals? This phase of the system is in place also. Scanners will read the chip as participants pass by, or as the right hand is presented. It will key to volumes of personal information: criminal record if any, marital status, religious affiliation, education, job training, current employment, social security number, driver's license number, digital photograph, etc., etc. All this and much more, including name, address, financial history, sex, known vices, date and place of birth, mother's maiden name, chemical dependencies if any, special training, buying habits, income source, credit history, medical records, political affiliation, probably a DNA print, bank, and more.

The government wants it all. Most is, at present, residing in various databanks. This advanced chip/mark providing access to it all, will make it available in one location. It will be the consummation of technical refinement in giving the government the ability to exercise vastly more control over many aspects of our lives. An expandable dossier on each world citizen; so very convenient! Our covert global government is progressing in baby steps. It, as a cat sneaks up on a canary, is steadily advancing. Soon it will be ready to devour the world, but as discussed earlier, the U.S.A will manage to elude the jaws of this ravenous beast to a greater extent than other nations of the world. To satisfy its insatiable appetite for money, the United Nations is now lobbying its world members to allow it to levy a world tax. It will begin low; but remember, the U.S.A started its income tax out at one percent to seven percent. (*Foot in the door!*)

As an example of the rigid control to be exercised over world populations when the global government is a complete reality and our world leader is in firm control, an identity chip will be created for each world citizen. This will be required of everyone wishing to buy or sell anything. Needless to say, this will work a real hardship on anyone who does not have the chip. For those who do accept it, though freedom as we know it today will be reduced, their ability to live a somewhat normal lifestyle, considering the constraints forced upon them by this people controlling dictatorship, will be generally intact. The future is not bright, however.

Now, for those who decide that accepting the chip really won't be so bad, the government plans to carry on a step further. This is set up as well, and ready to go into effect as soon as the chips are integrated into all societies. World populations will, for the most part, accept them. Why not? They will epitomize convenience and cutting edge technology in the war on terrorism. The world will feel safer and more upbeat as well, knowing that the global government will be more able to combat terror and offenders of the new hate crimes laws!

The chips will be pressed upon the public as a necessity, and a convenience by major media hoopla, and as the result of urging by the false prophet backed by the loosely knit confederation of religious entities that will make up the new one world united religion. This new cooperative effort of mankind to bring order out of religious diversity will parallel the United Nations in its organizational structure. As discussed earlier, it will water down Christianity in order to accommodate other religions and beliefs to form a big tent, anything-goes, feel-good religious system. This religious extravaganza will include apostate Christian groups, cults, Jews, and various forms of paganism and the new age, steeped in reincarnation.

All associated with this united religion will have few, if any, reservations about accepting the chip which will be explained as the solution to ever-mounting danger from within and a great asset in eliminating counterfeit currency and in fighting and preventing pathogenic disease epidemics. It will be promoted as the terminator of an outmoded form of financial commerce, and shall represent the latest threshold of the long-anticipated cashless society.

In order to make it a success, all will be required to make themselves available for insertion of the tiny chip, especially prepared in advance for each world citizen, and provided in infant format in cases of new births. Just under the skin in a painless and simple injection; the choice of location, either the forehead or the right hand, would be determined either by individual anatomical constraints or by personal preference.

Those who have studied any ancient history in school, or elsewhere, will recall that the rulers of ancient Rome and for that matter, rulers of other early nations and empires were worshipped as gods. This new world leader will wish to reinstate this early practice as he occupies God's temple. The world will be adjusting to domination by the United Nations and its secretary general. This man's world status will be much greater than that of all previous leaders of this world body. He will, for all practical purposes, be the ruler of the world. He is an experienced politician, having proven himself in the backroom political climate of presidential politics associated with being president of the United States of America. As such, and as the most powerful political leader on the world scene, he has built and is continuing to build relationships, make deals, and generally influence world leaders in preparation for positioning by his globalist backers for installation into this United Nations world leadership position.

This new world ruler will be backed and supported vigorously by his religious counterpart, leader and high priest of the new united religion, wielding all the power and influence of the papacy. Catholicism, born in the early years of Christianity, and with popes down through the years having had strong influence over many national leaders and populations, will produce this final pope, whose worldly prestige and religious stature will be greater than any other in recent history!

Now, to continue with the other people controlling aspect of the final divided world empire, we will preview the crown jewel of the citizen protection program featuring the chip/mark!

Not only will all personal information be readily available by way of the embedded chip to be carried around with them, but it will be tracked by a system of satellites that will be able to pinpoint the precise location of every single person who receives this chip. That is correct—pinpoint each person's location twenty-four hours a day, three hundred sixty-five days a year. Each chip will be identifiable in a database and trackable by satellite. The result will allow the powers that be the ability to pull up any individual file whenever desired, and know the exact location of that person, no matter where on earth he/she happens to be at any given time. Goodbye privacy—hello surveillance!

This technological excess is but one control technique waiting for an unsuspecting public, who, like lambs being led to the slaughter, follow the pied pipers of globalism into a Cubanesque, Red China-oriented, Marxist dictatorship. To use a Hollywood movie title: with *Their Eyes Wide Shut*. This satellite system is well underway at this time; and so all technology for the mark of the beast, as prophesied in Revelation 13:16–17, is in place; ready for fulfillment with this satellite rider attached for good measure.

Now, here we must ask: what about those people who will not allow themselves to be recipients of this chip/mark? Pressure will be great to take it; worldly prospects will appear bleak, and the thought of not being able to buy anything or sell anything will be chilling. The government may not have all the information on objectors that it will possess on the others, and satellites will be unable to track them. There is, however, the developing technology and practice of placing traceable tags in manufactured products that can be tracked, called "Radio-frequency identification" (RFID), intended for tracking merchandise from point of origin to retail destination. Desirable for large retailers who wish to reduce warehousing costs and rely on an "order as needed basis", but which provides the means to track the merchandise beyond point of purchase. For example, the tires on your car, and even things as personal as items of clothing. This practice, though in its infancy, is sure to expand, thereby growing the surveillance mentality that is already well advanced in some societies. But, even so, as with the radar detector, for some people controlling surveillance measures there will be developed countermeasures to bypass or override them. These limited advantages, however, are not the complete answer.

It will come down to who we know, as well as just what we know. If we know God the Father and Jesus His Son as Lord and Savior, He will provide guidance and direction to persevere. We will be reading the signs, preparing in advance, and trusting the Lord.

Revelation 14:9–11 makes it very clear that mankind is not to accept this mark. The Scriptures read as follows:

> Then a third angel followed them, saying with a loud voice, "If anyone worships the beast and his image, and receives his mark on his forehead or on his hand, he himself shall also drink of the wine of the wrath of God, which is poured out full strength into

the cup of His indignation. He shall be tormented with fire and brimstone in the presence of the holy angels and in the presence of the Lamb.

And the smoke of their torment ascends forever and ever; and they have no rest day or night, who worship the beast and his image, and whoever receives the mark of his name."

These passages can weigh heavily on our mind. One meaning to be derived is that taking the mark is the kiss of death to the eternal soul of anyone who capitulates to the requirements established by the false prophet. Antichrist, of course, a dedicated opportunist with a large ego, will integrate this valuable chip (no buying or selling without it), into his people-controlling agenda, with the stipulation that he is worthy of worship as God.

Not surprisingly, this person (indwelt by Satan) will exude a mystical spiritualism in combination with a charismatic personality. Many will blindly follow him, and not understand why! We know who he is, Antiochus IV Epiphanes. We know where he comes from; as Revelation 17:8 explains:

The beast that you saw was, and is not, and will ascend out of the bottomless pit and go to perdition. And those who dwell on the earth will marvel, whose names are not written in the Book of Life from the foundation of the world, when they see the beast that was, and is not, and yet is.

John's reference point was his time, circa A.D. 80. "The beast that was" clearly tells that he lived before John's time. "He is not" tells us that this beast did not live at the time of John's writing. "And will ascend out of the bottomless pit" puts his reentry upon the world scene at some future time. This statement also clearly tells where the beast was at the time of John's writing; that being in the bottomless pit, another name for hell. So the antichrist comes to us from another much earlier time period by way of hell, the bottomless pit, having been restrained there after his death as Antiochus IV until his rebirth *as the person he is today!*

135

Revelation 13:1 is quite revealing in its form and provides a telling description of this first beast (Antichrist):

> Then I stood on the sand of the sea. And I saw a beast rising up out of the sea, having seven heads and ten horns, and on his horns ten crowns, and on his heads a blasphemous name.

Verse 2 describes him further:

> Now the beast which I saw was like a leopard, his feet were like the feet of a bear, and his mouth like the mouth of a lion. The dragon gave him his power, his throne, and great authority (Revelation 13:2).

This beast, described as being like a leopard, confirms that it, in fact, portrays Antiochus IV. This assertion refers back to Daniel 7:6, where Daniel was describing a vision of four great beasts, which represented a quartet of future empires (future in reference to his time):

> After this I looked, and there was another, like a leopard, which had on its back four wings of a bird. The beast also had four heads, and dominion was given to it.

This leopard was the third beast in Daniel's vision and represented the Greek Empire. The first two beasts also represented empires. The first being the Babylonian, which was conquered by Medo-Persia, which in turn was conquered by the Greeks under Alexander the Great. This Greek Empire, as we know, was divided into four parts after Alexander's death, and ruled by four of his generals. These four parts of the divided empire are represented by the leopard's four heads. The leopard's four wings could be looked at as representing the four generals who carried Alexander and his empire to speedy victory over the Medo-Persian Empire and other parts of the then-known world. All conquered by Alexander and his Greek leopard forces.

Antiochus IV Epiphanes comes out of the old Seleucid Dynasty of ancient Syria, representing one of the four heads and one of the four wings of the Greek (leopard) Empire. Revelation 13:2, which describes the first beast, Antichrist (Antiochus IV Epiphanes) as being like a leopard, can now be understood. To build on that foundation, we see in the same verse that the leopard's feet were like the feet of a bear, and his mouth like the mouth of a lion.

Antiochus, representing the Greek (leopard) Empire, is here, symbolically shown partially composed of the two previously conquered empires; the bear conquered by the leopard, and the lion conquered by the bear. This would explain why the fourth beast, dreadful and terrible, and exceedingly strong, having ten horns (Roman Empire), was not included in the montage description of the leopard. This is true simply because Rome conquered the leopard (the divided Greek Empire), and was not part of it; but rather, the leopard became a part of the fourth beast, the Roman Empire.

This then explains Daniel 7:23–24:

Thus he said: The fourth beast shall be a fourth kingdom on earth, which shall be different from all other kingdoms, and shall devour the whole earth, trample it and break it in pieces.

The ten horns are ten kings who shall arise from this kingdom. And another shall rise after them [again, himself]; He shall be different from the first ones, and shall subdue three kings.

This other horn (king) that arises again, himself and subdues (plucks out, Daniel 7:8) three of the ten kings is, of course, Antiochus IV Epiphanes, known as Antichrist at the time he arises in the prophecy.

Now, about the words "after them": The Hebrew and Greek words used here can just as well mean "again, himself". It seems that this fact may be of some importance since current events surrounding the identity of the ten horns seem to be lagging the apparent, soon to be confirmed identity of the other horn (Antichrist).

Strong shows the Hebrew word for "after" as being (achar). This word can be used in various senses; as in: after that; afterwards; behind; besides; again, etc.

The same concordance renders the Greek word for "them" as (autos). This word means self as in: her-self; him-self; my-self; your-selves; them-selves.

This raises the question: "Why would a Greek word be used in a Hebrew text?" The obvious answer is that it was not in the original Hebrew Scripture, and was added later by Greek speaking transcribers to clarify the meaning of the Hebrew word (achar) which was meant to convey that the other horn (Antiochus IV Epiphanes) would again, himself rise up. This time his appearance would be in his second life, as Antichrist; and his involvement would be with the ten horns (entities) that would descend down from the old Roman Empire (Daniel 7:23–24).

The fact is, it seems that the misconstrued meaning though unintentional, locked up the intent until the time of the end, when prophecy would then fall into place and its accuracy would of necessity, be of paramount importance (Daniel 12:4).

Daniel's prophecy here, that has Antichrist expelling three of the ten horns/kings, is problematic for anyone attempting to relate Daniel's ten kings as being the same ten kings as those revealed in Revelation 17:16 (which they are!). This verse, Revelation 17:16, clearly points out that ten, not seven horns/kings/trading blocs will attack and destroy the great harlot. The question then becomes: what about the three horns?

# CHAPTER TWENTY

# THREE REBELLIOUS HORNS

The answer has to lie in identification of the three blocs, represented by the three horns to be plucked out by the roots from the global empire by Antichrist and, the reason why? The books of Ezekiel, Daniel, and Revelation hold the answers, and so pertinent verses must be examined.

Ezekiel 38:2 mentions the land of Magog (Thought to be ancient Scythians, who lived in what is now southern Russia). They were notorious for their cruelty and barbarism.

The verse reads as given here:

> Son of man, set your face against Gog, of the land of Magog, the prince [leader] of Rosh, Meshech, and Tubal, and prophesy against him.

Here we see that Gog is the authority over three named members of the trade bloc: Rosh (a northern people), and Meshech (thought to be an early Aramean tribe, which occupied the area of modern Syria). This leaves Tubal (a people that lived in eastern Asia Minor—modern Turkey). So here we have reason to believe that Russia, along with several Islamic, old Soviet Union nations, referred to as (Rosh), along with Syria and Turkey will form a trading bloc. This bloc may very likely be called "the Eurasian Empire" (The McAlvany Intelligence Adviser, January 2005, p 8, 800-528-0559).

Ezekiel 38 and 39 concern a military incursion by these nations and others, into the Mid-East and Israel. Ezekiel 38:5 names another group that is with them. This would be another trading bloc that will go along with the Russian-controlled bloc in the attack, which, in Ezekiel 38:39, deals specifically with entry into Israel. Ezekiel 38:5 reads as follows:

> Persia, [Iran] Ethiopia, and Libya are with them, all of them with shield and helmet.

These three will be part of a Mid-East/North African oil producing bloc, the second of the three horns/blocs to be expelled by Antichrist. This bloc will be separate from the group of seven heavy oil-producing nations of the Arabian Peninsula. Ezekiel 38:6 continues:

> Gomer [An early people living north of the Black Sea] and all its troops; the House of Togarmah from the far north [Thought to be Armenia] and all its troops; many people are with you. [12]

Location marks both of these peoples as being of the old Soviet Union. They would then be included in the Russian-led, "Eurasian Empire" bloc.

Since this attack into Israel figures prominently in prophesied end time events, it will be dealt with in greater detail a bit later. For now it is sufficient to use it to identify two of the three horns to be expelled by Antichrist from the global union (with good reason), and at which time the neophyte world government will be experiencing God's wrathful judgment.

One bloc will be made up of Russia and several others, probably Islamic nations of the old Soviet Union, referred to today as being in Central Asia. Syria and Turkey, it seems, will throw in with them rather than with a Mid-East oil bloc.

This second bloc, consisting of radical Islamic oil nations of the Middle East and North Africa, while controlling a modest portion of world oil production, will be separate from the heavy oil producers of the Arabian Peninsula. Political considerations will separate them from these heavy producers. The radical nations will be generally attracted to their union by a shared, unrestrained hatred of Israel. This bloc will include a new Palestinian state cut out of Israel, Iran, Libya, and Ethiopia. It could also include the North African nations of North Sudan and Algeria. The Bible includes Persia (Iran) as being in the attack into Israel. Iraq is not mentioned. So then, it seems that America's war to free Iraq from its tyrant dictator will result in a more global friendly government there. Of course, God knew this would happen; so He did not include Iraq with the radical attacking nations.

With two blocs identified, the third is easy: an eastern bloc to include China. News reports have stated that China plans to build an oil pipeline into the Mid-East oil fields. This facility would provide strong motivation for China to protect her interests in this important part of the world. Whether the pipeline is built or not, China and other free market nations of the east will have a vital interest in this area.

These are the three nonconforming unions that will be expelled from the final divided global empire, by a near-future secretary general of the United Nations. This also provides identification of two of the three invading armies to be involved in this last great war. The third, of course, will be the international community forces under Antichrist. This remaining body of seven cooperating trading blocs will have at its disposal the military might of the United Nations. This force may likely control a substantial portion of U.S. military power, freely and unilaterally given prior to the perceived

America threat being nuclearly neutralized. This acquisition would greatly strengthen the UN military.

The stage is now set for the prophetic final world war; we know who will be involved and where it will center. As we progress here, we shall learn more of why it will occur; and that it shall be seen as being the period at the end of the last sentence of the last chapter of the book of human knowledge. We will now look at Israel's prophetic response to this unprovoked attack and entry into God's glorious land by basically all nations of the earth.

# CHAPTER TWENTY-ONE

# ISRAEL'S RESPONSE

Modern Israel has built an astonishing record in the wars with her Islamic neighbors. In 1948, the year of her rebirth, Islamic nations representing a combined population of sixty million, sought to push this tiny enclave of six hundred-fifty thousand God-led souls into the Mediterranean Sea. God gave Israel victory then again in 1967 and again in 1973.

We have seen in Revelation 16:12–16 how demon spirits went out from the mouths of Satan, Antichrist, and the false prophet to summon the kings of the earth to battle at a place in Israel called Armageddon. We saw in these verses how the Euphrates River will be dried up at just the right time to allow the army of the kings of the east to cross over and thus take part in this great destruction.

Zechariah 9:13–14 tell how God will bend Judah His bow, fitted with Ephraim (House of Israel) His arrow, and will raise up the sons of Zion (modern day Israel) against the sons of Greece (forces of Antichrist and other armies at Armageddon).

Verse 15 continues:

The Lord of hosts will defend them; they shall devour and subdue with sling stones. They shall drink and roar as if with wine;

they shall be filled with blood like basins, like the corners of the alter.

Verse 16 says:

The LORD their God will save them in that day, as the flock of His people. For they shall be like the jewels of a crown, lifted like a banner over His land; (Zechariah 9:16).

Zechariah 12:2–3 continues:

Behold, I will make Jerusalem a cup of drunkenness to all the surrounding peoples, when they lay siege against Judah and Jerusalem.

And it shall happen in that day that I will make Jerusalem a very heavy stone for all peoples; all who would heave it away will surely be cut in pieces, though all nations of the earth are gathered against it.

Then Zechariah 12:8 says it so well:

In that day the LORD will defend the inhabitants of Jerusalem; the one who is feeble among them in that day shall be like David, and the House of David shall be like God, like the Angel of the LORD [Jesus] before them.

So here we have laid the groundwork for looking at another prophesied account of a portion of this last war, World War III, that will be the cornerstone of God's wrath in ending our present time prior to ushering in His kingdom on earth.

# CHAPTER TWENTY-TWO

# A GIGANTIC TREACHERY

Ezekiel 38 and 39 hold many of the details of this next episode of end time insanity, given to us as warning by a loving God to draw to Himself as many as will come while they can.

We know that spirits will go out from Satan, Antichrist, and the false prophet to work the power of the supernatural just under the surface of the natural realm. This force behind the scenes will be a contributing cause of the invasion of Israel. Antichrist will already be there. Daniel 12:11 tells us:

> And from the time that the daily sacrifice is taken away, and the abomination of desolation is set up, there shall be one thousand two hundred and ninety days.

Antichrist in the temple will define the "abomination of desolation."

So then, since Antichrist will be in Jerusalem, we can be quite sure that armed forces under his control will also be there. In fact, he will control all the United Nations' new global empire armed forces wherever they may be stationed. The ten political economic trading unions, though under his control, will be a new experiment in global cooperation. Not since the Tower of Babel has the world been united, and this collection of trading blocs will contain three that will act independently of the whole to advance their own individual interests. We have seen them and know who they are.

There will be three triggers, cocked and set to fire, that will propel this repudiation of the, at that time, recent Antichrist strengthened Mid-East peace accord into instant reality. First and foremost of these will be a cosmic attack on earth that will literally shake the planet to its foundations. We shall see it ahead in full relief against a backdrop of terror and encroaching darkness that will traumatize the world, and hold in the cold grip of fear and panic those upon whom it will come as a thief in the night! In Isaiah 24:19 the prophet said, regarding this occurrence:

> The earth is violently broken, the earth is split open, the earth is shaken exceedingly.

The resulting circumstances of the violence that will overwhelm the planet include, among others, atmospheric contamination, which will progress to shut out sunlight, thus inviting a myriad of troubling consequences to follow. This great catastrophe will serve to sharpen the somewhat placated instinct for survival among the participants of the newly formed global community. The glue holding them together in a cohesive union will not have hardened sufficiently by then, and some will act independently in their own interests.

All of this and more will be surveyed in its entirety when we look at the seal, trumpet, and bowl judgments. Two more triggers for the uninvited break-in of the Middle East await. Though they are secondary in some respects to that mentioned above, they shall play their parts in bringing completion to the awesome and terrible Day of the Lord. We shall see them fully exposed in their own right as accelerators of prophetic end time activity.

The Ezekiel 38 through 39 account, prophesied in great detail, deals with a massive unprovoked attack spearheaded from the far north. Daniel clarifies certain aspects of this raid to show that other nations will be entered, and the attackers will pass through and on into Egypt. We can identify these other countries as the heavy oil producing nations of the Arabian Peninsula. God's glorious land will be bypassed at that time. Some troops will remain in each of the conquered nations, and the onslaught, bypassing Israel at this point, will move into Egypt. Here, the attackers will be met by Antichrist and his international community forces. We shall see later that they will be defeated by the attackers there, and the insurgents will then move in force into Israel. Daniel shows that Antichrist's remaining military will also enter Israel after Egypt for the final showdown. Both Daniel and Revelation give cause to believe that the armies of the kings of the east will be fully represented in Israel as well, thus filling the winepress for treading of the grapes of wrath.

Ezekiel 30 deals with the destruction of Egypt in the time of God's wrath—the Day of the Lord. It credits Nebuchadnezzar, King of Babylon, as the main instrument of destruction. It shows some of the same nations as being involved, that Ezekiel 38 lists as being with Gog of the far north. There can be little doubt that this is one and the same attack into Egypt referenced above, but with Gog of Magog (Russia) here being called Nebuchadnezzar, King of Babylon. This is yet another example of Bible prophecy referring to a then-well-known nefarious leader or world power to represent a distant future last-days entity of ill repute.

Daniel 11:40–45 presents the sequence of this attack into the Mid-East, which was sketched above. Daniel 11:40 indicates that Antichrist will be a prominent target of the Russian-led invasion. The position taken here is that the main thrust of the attacking armies will focus on Egypt, and shall defeat Antichrist and his UN forces there. It is at this point that Ezekiel 38:4, speaking to Gog of Russia, says the following:

I will turn you around, put hooks into your jaws, and lead you out, with all your army, horses, and horsemen, all splendidly clothed, a great company with bucklers and shields, all of them handling swords.

This is the New King James version. The King James Bible says it this way:

And I will turn thee back, and put hooks into thy jaws, and I will bring thee forth, and all thine army, horses and horsemen, all of them clothed with all sorts of armour, even a great company with bucklers and shields, all of them handling swords (Ezekiel 38:4 KJV).

We have seen earlier some of the nations that will be involved in the initial attack by two of the three trading blocs to be expelled (plucked out) by Antichrist.

Ezekiel 38:8 says that:

After many days you will be visited. [demon spirits] In the latter years you will come into the land of those brought back from the sword [holocaust] and gathered from many people on the mountains of Israel, which had long been desolate; they were brought out of the nations, and now all of them dwell safely.

Ezekiel 38:9 continues:

You will ascend, coming like a storm, covering the land like a cloud, you and all your troops and many peoples with you.

What we have read so far deserves some discussion:

1.  Verse 4, in saying: "I will turn you around," or as the KJV says, "I will turn thee back," gives the distinct impression that God is taking the intruders back in the direction from which they had come. These troops will have swarmed down from the north, all around Israel—down from Syria

148

and Turkey, down from Iran, down from Russia and the far north by sea and into the Mediterranean and the Red Seas, all around Israel, but not into Israel at that time. Israel's time will come later.

2.  Verse 8 sets the stage for the entire operation—that of the military take-over of Mid-East oil fields by Russia, her northern bloc members with Turkey, Syria, and their trading partners in the radical Islamic bloc that hate Israel. Russia could benefit also from the pilfering of Israel's high-tech sector as she did from Germany's technology and industrial sectors after World War II.

Daniel has stated that the Russian axis, in its flanking raid on Antichrist (perceived to be) in Egypt, will coordinate their assault from the north simultaneously with the attack by the king of the south. Both Libya and Ethiopia will, as Ezekiel 38:5 tells us: "be with them." That is, with Russia and company, as partners in the entire scope of operations. So either Libya or Ethiopia would qualify as the king of the south with the other adding assistance. Daniel says also that in this attack, headed toward Antichrist in Egypt, that Russia and company "shall enter the countries, overwhelm them, and pass through" (Daniel 11:40). It doesn't name the countries, but verse 41 says that Jordan will escape. Not much imagination is required to see those not named by Daniel are heavy oil producers of the Arabian Peninsula, just beyond Jordan and on the way to Egypt.

In the stampede down from the north two rules will be operational. First, Jordan, a friend, will be skirted or shall give permission for troops to move across her borders on their way into the Arabian Peninsula. The other consideration will be that with Israel's military capability she must be avoided until Antichrist and the international community forces are dealt with in Egypt to prevent stirring up a hornet's nest and second front at their rear. Gog/King of the North/Nebuchadnezzar and all will prevail in Egypt.

Daniel 11:43 goes on to say:

> He shall have power over the treasures of gold and silver, and over all the precious things of Egypt; also the Libyans and Ethiopians shall follow at his heels.

In comparing the two accounts of this attack into the Mid-East, Daniel, though much more short on detail provides the full scope of operations, while Ezekiel lavishes considerable detail on only the final major attack on Israel from Egypt.

3.  Ezekiel 38:9 deals with Gog and those with him being turned back by God after victory in Egypt for a strike into Israel. It says:

> You will ascend, coming like a storm, covering the land like a cloud, you and all your troops and many peoples with you."

This seems to be in reference to an airborne operation ascending, to come like a storm, covering the land like a cloud. The original thrust into the Mid-East spoken of in Ezekiel 38:15 says this:

> Then you will come from your place out of the far north, you and many peoples with you, all of them riding on horses, [military vehicles] a great company and a mighty army.

Above, we have seen that the original thrust into the Mid-East strikes out from the north, with Gog and all the peoples with him riding on horses/military vehicles. This attack skirts Israel, respects Jordan, and picks off major oil producing nations of the Arabian Peninsula on its southward sweep to Egypt. As Daniel 11:40 describes it:

> At the time of the end the king of the South shall attack
> him [Antichrist]; and the king of the north shall come
> against him like a whirlwind, with chariots, horsemen,
> and with many ships; and he [king of the north] shall en-
> ter the countries, overwhelm them, and pass through.

This clearly describes the scene in that not-too-distant time,
of a darkening atmosphere resulting from a major natural
cataclysm to strike earth. This will propel oil and its avail-
ability to the forefront of the collective conscience of each
of the ten world trading blocs, and of a likely independent
U.S.A as well. After The Harlot is destroyed two blocs will
act in concert out of greed and hate; the third will act in
self-interest. The initial thrust will be by the Russian-led
and the radical Islamic blocs, with their whirlwind attack
eventuating in Egypt. Antichrist and his international community forces will be caught in the jaws of a coordinated
pincer movement between the armies of the king of the
north/Gog/Nebuchadnezzar and the troops of the king of
the south.

God, through His prophets many years ago, told of this ground
attack into the Mid-East and Egypt, an attack with offshore support
vessels, no doubt awash in helicopters, troops, and equipment,
to sustain an air and land invasion of tiny, but mighty Israel, the
technological crown jewel of the Mid-East.

With the first notice of ominous troop movements from the
north heading south, Ezekiel 38:13 deals with targets of opportunity in their path:

Sheba, [ancient people on the shores of the Persian Gulf and
southern Arabian Peninsula (small, heavy oil producers and
Suadi Arabia)] Dedan, [Jordan] the merchants of Tarshish, and
all their young lions will say to you, "Have you come to take
plunder? Have you gathered your army to take booty, to carry

away silver and gold, to take away livestock and goods, to take great plunder?"[13]

Here we have a scene at the outset of the incursion, at a point just prior to the outbreak of hostilities, with troops on the move, and armies marshalling in various places. Troopships in the Mediterranean and Red Seas, northern overland armies drawing up in Turkey and Syria along with these nations' own armies at the ready; Iran (Persia), another avowed enemy of Israel, boiling over with hatred and dedicated to the eradication of Israel; equipped by Russia and probably already at this point, on the move. Comment: No U.S.A presence equates with no restraint. (When the cat's away, the mice will play.)

This will approximate the situation at the time of inquiry by the concerned nations of Ezekiel 38:13. They will see the ominous signs of a gigantic treachery in the process of forming and about to be launched at who else, but them? So they ask the obvious questions of the intruders: Have you come to take booty and steal our wealth (oil)? But besides the nations of the Arabian Peninsula and Jordan being concerned for their safety and asking questions, verse 13 mentions the "merchants of Tarshish, and all their young lions" as being concerned and asking questions also.

Ancient Tarshish, on the southern coast of Spain, represented the best in high-tech trading vessels that plied their trade throughout the then-known world. The name *Tarshish* was synonymous with *trade*; this seaport community carried on a considerable trade with Phoenician Tyre. The obvious conclusion to be drawn here is that "the merchants of Tarshish, and all their young lions" represent the final divided global empire; the international community, built upon and held together by commercial trade. The juncture, at which time this inquiry by the concerned parties is made, will quite likely represent the point at which *two of the rebellious blocs will be expelled from the union they are about to attack, with the third bloc's detachment to come very soon thereafter!*

*At this near future point in time, Jesus Christ will have returned, the Resurrection will have occurred, Mystery Babylon the great will have been destroyed by the group of ten, and darkness will shroud the earth.* Regarding the massive strike to America by the then-group of ten: Russia will most likely serve as the primary instrument of destruction. [Russia has the nuclear capability, and has also the avowed commitment to win a nuclear war with America based on a first strike agenda. America, on the other hand, has the *Clinton Presidential Decision Directive Number 60* (PDD-60). This requires America's military to absorb a nuclear first strike in place of responding in kind at the first sign of a potential Russian missile launch with America factored as ground zero. This procedure provokes the question: how effective will America's response be with what remains of her military deterrent capability? PDD-60 insures a weakened American nuclear response, not to mention the potential for millions of civilian casualties.] Bracketed commentary paraphrased from *The McAlvany Intelligence Advisor*, February 2002, p 18. Ph 800-528–0559.

America will have been destroyed in the name of equitable global survival in the face of the darkening aftermath of an earth-shaking disaster on a scale not seen by so-called civilized man. We will now return to the wielder of the bloody sword and her inequitable act of aggression against the oil-rich nations of the Arabian Peninsula, Egypt, and Israel. The deed will be a crude, broad-scoped attempt using a meat-ax approach to accomplish that which America will have attempted to attain in a less uncivilized way; that is, grab the oil.

The attack into the fields of energy will progress rapidly. Major oil fields will be locked up; the men of the east working there will be scattered, and on to Egypt as a whirlwind to confront Antichrist and his loyal international community forces there. Ezekiel 30:3–5 provides a picture of the attack:

> For the day is near, even the day of the LORD is near; it will be
> a day of clouds, the time of the Gentiles.

The sword shall come upon Egypt, and great anguish shall be in Ethiopia, when the slain fall in Egypt, and they take away her wealth, and her foundations are broken down.

Ethiopia, Libya, Lydia [Turkey], all the mingled people [Russian, radical Islamic axis], Chub, [Early people, probably of North Africa, or of the Lands near Egypt to the south], and the men of the lands who are allied [international community], shall fall with them by the sword.[14]

Verse 6 continues:

Thus says the LORD: "Those who uphold Egypt shall fall, and the pride of her power shall come down. From Migdol to Syene those within her shall fall by the sword," says the Lord GOD (Ezekiel 30:6).

The ancient cities of Migdol and Syene were along the Nile River; Migdol north at its mouth in the Nile delta, and Syene in the south at present site of Aswan. These verses verify that the forces of the international community will fight for Egypt (the men of the lands who are allied). The battle will rage in the Nile Valley, and many will fall on both sides. The victor, Russian axis, will control the wealth of Egypt (Nile basin, the Sumed oil pipeline, and strategic Suez Canal).[15]

The Russian-led onslaught will not destroy Jordan, as it will Egypt (Daniel 11:42). Ezekiel tells who will destroy Jordan. Ezekiel 25:4–5 in prophesying judgment on Ammon (Jordan) says:

indeed, therefore, I will deliver you as a possession to the men of the East, and they shall set their encampments among you and make their dwellings among you; they shall eat your fruit, and they shall drink your milk.

And I will make Rabbah a stable for camels and Ammon a resting place for flocks. Then you shall know that I am the LORD.

So the area in Jordan just east of the Jordan River, in the north-western portion of the country will be pillaged by the men of the east. These, as already surmised, will almost certainly include China. Who the others will be can only be guessed at, but prob-ably best determined by judging which eastern nation's economies would be seriously threatened if their supply of oil were to be substantially reduced. All of the manufacturing nations of the Far East, especially South Korea, Taiwan and Japan, would suffer se-verely with interrupted or sharply reduced oil supply. Then there is the current friendship between China, North Korea, Vietnam, Pakistan, and Indonesia. These could constitute a bloc, or part of one that would be in the Mid-East oil fields, peacefully going about the business of operating their pipeline, ocean going tanker transport facility, overland tanker truck lines, etc.

When the Russian-led attack takes place, the eastern bloc's on-site technician teams and their facilities are overrun and personnel scattered. Will this bloc react with its own military force? The Bible seems to be saying, *Yes it will!*

We now need to disqualify Iran as being *the men of the east*. Iran (Persia) is included with those nations, associated with the Russian invasion. Iran, too, would not harm Jordan due to Jordan's loyalty to Iraq in the 1991 Desert Storm War. Iran will be fully cooperat-ing with the attack from the north; according to Ezekiel 38:5. Iraq is not mentioned in this incursion and, of course, we now know why. God knew it two-and-a-half millennia ago, and so deleted Iraq (Babylon) from the prophecy.

God has, however, sealed Jordan's fate with pronouncements against three early peoples of that region: Ammon, Moab, and Edom; all in context of World War III. Ezekiel 25:9–11 makes this prophecy:

> therefore, behold, I will clear the territory of Moab of cities, of the cities on its frontier, the glory of the country, Beth Jeshimoth, Baal Meon, and Kirjathaim.

To the men of the East I will give it as a possession, together with the Ammonites, that the Ammonites may not be remembered among the nations.

And I will execute judgments upon Moab, and they shall know that I am the LORD.

God's judgment on the third people of what is now Jordan is given in Ezekiel 25:14:

"I will lay My vengeance on Edom by the hand of My people Israel, that they may do in Edom according to My anger and according to My fury; and they shall know My vengeance," says the Lord GOD.

Edom was located south of the Dead Sea and just east of Israel.

After the rout of their people and takeover of the oil by the invaders, the kings of the east will send military forces to the Mid-East and encamp in western Jordan, the fertile area that was at one time occupied by the small nations of Ammon and Moab. They will take what they want and destroy much of what will remain. This location places them in a strategic position to oppose the Russian-led invaders that will have by then invaded Israel in full strength. The international community forces will have regrouped from their defeat in Egypt and will also have entered Israel. Daniel 11:45 confirms that Antichrist will be there:

And he shall plant the tents of his palace between the seas and the glorious holy mountain; yet he shall come to his end, and no one will help him.

This places him in the area of Megiddo, about fifty-five miles north of Jerusalem.

Antichrist and his international community forces will be encamped on the Plain of Jezreel in Israel. The Russian-led armies will also be in Israel, according to Daniel 11:41 and Ezekiel 38:8;

and so the battle lines will be drawn. With all the hostile activity resulting from the massive number of foreign troops and equipment assembled in and around tiny Israel, how will God deliver His holy Jewish remnant intact, safely into the kingdom of God? Jerusalem will be raided in a door-to-door vendetta of retribution against Jews for daring to exist.

Even though God will allow the area of Moab in the nation of Jordan to become a bivouac area for the kings of the east, He will elevate it to His own use in having it serve as a sanctuary for His remnant of Jewish survivors from Israel: "everyone who is found written in the book" (Daniel 12:1).

Zechariah 14:4–5 tell how the Jewish remnant will be saved from Jerusalem after Jesus' return early in the wrath of God:

> And in that day His [Jesus'] feet will stand on the Mount of Olives, which faces Jerusalem on the east, and the Mount of Olives shall split in two from east to west, making a very large valley; half of the mountain shall move toward the north and half of it toward the south.

> Then you shall flee through My mountain valley, for the mountain valley shall reach to Azal [unknown location east of Jerusalem leading to safety]. Yes you shall flee as you fled from the earthquake in the days of Uzziah king of Judah.[16]

Zechariah 14:2 tells more about this nation of God's chosen people, just before their power will be completely shattered (refer to Daniel 12:7). Even though much of Israel's civilian population will be vaniquished, her armed forces will be viable and deadly; and as we have already seen, Jesus, after His return, shall use them as the sword of His mouth to defeat the nations, as He spoke the universe into being (Genesis 1:1–31).

Zechariah 14:2 says the following:

For I will gather all the nations to battle against Jerusalem; the city shall be taken, the houses rifled, and the women ravished. Half of the city shall go into captivity, but the remnant of the people shall not be cut off from the city.

This explains that those of God's people to be saved, the Jewish remnant, shall not all originate from Jerusalem, but from elsewhere as well. From all over Israel; and with some having been more recent arrivals to Israel from other nations around the world. Jerusalem will be used by God as a staging area for His holy remnant to gather for evacuation before the city is sacked and the great battle commences. The Mount of Olives shall be split asunder at Christ's return. Confusion shall reign, as a great earthquake (the cause of which will become clear), parts the mountain elevates the city, which shall later be divided into three sections and takes seven thousand lives in the same hour that Jesus will be seen on the clouds of heaven with power and great glory. These events will serve as a great distraction to mask the ingathering of participants in the remnant, as they assemble in Jerusalem and exit the city by the valley; knowing that the abomination continues in the holy place!

Isaiah 16:3–5 clarifies details of the escape:

Take counsel, execute judgment; make your shadow like the night in the middle of the day; hide the outcasts, do not betray him who escapes.

Let My outcasts dwell with you, O Moab; be a shelter to them from the face of the spoiler. [Russian-led invaders] For the extortioner [Antichrist] is at an end, devastation ceases, the oppressors are consumed out of the land.

In mercy the throne will be established; and One will sit on it in truth, in the tabernacle of David, judging and seeking justice and hastening righteousness.

It could not be more clear as to how God intends to save His holy Jewish remnant. So back to Ezekiel 38 and 39, which deal with Gog of Russia and the attack into Israel. All nations of the earth will be represented in the conflict, as God's Word proclaims. This war will be the final episode in God's wrath to be inflicted on lost mankind. Ezekiel 38:18–19 confirm this as they reference God's fury and the fire of His wrath:

> "And it will come to pass at the same time, when Gog comes against the land of Israel," says the Lord GOD, "that My fury will show in My face.
>
> For in My jealousy and in the fire of My wrath I have spoken: 'Surely in that day there shall be a great earthquake in the land of Israel.'"

A mountain shall become a valley; as we have just seen above.

God will infect the invading armies with confusion, so that they will fight among themselves. Besides inflicting heavy losses on one another, they will become easy targets for the Israeli defense forces, with the help of Jesus Christ, to pick them off at will with neutron weapons. God shall also use forces of nature, harnessed to His will, to impose punishment on all. In Ezekiel 38:22, He tells about this:

> And I will bring him [Gog] to judgment with pestilence and bloodshed; I will rain down on him, on his troops, and on the many peoples who are with him, flooding rain, great hailstones, fire, and brimstone.

The fire and brimstone, however, suggest tactical bombs.

In Ezekiel 38:21 God says this:

"I will call for a sword against Gog throughout all My mountains [governments]," says the Lord GOD. "Every man's sword will be against his brother."

Besides the great battle to be waged at Armageddon, nations and cities will be devastated by nuclear weapons of mass destruction. God alludes to this in Ezekiel 39:6:

And I will send fire on Magog and on those who live in security in the coastlands. Then they shall know that I am the LORD.

This last entity very likely represents America; as we know from Revelation 17:12–17, America (Mystery Babylon the Great) will be attacked and destroyed by the ten kings/trading blocs prior to expulsion of the three that will rebel.

The picture that emerges from all that we have seen up to now is this: the United Nations, exercising newly acquired control over the nations of the earth, will be headed by a powerful political figure. This individual will be empowered by Satan and his fallen angels, demons. He will be propped up, supported, built up, protected, lionized, and even worshipped by the mass media of the world. He will be made to look worthy of worship by the one described in Revelation 13:11–18, and called the false prophet in Revelation 19:20. As a result of all the propaganda and falsification surrounding and contributing to the persona of this seasoned and charismatic political despot, mankind will look to him for leadership in bringing the world to a place where strife, contention, and hostility will no longer plague nations and peoples.

The new civilization will result; the international community, with a new world religion, a strong military, and a celebrated leader. At last, man will have achieved what he has been striving for, for many long years: oneness—one government, one leader, one religion. How can there be any more wars? How can there be any more national territorial disputes, especially after peace is finally established in the Middle East and the Palestinians at long last have their own homeland, all, of course, complements of the secretary general?

It seems that the peace accord for Israel and her enemies, seen in Daniel 9:27 will coincide with a concerted effort at elevating the UN to a position of control over the international community. It is reasonable to expect as well that Antichrist will have consolidated his power, and as confirmer (strengthener) of the Middle East peace accord, will use the momentum of his personal victory over all diverse factions of discord to position himself as leader of the world. It is quite likely that he will use the Mid-East peace solution to symbolize the spirit of world government for achieving a state of peaceful coexistence among all nations. This would be his gift to the world, nicely wrapped and tied with a ribbon representing unity, and containing the prescription for achieving at last that which has always eluded mankind—a peaceful world.

The fallacy of this presumption will become apparent about three years and four months after commencement of the now running Rice accord (See Table #1), as Daniel 9:27 prophesies an occurrence in the middle of the seven-year peace effort that will be the spark to ignite suppressed passions and result in a world holocaust. Here again lies treachery:

Then he [Antichrist] shall confirm a covenant with many for one week; [seven years] but in the middle of the week he shall bring an end to sacrifice and offering. And on the wing of abominations shall be one who makes desolate, even until the consummation, which is determined, is poured out on the desolate.

In examining this verse more closely, we find first of all that it is given to Israel, the Jews, for the very last seven years of their allotted time, and includes Messiah's return. Second, in the middle of the seven-year period, Antichrist, later hero of the accord/covenant, will himself break it by his order for Israel to cease sacrificing to God and evacuate the temple.

Third, he, after preventing Jews from sacrificing and providing offering to God, will move into the temple and seek to establish himself as God. This attempted takeover of God status will transpire over the following 1,290 days (approximately three-and-one-half years).

Before proceeding, there is one point that needs to be cleared up concerning the last statement above. Daniel 12:11 might appear to contradict the third point. It does not, however, and deserves an explanation. Daniel 12:11 reads as follows:

> And from the time that the daily sacrifice is taken away, and the abomination of desolation is set up, there shall be one thousand two hundred and ninety days.

The problem lies in how the words *set up* are interpreted. At first glance, one might assume that their meaning is *begun*, or *started*. This is not the case here; in fact, the meaning is just the opposite. The dictionary provides the answer. It asserts that the word *establish* means *to set up, to cause to be widely or unquestionably recognized and accepted.*

This interpretation then, of Daniel 12:11, provides continuity to Daniel 9:27, and shows that upon expelling the Jews from the temple, Antichrist, in the mid-section of the seven years, will enter and attempt to establish himself as God during the next 1,290 days (3 years and 6 1/2 months). Both Daniel 9:27 and Daniel 12:11, in their own way, detail the same portion of the same seven years. Daniel 9:27 refers to it as beginning in the middle of the accord, while Daniel 12:11 provides a specific number of days that Antichrist will be in the temple, establishing himself as God. The one, being specific in number of days, while the other verse, being general in nature, is in large part, presented as half of a given period of years.

These verses both point to the same coming event: the fracture of a coveted treaty, the Mid-East Rice peace accord, the final seven years. The end of which, in both Bible prophecy and Maya-engendered new age enlightenment, will be a climactic time in human existence in preparation for the beginning of: "The Kingdom of God," "the new Mayan long cycle," or "the age of Aquarius." Take your pick! The point being that Antichrist's act of treachery in prohibiting Jews from using the temple, will likely be followed at some later point, by the termination of Palestinian control over East Jerusalem. This additional treachery, and Israel's insult, will have serious future consequences.

Islamic nations will become inflamed, thus being instrumental in bringing an attack upon Antichrist in Egypt very soon after (the 1,290 days that he will be in the temple.) This attack will come shortly thereafter with Antichrist foreseeing imminent invasion of the Mid-East eventuating in Egypt. He will withdraw from the temple to lead a hasty defense of the vital Suez Canal in Egypt. This battle will proceed in the early portion of the last forty-five dark and dismal days of the 6,000 years and will culminate in the great winepress of Armageddon, the conclusion of which will mark the end of the same forty-five days. (See Table #1)

Again the Palestinian question: which part of the seven-year peace will be theirs to exercise control over East Jerusalem (tread the Holy City underfoot), the first or the last? Considering all aspects of circumstances as we now see them, it seems more probable that the Palestinian Authority will gain their control of the old city of East Jerusalem sometime in the mid-section of the first half of the negotiated peace. We know that the accord will affect a period of seven years, and we know also that the Gentiles (Palestinians) will have their government authority there for forty-two months. When God's Word refers to months, they are 30-day months, making these 42 months equal to 1,260 days. Seven 365-day years plus two leap year days equals 2,557 days. Antichrist will be in the temple 1,290 days with 45 additional days to the end of the war (World War III). This totals 1,335 days—see Daniel 12:11–12. When we subtract these 1,335 days from the 2,557 days of the seven years;

we have 1,222 days counting back to the beginning of the accord. So there will be 1,222 days from the start of the peace to when Antichrist will expel the Jews and take the temple for himself. This point is 1,222 days after the start of the treaty of peace; with the Palestinians taking control of Ancient Jerusalem in the mid-section of the 1,222 days portion of the treaty, their 1,260 days will end well before the end of the seven years.

But how can we be sure that Palestinian control of the old city will commence in the first part of the negotiated peace? Of course, we can't know for sure. The reality of the situation simply is weighted more heavily for this to be the case. Then, too, we know that the Palestinians will not be in Jerusalem when the invaders focus on Israel. This adds weight as well.

If, however, a variation of Palestinian control of East Jerusalem is not phased in by the terms of the treaty until sometime later, then the Bible's prophesied three-and-a-half years of Gentiles treading the Holy City underfoot might necessitate a rapid withdrawal of the Palestinian government and its general population. This would result as the storm clouds of imminent invasion of God's glorious land looms on the immediate horizon, and the hammer (and the sickle) are about to strike the anvil.

Radical Islamic nations that are with Russia in the attack into Israel will not come against their brothers, the Palestinians, nor would Russia. Considering this realism, we can, therefore, safely judge that the Palestinians will not be in Jerusalem in either case when the attack comes. The first scenario appears the most plausible, especially when one considers what seems to be the retaliatory nature of the whirlwind attack by the Islamic nations along with Russia and others, eventuating against Antichrist and international community forces in Egypt.

Now, to clarify: after Antichrist violates the terms of the treaty, Israel will be seen by the world as enjoying less support by the international community, and so will appear more vulnerable. Israel's allegiance to the global community then, too, will have plunged in response to Antichrist's treacherous act. So, God's prophetic Word demonstrates that treachery has consequences. With Israel being forced to refrain from offering sacrifices to God and with Antichrist's takeover of the temple for elevation to deity status, Israel will be free of all reservations in her deadly response to his then-future military breach of her national borders and invasion into her hard-fought homeland.

In reference to Russia: despite her meager economic status, Russia does now and will then have control over one of the largest stores of military hardware on earth. In this arsenal will be air, sea, and land-based equipment; some of it incorporating the latest technology. She will also have the largest cache of nuclear, bacterial, and chemical weapons of mass destruction in the world. Russia is and will be a force to be reckoned with.

A very conspicuous target of the invaders in their liberating attack into the oil fields will be the men of the east. The Bible places them in Saudi Arabia. We can expect that they will be in other oil-rich nations of the Arabian Peninsula as well. China has for years, been positioned at both ends of the Panama Canal, and has gained a port in the California City of Long Beach. Building their global infrastructure is what the Far East bloc will be about. Jeremiah has the men of the east in Saudi Arabia, with Nebuchadnezzar (Gog) attacking them there. These Arabian Peninsula oil fields may sound the death-knell for America as well. If it turns out that in the wake of the natural disaster, and the resulting darkening atmosphere, she makes a move on the oil, this would be anathema to the still, at that time, cohesive group of ten. So, both the men of the east, already positioned in the Mid-East oil fields, and a likely move by America to stake out a position on a portion of Mid-East oil, could be considered to be the *other two triggers*. Both being secondary to the cosmic, light-restricting event that in changing the atmospheric face of Planet Earth, will bring these secondary triggers into play.

God's Word uses Nebuchadnezzar, king of old Babylon, to symbolize villains. The following again demonstrates this being done with Gog of Magog. Jeremiah 49:28–29 says this:

> Against Kedar [north Arabian desert] and against the kingdoms of Hazor, [unknown Arabian area][17] which Nebuchadnezzar king of Babylon shall strike. Thus says the LORD: "Arise, go up [high, overhead] to Kedar, and devastate the men of the East!

> Their tents and their flocks they shall take away. They shall take for themselves their curtains, all their vessels and their camels; and they shall cry out to them, "Fear is on every side!"

Regarding these verses, could curtains in our day be radar or sonar? Could vessels be oil tanks mounted on camels (trucks?) Answer: no question about it (Helicopters also are involved.)!

That the men of the east will be in the Mid-East is borne out by Ezekiel 25:1–11. Since it appears that these far east (technicians) will be forcibly expelled from the oil fields by the unprovoked attack, it is not surprising that they will seek refuge in Jordan. It is also realistic to expect that they will be joined there by supporting troops in preparation to engage Russia and friends, who will by then be in Israel, just across the River Jordan. The intent of the far east forces will be a showdown for right of access to the oil fields. After defeat in Egypt, Antichrist and his remaining mauled and probably reinforced military will cross Israel's sovereign border for another chance at survival of his global control status.

Russia and China, presently having a mutual cooperation pact in force, has very little or nothing to do with what the situation may be then. Recall that Nazi Germany and Russia had a similar pact in force at the time of Hitler's massive invasion of Russia during World War II.

America is a wild card in the coming confluence of predestined, out of control, desperate, and chaotic activity that will rip the fabric of global unity. America today is a mighty nation relative to the rest of the world. By maintaining an arms-length relationship with the intricacies of control that will dictate the character and workings of the UN dominated global union, America will become a distrusted outsider. She will exert her own force in the world; and after the darkening, threatening days of the first, second, third, and fourth cosmic strikes to earth, global unity will be seriously strained. America, with her insatiable appetite for oil, huge dependence on Mid-East crude, and with her perceived first right of refusal to the oil—American and British corporations having found and developed the oil fields in the first place–may well threaten a military takeover of the Mid-East oil fields. Under the extreme turmoil of this progressively darkening time, a threatened act of U.S. aggression could likely (will) trigger a global nuclear response.

Immediately after the attack on the U.S. by the then-ten blocs still loyal to the politically astute, but increasingly neurotic secretary general, calling himself God in the temple of God, cracks will become apparent in the foundation of the global union. The radical Islamic bloc and the Russian-led bloc will look upon Israel, dwelling safely without walls, and the men of the east, working in the Arabian Peninsula oil fields as targets of opportunity. Egypt's strategic Suez Canal, Sumed pipeline and Antichrist's antics will place them in danger as well.

The harlot will perish early in the Day of the Lord; six months of terror like none other. With military bases in Iraq, she will be in an ideal position to preempt whichever major oil fields on or around the Arabian Peninsula that she so desires. After the cosmic attack on earth, and the heavenly lights begin to dim, will she make a move on the fields of energy surrounding her Mid-East military position? Is there any doubt? Black gold will be more valuable than yellow gold, and without the sun, the prognosis for pain will be off the chart. Oil and natural gas for electric power generation and transportation, must be had at all costs. Modern civilization cannot function without in normal times; a sunless world will be something else altogether. Oil must be had. He who controls the oil will control the world. So then—a stampede into the oil fields.

A short time before Jesus' return, God's wrath will affect the planet in a variety of ways. These will include: earthquakes, advancing intensity of atmospheric darkening, raging fires, extremely high tsunamis crashing over islands and into costal areas, and great hail. We will see later that this great hail may be something other than ice. Following that, there will be famine and then scorching ultraviolet sunrays.

If wrath will begin before Jesus returns, how will God's people, the saints and the Jewish remnant be saved? We can rest assured, for God has provided for and put in writing a clever means of escape from wrath for each of these. A loophole through which both will escape these events during the short time until Jesus shall return and the Resurrection take place. Then, at the same hour, a mountain will part, forming a valley through which the remnant will later escape to safety in Jordan to be saved from all wrath. Full disclosure ahead!

Much of the above havoc will come upon the earth in the short period between the beginning of wrath, marked by a cosmic attack on earth's atmosphere, to be followed in close succession by three earth strikes and an atmospheric sign, which will announce the magnificent return of the Lord Jesus Christ. This second advent will occur shortly after the wrath will have begun (Matthew 24:29–30). Christ Jesus' return will set in motion the Resurrection of the dead in Christ and the translation of those living in Christ, from mortal to immortal. They will all rise to meet the Lord in the air and, thus will always be with the Lord (1 Thessalonians 4:16–17; 1 Corinthians 15:51–54). Saints shall be brought through initial wrath unscathed; the remnant saved through all of the wrathful Day of the Lord!

The Bible tells of devastation to the nations that hate Israel. These accounts are all in the context of God's wrath in the near future, and involve Armageddon, World War III. They include the Palestinians of Gaza (Zechariah 9:5), and in the West Bank (known earlier as Samaria and Ephraim; Zechariah 9:10), Syria (Damascus; Zechariah 9:1), Iraq (Assyria; Ezekiel 32:22), Iran (Elam; Ezekiel 32:24), Jordan (Edom; Ezekiel 32:29), Turkey (Lydia), Ethiopia, and Libya; (Ezekiel 30:5), and Lebanon (Sidon; Ezekiel 28:22–23). These are all familiar names today.

Ezekiel 39:2, as rendered by the King James Version of the Bible, is somewhat at odds with more recent versions, including the New King James Bible. All versions in the first part of Ezekiel 39:2 agree that Gog is to be turned around. The implication is, back in the direction of Israel from Egypt. The departure in the King James Version from other Bibles indicates a depth of understanding missing in other versions. To see the difference clearly we will read Ezekiel 39:2 in the King James Version:

> And I will turn thee back [Gog], and leave but the sixth part of thee, and will cause thee to come up from the north parts, and will bring thee upon the mountains of Israel (Ezekiel 39:2 KJV).

The New King James Version states in Ezekiel 39:2: "and I will turn you around and lead you on, bringing you up from the far north, and bring you against the mountains of Israel." Ezekiel 38:15 gives a picture of the departure of Gog and all the troops with him from the Far North. It is worth noting and tells us this:

> Then you will come from your place out of the far north, you and many peoples with you, all of them riding on horses, a great company and a mighty army. (Ezekiel 38:15 NKJV)

The horses would be, in our time, military vehicles of various kinds. The point here is that they are coming by land. We will now look at Ezekiel 38:16, which paints a different picture of their entry into Israel.

> You will come up against My people Israel like a cloud, to cover the land. It will be in the latter days that I will bring you against

My land, so that the nations may know Me, when I am hallowed in you, O Gog, before their eyes.

We see here that God claims this land (Israel) as His own.

Verse 16 strongly suggests that they will enter Israel, at least in part, in an airborne attack. We will now look more closely at the word *up* as used in: *you will come up against My people.* The Hebrew word used here for *up* is *maal.* It has a number of meanings, several of which are: *the upper part, upward, above, overhead, and very high.*

So Ezekiel 38:15 says Gog and all will commence the attack from the far north, into the Middle East by land. Then the next verse, Ezekiel 38:16, strongly suggests that Gog and all will attack Israel from the air (very high overhead). Something is missing here. As we have seen before, this would not be the first time that a pair of Bible verses were separated by a span of time in transition from one time period and set of circumstances to another. So, what belongs between these two verses (Ezekiel 38:15 and Ezekiel 38:16)? This writing suggests that Daniel 11:40–45 fills the void realistically and does, in fact, tell the rest of the story. We will summarize here:

King of the North (Gog), with a great army, will come by sea, by land, and with helicopters, as a whirlwind, will enter the countries (heavy oil producers), and pass through on their way to Egypt for a coordinated two-front attack with the king of the south (Libya, Ethiopia, or both) against Antichrist and international community forces. Antichrist's forces will be in Egypt secondarily to protect this nation from retribution by the radical blocs for probable continued friendship with Israel. The radical blocs will prevail; and Daniel 11:43 says:

He [King of the north/Gog] shall have power over the treasures of gold and silver, and over all the precious things of Egypt; also the Libyans and Ethiopians shall follow at his heels.

The precious things of Egypt would refer to the irrigated Nile basin, the pipeline and the strategic Suez Canal. This priceless link between the Red Sea and the Mediterranean is of immense value if you control all the oil of the Arabian Peninsula. These precious things are the primary reason that the International Community forces will intervene in Egypt!

The battle in Egypt, prophesied in Ezekiel 30, provides considerable detail as to those involved, and how it will end. Knowing that Gog and those with him will be victorious is balanced by Ezekiel 39:2 in the KJV, seen earlier, and which says in part:

And I will turn thee back, and leave but the sixth part of thee,

So it appears that Gog/king of the north and the radical axis forces will be victorious with moderate losses of one-sixth leaving them there in Egypt. He/they will then be turned back/around, and will enter Israel from on high. Daniel 11:40 clarifies that when the king of the north comes against Antichrist and his forces, this king, as well as coming by land, will have many ships. These ships would explain the presence of helicopters to attack the men of the east in the oil fields on the way to Egypt, and to transport troops, equipment, and supplies from Egypt to Israel, for as God's word says:

You will ascend, coming like a storm, covering the land like a cloud, you and all your troops and many peoples with you (Ezekiel 38:9 NKJV).

After defeat in Egypt, and after the raider's rapid pullout to make their presence known in Israel in a meaningful way by a combined land, sea and air invasion, Antichrist will receive word in Egypt of two troubling events. One will concern a large army or armies headed toward the Middle East from the east. The other will confirm his already forming conclusion that the axis forces will be entering Israel for the purpose of committing maximum havoc and harvest of technology and supporting infrastructure. Antichrist will regroup and probably receive reinforcements. He then shall react to this latest communique:

But news from the east and the north shall trouble him; therefore he shall go out with great fury to destroy and annihilate many (Daniel 11:44).

Then Daniel 11:45 has him bivouacked between the seas and the glorious holy mountain (Jerusalem) on the plain of Jezreel, Israel. This is the location of biblical Armageddon.

# CHAPTER TWENTY-THREE

# ISRAEL,
# THE DOUBLE-EDGED SWORD!

When Antichrist and the remaining forces of the UN global union go into Israel, as Daniel says "with great fury to destroy and annihilate many" after the Egypt debacle, it will not be to protect Israel. It will be for their own survival. If they allow the attackers to keep the victory, their cozy global dictatorship will be turned upside down. With the entry into this tiny nation of these three separate forces, the Russian-led armies, the army of the kings of the east, and the remaining UN global union forces, the entire world will be represented there. Isn't this what God said was going to happen?

In this very awkward position that Israel will find herself in, if she were to be operating in her own power, she would find that her luck will have run out. The odds against her would be too great. All the military might of the entire world will be right there in her midst. That which will not be attacking her directly will not be especially concerned for her welfare. The picture that emerges is similar to that of western Jordan being overrun by the forces of the kings of the east. These armies in Israel will be eating, drinking, and plundering, and whatever else invading armies do when they occupy a nation. This is not to mention the Russians and the radical Islamic forces, there for the express purpose of ripping Israel apart. This tiny nation will need immediate aid, and the United States of America will not be able to supply it even if she wanted to, which she did not in the three prior invasions by Israel's Islamic neighbors. God, however, did supply it; and Israel, as we know, in the power of the Lord, emerged victorious each time. This time will be no different in its ultimate conclusion, except for the heavy losses on all sides. The intruding armies will be completely annihilated. Zechariah 13:8–9 tell, in the context of World War III, how Israel will fare:

> "And it shall come to pass in all the land," says the LORD, "that two-thirds in it shall be cut off and die, but one-third shall be left in it (verse 8).

> I will bring the one-third through the fire, will refine them as silver is refined, and test them as gold is tested. They will call on My name, and I will answer them. I will say, 'This is My people'; and each one will say, 'The LORD is my God'" (verse 9).

Now, about the destruction that will prevail in the Day of the Lord: if we go back to the first destruction, the time of the flood, we will see God's thoughts on the matter. Genesis 6:5–7 shows God's heart:

> Then the LORD saw that the wickedness of man was great in the earth, and that every intent of the thoughts of his heart was only evil continually.

> And the LORD was sorry that He had made man on the earth, and He was grieved in His heart.

> So the LORD said, "I will destroy man whom I have created from the face of the earth, both man and beast, creeping thing and birds of the air, for I am sorry that I have made them."

The account of Noah and the ark is well known, and does not need repeating here. The situation, however, at this time is similar, but to a lesser degree. Christ came to bring the light of repentance and salvation to a dark and dying world. Those who accept the offer of repentant salvation receive it. God's chosen people, who earnestly adhere to His Mosaic Law and who accept Christ at His return, shall, it would seem, be in the remnant that God will save and take physically into the millennial kingdom. Revelation 9:15 says that a third of world population will not make it alive into the millennial kingdom of God. Nevertheless, many will make the physical transition from the eternal death of man's destroyed kingdom to a new beginning and opportunity for a new way of life in the millennial Sabbath, Christ's earthly kingdom.

We see then that this destruction will differ greatly from that brought about by the Flood. This time it will be focused more on doing away with man's new idol; world government of man, by man, and for man. With mankind seeking God-status to the ex-clusion of God the Father, God the Son, and God the Holy Spirit, man's days are surely numbered with His millennial Sabbath right at the door.

We remember how God defeated the pagan giant Goliath, who represented the entire Philistine nation at war with Israel, by pit-ting the young shepherd boy, David, against him, and how David, with one of five smooth stones for his sling, slew the giant before the eyes of both nations' armies. Because of this single victory, the Philistine army fled in panic and was cut down in flight by the Israelites.

This defeat of the Philistines, engineered and carried out by God, using one shepherd boy as his double-edged sword, is a mi-crocosm of how God defeated the enemies of modern day Israel in 1948, 1967 and again in 1973. Israel received no other assistance and, of course, didn't need any. Now it will happen again, even on a larger scale. As we have already seen reference to, modern Israel will become God's bow and arrow. Zechariah 9:13 pictures Israel being used as the sword of a mighty man. Zechariah 9:15 has Israel being defended by the Lord of hosts, and going forth to devour and subdue with sling stones. All of this is in the context of the last invasion and attack on Israel by all the nations of the world.

In this last great conflict it seems that many in Israel's military will be God worshipping Jews and/or will turn to Christ when they see Him return for His saints. Since Israel's military will remain sufficiently strong to inflict the serious damage on the invaders intended by God, those in the armed forces who survive this intense fire storm will become a part of the remnant that will be saved through the fire, refined as silver, and tested as gold (Zechariah 13:9).

Jeremiah 51:20 goes on to say:

You are My battle-ax and weapons of war: for with you I will break the nation in pieces; with you I will destroy kingdoms.

So the plan is made; the trap is set. God will be known by the nations. All the nations in the world, atheistic, secular, and those that worship their own gods whoever or whatever they may be, will see the power of almighty God. The entire world will be a witness to His power and His fury. For once and for all, He will be known by the nations of the world. Ezekiel 38:23 has God making this statement:

Thus I will magnify Myself and sanctify Myself, and I will be known in the eyes of many nations. Then they shall know that I am the LORD.

God's attitude toward the lost is just that—they are lost! If they haven't accepted His Son before His return, or their own death, they have played out their losing hand only for what pleasure it may have afforded; *then the game is over!* Just being a good person can not do it—Jesus is the only way.

Many believe mankind to be basically good. Christians know that man is inherently bad, evil. It happened in the Garden of Eden and has been passed down generation to generation.

Christians know that the nature of mankind is to partake of sin. They know this because they themselves must deal with it each day of their lives. What they know also is that sin is not a death sentence for them as it once was. The Christian life is one that intentionally avoids sin. When sin occurs in a believer's life, and it does from time to time, the Christian sinner asks God's forgiveness through Jesus Christ. Christ's blood bought forgiveness, upon repentance, for all who follow and believe in Him. The sin is *forgiven* and *forgotten*. The apostle Paul, in his letter to the Ephesian church clarifies this:

And you He made alive, who were dead in trespasses and sins,

in which you once walked according to the course of this world, according to the prince of the power of the air, the spirit who now works in the sons of disobedience (Ephesians 2:1–2).

In God's eyes according to His word, all are lost who ignore His Son Jesus Christ and instead, allow themselves to be drawn away to eternal death by, as Paul says: "the spirit who now works in the sons of disobedience." More about this spirit just ahead.

# CHAPTER TWENTY-FOUR

# THE SPIRIT REALM

Many people today have come to realize that we are not alone in our physical world. Christians, of course, have been aware of this other world ever since the days of Jesus' earthly ministry. Jesus, in the power of the Holy Spirit, cast out unclean spirits, demons, fallen angels who follow Satan. There are a number of instances of this phenomenon recorded in the Scriptures of the New Testament: Mark 1:23–26, 5:2–13, 7:25–30; Luke 9:38–42, to name some. Both Paul and Philip are recorded as having cast out unclean spirits by the Holy Spirit: Acts 8:5–7, 16:16–18.

References to unclean spirits are found throughout the Old Testament. Zechariah tells that we can look forward to the time when the kingdom of God will be in place on this earth, the millennial Sabbath; then God will expel unclean spirits from the land (Zechariah 13:2). Demon spirits were a fact of life in Bible times. They are as well a fact of life in our time. This phenomena may be observed to a high degree in the new age community. Interaction of humans with demon spirits is now an art form among many new age gurus and channelers, with demons calling themselves spirit guides and masters of the universe, and being called up at will by the individual involved. In other relationships, demon spirits pass themselves off as aliens from another galaxy. These interactions take the form of alien abductions; with episodes occurring as a result of individuals leaving themselves open to various kinds of demonic activity. Invitation for possession by or contact with demons usually occurs innocently through involvement with fortune tellers, psychics, astrology, attempted contact with the dead, witchcraft, ouiji boards, role-playing fantasy games such as Dungeons & Dragons, etc. These activities, though they may be considered harmless, serve as an open door through which demonic contact can occur. Intense meditation can also serve as a medium for contact.

The result of all of this interaction has served to advance the cause of the new age mentality. It is obvious that there is a power involved. In new age circles it is referred to as the force. This force is the essence of occultism, which in turn is diametrically opposite of the righteousness of Jehovah God Almighty. In this end time in which we live, the prime objective of this satanic force is the abolishment of the power of the gospel of Jesus Christ. All demonic activity is directly or indirectly focused on this effort.

Yes, the power source of this force is Satan (Lucifer), the powerful rebel leader of fallen angels (spirit beings). Satan, though he masquerades as the angel of light, in reality is the embodiment of evil. Satan exemplifies the apex of moral degradation. He has dominion over all the earth. Though unseen, he exerts his dark influence from behind the veil that separates the physical world from the spiritual world. Satan enjoys abundant assistance from his hoard of fallen, judged, and convicted angels who, like him, know that their time is growing very short. The tempo of their negative activity, therefore, is accelerating. Evidence of this heightened level of human/demonic involvement is all around us.

The coming of the lawless one is according to the working of Satan, with all power, signs, and lying wonders (2 Thessalonians 2:9).

No prophecy could be more accurate, concise, and to the point. The key word, though, is accurate. This prophecy describes perfectly what is happening today in new age circles in the U.S.A and all around the world.

Demonic manifestations resulting from channeling, meditation, and unsolicited contact brought on by unintentionally opening one's self to it, are only part of the current scene. Alien abductions occur with abductees taken to supposed space ships to undergo physical examinations; sometimes to receive a tiny implant under the skin. These procedures are administered by beings who closely resemble our concept of how outer space aliens should look. Other abductee encounters involve a race of creatures appearing to be part reptile and part human; thus the name reptilians. Sexual activity is reported to result *between these creatures and human abductes. The outcome produces an offspring cross between the two that is referred to as grays.* Is this real or delusion, a demonic lying wonder?

Crop circles, animal mutilations, bigfoot, out of body experiences and UFO's also belong in the category of signs and lying wonders. These are manifestations of Satan's power; preparatory to ushering onto the world scene the lawless one, the beast of Revelation 13:1, Antichrist, the archenemy of Jesus Christ!

The Bible tells in the book of Genesis of a strange occult occurrence that prevailed on the earth preceding the Flood. It has relevance for today with reports from new age circles of sexual encounters between so-called aliens (demons) other than reptilians and humans. These unions are said to produce offspring called hybrids that appear human.

Genesis 6:4 says:

There were giants on the earth in those days, and also afterward, when the sons of God came in to the daughters of men and they bore children to them. Those were the mighty men who were of old, men of renown.

So these mighty men, men of renown, were the progeny of a demon/human relationship. The fallen angels then, materialized robust physical bodies with which to procreate offspring with humans. These offspring had some definitive paternal characteristics such as large size, great endurance, and warrior qualities. The verse also says that they were on the earth after the Flood as well as before. Though the Flood did not stop the demonic practice, God did stop it later.

These giants are mentioned in the Bible as existing long after the Flood. One example concerns the Israelites when they were preparing to enter the Promised Land on the west side of the Jordan River. Moses sent spies across the river to investigate the land, its people, and its produce. Numbers 13:33 records part of the report given to Moses and the children of Israel upon return of the spies. The verse tells of the giants in this way:

> There we saw the giants [the descendants of Anak called the Anakim]; and we were like grasshoppers in our own sight, and so we were in their sight.

Another biblical record of giants after the flood refers to the time shortly prior to the one mentioned above. It involves the Israelites warring against Og, King of Bashan in what is now western Jordan. They defeated Og and all sixty of his cities (Deuteronomy 3:1–10.) King Og was the last remaining giant in the land of Bashan. An interesting reference is made to him in Deuteronomy 3:11:

> For only Og king of Bashan remained of the remnant of the giants. Indeed his bedstead was an iron bedstead. Is it not in Rabbah of the people of Ammon? Nine cubits [13 1/2 feet] is its length and four cubits [6 feet] its width, according to the standard cubit.

The giant Goliath was one of the dwindling number of post-flood giants remaining west of the Jordan. He was from the city of Gath in what is now western Israel. At the time David slew him, Gath was home to one of three remnant collections of giants called

Anakim. All three of these cities of the Anakim giants are mentioned in Joshua 11:22, which tells us:

> None of the Anakim were left in the land of the children of Israel; they remained only in Gaza, in Gath, and in Ashdod.

This area is in and around the present day Gaza Strip occupied by the Palestinians, but in those days it was the land of the Philistines. Joshua's Israelites had destroyed all the remaining giants except those in the land of the Philistines, Joshua 11:21. God had given the Philistine's paganized land to Israel along with that of their neighbors, but Israel had difficulty taking it.

So with these giants being descendants of demons and humans, God tolerated their existence for a time, and then removed them from the earth. If these human/demon cross offspring are other than satanic smoke and mirrors that is; if, in fact, they do exist in the physical or possibly the spirit world, their days are strictly numbered. They are, nevertheless, part of the physical/spiritual, or imaginary imagery of the end time orgy of:

> . . . the working of Satan, with all power, signs, and lying wonders (2 Thessalonians 2:9).

There are two new age human/demon relationships that are attained by mutual agreement. One is channeling. This occult affair results after a relationship between a human and a demon has been consummated. The relationship involves a deceiving spirit making contact with a human target, usually through the person having opened himself or herself to it by an occult activity, some of which have been discussed.

The demon spirit will pass itself off as something it is not. The deceived human, not knowing better, then accepts the lies at face value. The relationship then progresses to the channeling stage where the person involved can call up the spirit at will. The lying spirit, upon being called, takes over the human body which will have gone into a trance. The spirit proceeds to impart information of one kind or another through the human's vocal cords for the benefit of any onlookers who may be present. Demons, being angels, although fallen and doomed, are knowledgeable on many subjects. Lying is a virtue with them. The fact is, they will usually give information on past events or on supposed future events, as well as intelligence of a highly technical nature involving the physical sciences. These subjects, of course, cannot be proven false or even slightly in error since the human channeler and the audience have no knowledge of the past or future spoken of, or of the highly technical subject matter. The flawed information is usually accepted as fact and the delusion continues.

The spirit, more than likely to build credibility, will have provided some information that would have been known as fact by the channeler and/or the audience. Give some truth for bait, and then switch to lies. Bait and switch, a time-proven method of deceptive manipulation.

The other new age human/demon relationship by mutual agreement is referred to as a walk-in. This arrangement involves a demon spirit masquerading as an enlightened universal being. This spirit, having been invited in, takes over the human body and then proceeds to impart flawed information to other humans. The potential for widespread satanic influence is quite great if the occupied human is a person of renown. He or she could be in the public eye through TV, magazines, etc., advocating unchristian, ungodly beliefs, and practices. Should it be a well-known media person, such as a television personality, movie star, rock music celebrity, etc., the fallout from worldwide exposure to counter-Christian mentality could be contagious. Should this person be a well-known politician working toward humanistic, one-world, global unification, he could have a pronounced worldwide influence.

This is not possession, but rather a willing surrender of one's self to supposedly higher beings, of another dimension from another world, an outer galactic presence calling itself a spirit guide, a universal presence, or masters of the universe. The human recipient of the imposter's masquerading lies is totally convinced, believing he/she is involved with and helping a genuine alien being. The goal of the benevolent entity can be varied, but generally deals with redirecting human thinking in the areas of ecology and spirituality. It occurs in the context of imparting higher levels of knowledge and understanding to earthlings. All these interactions with humans are, of course, aimed at filling the senses with humanistic, worldly trivia through preoccupation with contrived ecological emergencies, pagan spiritual nonsense, and things of the flesh (i.e., *sex*).

The truth of the matter is that the demon spirit is trying to eradicate every vestige of God the Father's and God the Son's influence on our earth, the goal being humanistic global government of man, by man, and for man. To diefy man as master of his own destiny with the ability to reach ever-higher levels of not only understanding, but to attain glorified eternal life as well through his own power—*this is the big lie!*

God Almighty, knowing the beginning from the end, through His apostle Paul in 2 Thessalonians 2:9, and as we have already seen, tells us that: "The coming of the lawless one is according to the working of Satan, with all power, signs, and lying wonders."

Paul expands on this in the next three verses, 10–12, which say: "and with all unrighteous deception among those who perish, because they did not receive the love of the truth, that they might be saved. And for this reason, God will send them strong delusion, that they should believe the lie, that they all may be condemned who did not believe the truth but had pleasure in unrighteousness."

So we see here that God, through the apostle Paul two thousand years ago, told what things would be like in regard to satanic lying wonders leading up to Antichrist's debut and entry upon the world scene. He not only warned of lying wonders, but told also of unrighteous deception that would be transmitted by the lost, those who refused to accept and believe God's truth, the gospel of Jesus Christ. He went on to explain also that these lost refusers of the truth would be condemned to eternal punishment for their denial and for their unrighteous activity in participating in the ongoing deception.

At this time (early 2006) Antichrist has not yet, but will very soon be revealed. Based on a theoretical understanding of God's prophetic Word as seen in Table #7, using June 19, 2012 as the potential end of WWIII and the six thousand years, this would indicate the treaty of peace commencing on, or about June 19, 2005. As we know, the treaty started in stealth, clothed in ambiguity precisely on that date! Deceptive wonders will continue, to and into his time of relevance. The intent seems to be that of rendering people's sensibilities numb to unusual and unexplained phenomena; with the expected result being that Antichrist and the charade surrounding his grand entrance onto the scene will be accepted without qualification by the majority. The unrighteous deception by and of those who will refuse to accept the saving truth will continue unabated. This time of heretofore unknown deception, though it will be a time of marvelous awakening, renewal, and reaching unhindered spiritual heights by the deluders and the deluded, will be a time of severe testing for Christians. Many nominal Christians will fall away, to be swept up in the excitement of the day—humanistic, new age spirituality. Christians will need to draw near to Jesus and stay there!

This last days deception—described by the apostle Paul as being propagated by refusers of the truth" is all about angels—fallen angels—demon followers who serve Satan.

# CHAPTER TWENTY-FIVE

# A SYMBOLIC LOOK AT PAST AND FUTURE SATANIC ACTIVITY

Lucifer, Satan, the great deceiver, once highly favored by God, turned on God, wanting to be greater than He. Revelation 12, using symbolism, gives a clear explanation of how Satan and his demons were given access to earth, with authority over the planet as well. It also describes how Satan and his angels will soon come to lose their access to heaven, a privilege to which they have grown accustomed; to be restricted to earth only, and how this action will stimulate earthly satanic activity and bring it to a fever pitch.

An important point to understand and keep in mind before entering into this area of interest is: the reason that Satan was given his free run of the earth in the first place, is that he had contaminated it with sin in the Garden of Eden.

Proof of strong delusion is today, all around us. With mass media served by world circling communication satellites, relatively few deluders can now infect the minds of multitudes!

In Revelation 12:4, it is shown that Satan and his followers were allowed to come down to earth: "His [Satan's] tail drew a third of the stars [angels] of heaven and threw them to the earth." This is a symbolic picture of the early event that occurred at or near the time of Adam and Eve's sin in the Garden of Eden. This expansion of Satan's hunting privileges resulted in his gaining sufficient authority on earth, that he was free, even to attempt to destroy the Christ child after Jesus' virgin birth (Revelation 12:4).

After a great old time on earth of deceiving mankind in ways that only the devil could dream up, and generally leading the unrepentant down the primrose path to eternal destruction, and then approaching God in heaven to accuse each foolish human of the resultant sins that he fell victim to, God will say, "Stop! That's enough!" It seems that which the Apostle John was shown is to happen in the end time is about to happen, and by the time you read this, may have already occurred:

> And war broke out in heaven: Michael and his angels fought with the dragon; and the dragon and his angels fought,
>
> but they did not prevail, nor was a place found for them in heaven any longer.
>
> So the great dragon was cast out, that serpent of old, called the devil and Satan, who deceives the whole world; he was cast to the earth, and his angels were cast out with him (Revelation 12:7–9).

With Satan and his companion deceivers about to have their first class travel arrangements between heaven and earth, not just downgraded, but canceled entirely, Satan's smoldering enmity toward mankind will erupt into violent rage.

More could be said of this activity in Revelation 12 about Satan directing his wrath against godly Jews and Christians after his exile to earth. This banishment will intensify Satan's already underway crusade against God's people. His rage will then boil in his ruthless attacks on them. The most severe persecution will begin three-and-a-half years just prior to Jesus' return (See Table #1). Revelation 12:12 paints this word picture:

> Therefore rejoice, O heavens, and you who dwell in them! Woe to the inhabitants of the earth and the sea! For the devil has come down to you, having great wrath, because he knows that he has a short time.

We will have more exposure to this satanic/demonic activity on earth as we proceed in this work, but now we will meet two angels who are very special to God!

# CHAPTER TWENTY-SIX

# TWO ARCHANGELS

We met the first of these in Revelation 12:7–9, where "war broke out in heaven; Michael [the archangel] and his angels fought against the dragon; and the dragon and his angels fought."

Another reference to Michael can be found in Daniel 12:1. This verse speaks of the time of God's wrath (time of trouble), when God's Jewish remnant will be saved through the holocaust of Armageddon. This is what it says:

> At that time Michael shall stand up [continue on], the great prince who stands watch over the sons of your people; and there shall be a time of trouble, such as never was since there was a nation, even to that time. And at that time your people shall be delivered, every one who is found written in the book.

The Hebrew words for "stand" and "up" can also mean "continue" and "on". So this verse apparently is saying that Michael's 1,260 days of protecting the remnant is not used up and will continue on and through the time of trouble like no other. Michael will lead the remnant through the valley to safety from Armageddon in Jordan!

In these verses we have seen that Michael is not only an authority in heaven, having been referred to as Michael and his angels, but he is also the protector of God's holy Jewish remnant. We will see another important reference to this great archangel, Michael, just ahead in connection with his companion archangel of the Bible, Gabriel. But for now, we will concentrate on Gabriel, who is central to two important biblical revelations, both of which are found in the book of Daniel. We will direct our attention to the first one now, and the second one further on. In the second, he is involved in the delivery of an important prophecy, which proves the year ending man's six thousand years; and yes, provides proof of the year of the Lord's birth and of His return as well!

Daniel, while captive in Babylon, was stricken by the gross sins of his people that had resulted in their defeat at the hands of King Nebuchadnezzar and captivity of most of the survivors. Daniel prayed fervently to God in repentance for his people and himself. God was highly impressed with Daniel, and wanted him to understand certain future occurrences that would impact his people. It was God's intent that Daniel record these prophecies for the benefit of future generations; but which would become fully understood only at the time of the end (Daniel 12:4).

We are concentrating here on Gabriel, and so will reference several prophecies only to establish the fact that Gabriel, as seen in them, has the appearance of a man. We shall establish this as fact, and then will proceed to uncover an important revelation that has been clouded by considerable misunderstanding. This, in turn, has lead to belief by some, in a completely false doctrine. So here we will attempt to clear up the misconception of who, or what, is restraining the appearing of the Antichrist. A common misconception has the church and Holy Spirit written into this role as Antichrist's restrainer. This then establishes a springboard for the pre-tribulation doctorine to take off (no pun intended), with its contention that the Holy Spirit is holding back Christian persecution, that when He is removed by God, then the church will be taken (raptured) in a pre-resurrection translation, and not until that time will the bad stuff begin; allowing the church to miss Antichrist's wild party, so to speak. Perhaps Christian killings, amputations, and slavery in Africa do not count yet.

In direct opposition to this doctrine of escape, Matthew 24:29–30 says that "immediately after the tribulation of those days, the Son of Man will be seen coming on the clouds of heaven." Since this escape doctrine is not found in the Bible, its adherents are forced to draw inaccurate conclusions from Scripture having no reference point, apparent or inferred, that in any way relates specifically to a pre-resurrection translation. They read into it what they want it to say. It is becoming more and more difficult to ignore what is going on in the world. Persecution of Christians is a fact of life the world over. China, India, most nations of Africa, all Islamic nations, all Communist nations, and all opposing political/spiritual factions within so-called enlightened Western nations, all engage in this activity to one degree or another. It is becoming increasingly problematic for sincere Christians to accept this questionable premise as factual.

Escape from difficult times is appealing, but Jesus did not say that following Him would be without loss. In this temporal time in which we live, only God's word is lasting and permanent; with all other as grass of the field, to wither and die. But permanence beckons just ahead! Now, back to Gabriel.

Daniel 9:21 specifically describes the angel Gabriel as having the appearance of a man. It reads as follows:

> yes, while I was speaking in prayer, the man Gabriel, whom I had seen in the vision at the beginning, being caused to fly swiftly, reached me about the time of the evening offering.

It is established here that Gabriel appeared to Daniel in the form of a man and gave him the prophecy of the seventy weeks. Prior to that, in Daniel 8:15–16, the angel Gabriel is identified as having the appearance of a man; and he then explained to Daniel the meaning of the vision of the ram, the goat, and the little horn (Antiochus IV Epiphanes) (Daniel 8:17–27). Then, in Daniel 10:5, we are told of another encounter. This time the angel is not named; but the strong inference is that this is also Gabriel. In Daniel 10:5 we read this:

> I lifted my eyes and looked, and behold, a certain man clothed in linen, whose waist was girded with gold of Uphaz!

We know that this man was an angel because in Daniel 10:11 we are told:

> And he said to me, "O Daniel, man greatly beloved, understand the words that I speak to you, and stand upright, for I have now been sent to you." While he was speaking this word to me, I stood trembling.

The statement "for I have now been sent to you," confirms that he is a messenger, an angel. The word *now* infers *as at other times*; that he had been sent to Daniel before. Who had sent him?

> Then he said to me, "Do not fear, Daniel, for from the first day that you set your heart to understand, and to humble yourself before your God, your words were heard; and I have come because of your words (Daniel 10:12).

Here we see Daniel's prayers to God were heard, and God sent this angel to Daniel to help him understand.

We too are about to understand that which seems to have fallen through the cracks, but is now found and will make its contribution toward clarity in understanding end time Bible prophecy. In the very next verse, Daniel 10:13, Gabriel, in explaining his belated arrival in coming to Daniel, reveals what it was that caused his delay. The verse says this:

But the prince [leader] of the kingdom of Persia withstood me twenty-one days; and behold, Michael, one of the chief princes, came to help me, for I had been left alone there with the kings of Persia.

Satan here is called prince leader of the kingdom of Persia; Persia here meaning the seat of anti-God activity. The kings of Persia refer to Satan's demon angels.

This reference to Gabriel has his job description in part, prioritized to Satan and his angels. Gabriel, being a prince (leader), will have a contingent of God's angels under his authority in accomplishing this task. For one reason or another, he was left alone with the enemy, which resulted in his being delayed in getting to Daniel by twenty-one days. It appears that his delay would have been longer had not Michael, and we can assume some of his angels, come to Gabriel's aid. The important point here is that Gabriel is God's delegated authority in dealing with Satan. We will see just ahead that Gabriel's authority in dealing with Satan is specific to a certain area of control that he, with assistance of his angels, exercises over Satan and his demons. But, Satan being Satan, representative of all that is evil in the world, by his very nature, we would expect that he and his followers would present a major challenge to Gabriel in the archangel imposing his will on them. For an account of what Gabriel had to say about this difficult job and a look at what we could say was "smoking gun" proof of who is restraining Antichrist's appearance, read on.

Gabriel's words to Daniel, in Daniel 10:20 are these:

Then he said, "Do you know why I have come to you? And now I must return to fight with the prince of Persia; and when I have gone forth, indeed the prince of Greece will come."

The prince of Greece indwelt by Satan was seen in (Revelation 13:4). Of course, the prince of Greece is Antichrist; returned

Antiochus IV Epiphanes, a Syrian king of the ancient Seleucid Dynasty, part of the divided Greek Empire. Gabriel is clearly seen here as being the one who is restraining the recognized appearance of Antichrist. *Mystery solved!*

In 2 Thessalonians 2:7–8, we find the following:

For the mystery of lawlessness is already at work; only He who now restrains will do so until He is taken out of the way.

And then the lawless one will be revealed, whom the Lord will consume with the breath of His mouth and destroy with the brightness of His coming.

Now, a comment about interpretation. The New King James Version of the Bible, used throughout this writing, makes the subjective decision to capitalize "he," inferring that Antichrist's restrainer is the Holy Spirit. Compelling evidence has shown this to be an error in subjective judgment. The *one who restrains* is unquestionably the powerful angel, appearing to be *Gabriel*, not the Holy Spirit, nor the church!

# CHAPTER TWENTY-SEVEN

# PRELUDE TO THE REBORN TWO WITNESSES

Revelation has the apostle John in his vision, being told by an angel to . . . rise and measure the temple of God, the altar, and those who worship there. But leave out the court which is outside the temple, and do not measure it, for it has been given to the Gentiles. And they will tread the holy city underfoot for forty-two months (Revelation 11:1–2).

This prophetic picture involving the next temple, but leaving out the court (outer court), allows for the existence of another structure in the outer court area. A building exists today in that very location. This present structure, the Islamic Dome of the Rock is a Muslim holy site, built long after the second temple of God was destroyed by the Romans. This temple destruction is that which Jesus referred to in Matthew 24:1–2, where He said: "not one stone shall be left here upon another, that shall not be thrown down." It all went down in A.D. 70.

Revelation 11:1–2 are very meaningful verses in their ability to focus directly on the Israel/Palestinian situation which exists in our time; that is, a final disposition of Jerusalem. The Palestinians claim the old section of the city (East Jerusalem) for the capital of their forthcoming homeland. This old city, however, is firmly in the hands of the nation of Israel, and is claimed by her as the ancestral capital of her godly inheritance. Many will remember the old 1970's song for its unique ability to portray hostile opposition between disputing parties when it referred to the "irresistible force meeting the immovable object." This is precisely the dilemma facing these two negotiating sides. Neither will bend very far. The bargaining will involve the delicate subject of Jerusalem; and who will receive what, and how much. On the other hand, what will have to be sacrificed in payment thereof, that in the eyes of each party will be of less real worth? The goal of each—to gain the most perceived value, while giving up the least— it used to be called horse trading!

It looks very much like the time is close at hand for the nation of Israel, with its strong religious community in hot pursuit of the right to rebuild the temple on the temple mount, to strike a deal with Islamic nations that will allow this important prophetic milestone to become a reality. Could Israel's final concession be a limited and controlled version of presently insurmountable Palestinian demands for unrestricted "right of return"?

One critical aspect of a potential joint occupancy of the temple mount that will not be lost on the follow-up strengthener of the peace accord, will be the powerful statement of cooperation to be made to the world: The side by side existence of the Jewish temple of God and the Muslim Dome of the Rock holy site together, on ground that shortly before had symbolized the height of religious and political opposition. Then, to become the poster child and focal point of the worldwide, trade sensitive, religious ecumenical movement to global brotherhood in a war weary world.

# CHAPTER TWENTY-EIGHT

# THE TWO WITNESSES

Revelation 11:3 foretells the following: "And I will give power to my two witnesses, and they will prophesy one thousand two hundred and sixty days, clothed in sackcloth [humility]." With Jesus' return prophesied to occur after the tribulation of those days, Matthew 24:29–30, and with Christians not appointed to wrath, 1 Thessalonians 5:9, we seem to have a conflict. We do not, however, since saints will be protected through initial wrath, up to the then, soon return of Jesus at the fourth trumpet! With the two witnesses' 1,260 day ministry ending at Christ's return and the Resurrection, it can be seen that these forty-two months are likely not congruent with the forty-two months (1,260 days) of the Gentiles trampling on Jerusalem. This Palestinian (Gentile) control of East Jerusalem, possibly shared with Israel, will probably begin with commencement of Antichrist's confirmation (strengthening) of the treaty. (See table #1.) Yes! No mistake! Jesus will return at the fourth trumpet. Absolute proof awaits!

Much speculation exists as to just who the two witnesses are/were. Their correct identification lends to the continuity of interpreting Bible prophecy. So then, we need to correctly identify them. We have already placed the time of their testimony as being the approximately three-and-a-half years (forty-two months), or 1,260 days just prior to the return of the Lord at the fourth trumpet. This will plunge Christ's return right into the middle of some very intense cosmic activity shortly after the wrath will have begun.

At the end of the witnesses' three-and-a-half years of introducing the gospel of Jesus Christ to a lost and dying world, Revelation 11:7 tells what will take place:

> When they finish their testimony, the beast that ascends out of the bottomless pit will make war against them, overcome them, and kill them.

What happens next is interesting, to say the least. Revelation 11:8–10 makes it clear that after the two witnesses are killed, their bodies will be left lying in a street of Jerusalem. The apostle John didn't know anything about television, but he said anyway that the people of the nations would see the dead bodies in the street and would not allow them to be removed for burial. He went on to say that the people of the world will rejoice over them, make merry, and send gifts to one another because these two had tormented them to such a great extent. Question: could it be that the making merry and sending of gifts, one to another, was actually due to our modern Christmas tradition being observed in the vision at the time of the witnesses' unceremonious lack of interment? John would have been unaware of our late December tradition, just as with our eye on the world (TV) for people of the nations to view the dead bodies. There would be joy for this Christmas gift to the world! Revelation 11:5–6 tell why the great joy:

> And if anyone wants to harm them, fire proceeds from their mouth and devours their enemies. And if anyone wants to harm them, he must be killed in this manner.

> These have power to shut heaven, so that no rain falls in the days of their prophecy; and they have power over waters to turn

them to blood, and to strike the earth with all plagues, as often as they desire. [Great joy; out of the way at last!]

After three-and-one-half days of viewing the bodies where they lay in the street of the holy city, something very spectacular will happen. Revelation 11:11–12 tell what it will be with this account:

> Now after the three-and-a-half days the breath of life from God entered them, and they stood on their feet, and great fear fell on those who saw them.

> And they heard a loud voice from heaven saying to them, "Come up here." And they ascended to heaven in a cloud, and their enemies saw them. [A dark cloud, growing ever darker!]

Something to consider: Matthew 24:30 clearly says "and they will see the Son of Man coming on the clouds of heaven with power and great glory." So when these two witnesses ascend to heaven in a cloud, as Revelation 11:12 says, it is being faithful to conditions as they will exist at the Lord's return in the commencement of the dark and cloudy Day of the Lord (Zephaniah 1:15). This is a microcosm and a part of the Resurrection! Revelation 11:13 follows in support of wrath at Christ's return:

> In the same hour there was a great earthquake, and a tenth of the city fell. In the earthquake seven thousand men were killed, and the rest were afraid and gave glory to the God of heaven.

We shall later see the cause of the great earthquake up close.

The loss of seven thousand lives in the earthquake, not to mention the encroaching, catastrophic darkening of the atmosphere, will make a strong statement in establishing the reality of God's wrath. It is realistic to believe, also, that they might be greatly afraid to have witnessed Jesus' return, and the resurrection of not only the two witnesses, but the resurrection and translation of all other saved Christians in their midst. It's easy to see why these people would give glory to God after witnessing this cataclysmic event. After all, most will be Jewish and many of these, in recognizing the return of their Messiah, will feel the weight of their disbelief weighing heavily on their hearts. The cold fingers of fear will tear at their conscience. They will give *glory to God!* The rest will be afraid.

Now, to face the question asked above, referencing the possibility that the circumstances of the witnesses' deaths as seen in the vision being a last days occurrence, actually coincided with the entrenched, worldwide tradition of sending gifts to one another at Christmas. If this assumption were true, we would find yet another reflection of Bible prophecy mirrored by Mayan long cycle tradition.

The Mayan long cycle, lasting more than 5,000 years, within which their 365 day calendar cycles, is not only ending in the year 2012, but on a specific day and in a specified month of that year. The month is December, and the day is the twenty-second.[18] If this day a year earlier (2011) happened to be the day that the witnesses' death sentences were carried out, their resurrection, three-and-one-half days later would occur on December 25! (See Table #7)

The Mayan long cycle calendar and its seemingly shadow relationship to God-inspired end time Bible prophecy is an interesting anecdote, but little more. We will then leave it for those who are interested in such things to ponder the relevance, if any, and move ahead with what appears to be a group of collaborators, closely associated with the two witnesses.

In God's wisdom and for His glory, He will create an effective last days force, which being associated with the two witnesses, will reap mightily in the final harvest of souls for Christ. This will proceed through bad and tumultuous times.

# CHAPTER TWENTY-NINE

# THE ONE HUNDRED FORTY-FOUR THOUSAND, AND THE NUMBER TWELVE

This is a puzzling group to say the least! Revelation 7:4–8 lists 12,000 servants of God to be sealed from each of twelve tribes of Israel. This comes to a total of 144,000 precisely. Now, the question begins to surface: why exactly 12,000 from each of twelve tribes?

The fact is, there are actually thirteen tribes of Israel. Joseph was removed, and his two sons, Ephraim and Manasseh, replaced him in the line of tribal fathers. So then, why not thirteen tribes having 13,000 servants of God sealed? The answer seems to be found in the number "twelve" itself. Twelve is a very special number in God's scheme of things. It is found over and over in the Bible, in both high-profile use and low-profile situations. It is startling when confronted with the high usage of this number in low-profile circumstances—common, and ordinary, mundane conditions.

Just for example, we use the number twelve every day ourselves. In fact, we live our lives around it. Twelve hours in a day, twelve hours in a night, and twelve months in a year. Twelve o'clock midnight, twelve o'clock noon, a dozen eggs, twelve inches to a foot, and twelve pre-college grades!

For a few examples of how the Bible uses the number twelve, we can cite the following:

A. Jacob's (Israel's) twelve sons as fathers of the twelve tribes of Israel; prior to the exchange of Joseph for his two sons in this line of tribal fathers (Genesis 48:3-5).
B. Jesus choosing His twelve disciples (John 6:70).
C. When Jesus was taken into custody by those sent from the chief priests and elders of the people, prior to His trial and crucifixion, He said to those who came for Him: "Or do you think that I can not pray to My Father, and He will provide Me with more than twelve legions of angels?" (Matthew 26:53).
D. After Jesus fed the five thousand with five loaves and two fish, and the people ate and were filled the twelve disciples took up twelve baskets full of fragments and of the fish (Mark 6:43).
E. New Jerusalem (future eternal heaven) will be laid out as a cube, with each of the three dimensions being equal at twelve thousand furlongs; its length, breadth and height are equal (Revelation 21:16).

   1. The New Jerusalem will have twelve foundations under its walls (Revelation 21:19–20).
   2. The New Jerusalem will have twelve gates, of twelve oversized pearls, (Revelation 21:21).
   3. The city had a pure river of water of life, clear as crystal, proceeding from the throne of God and of the Lamb (Revelation 22:1). On either side of the river was the tree of life which bore twelve fruits, each tree yielding its fruit every month—twelve times a year (Revelation 22:2).

F. About Abraham's first son, Ishmael, God said: "Behold, I have blessed him, and will make him fruitful, and will multiply him exceedingly. He shall begat twelve princes, and I will make him a great nation" (Genesis 17:20). All Arab peoples today claim to be descended from Ishmael.

And so it goes. It's like the Bible is built around the number twelve. In the Old Testament, the trend in the use of twelve seems to center around the twelve sons of Jacob. In the New Testament, the trend is around the twelve disciples and the twelve tribes (sons) of Israel. Again the impression is that these trends honor the twelve tribes of Israel, even to the extent that the twelve disciples themselves rise to the status of honoring the twelve original tribes.

Comment: God made man and woman on the sixth day (Genesis 1:27-31). Man's number is therefore six. The very first two humans, Adam and Eve, the progenitors of human kind, each representing six, together yield twelve, *the fullness of mankind!* Does the year 2012, then have connotations of the fullness of mankind's free will?

With this said, we can see that the selection of twelve thousand from each of twelve tribes of Israel in Revelation 7 is a symbolic gesture aimed at honoring the concept of twelve, the fullness of Christ's church. So then, is the one hundred forty-four thousand a symbolic figure, which represents something else? Or is it an actual total of exactly twelve thousand individuals from each of twelve tribes that leaves out one of the actual thirteen tribes of Israel?

It appears that we may have already answered the question! With the number twelve used symbolically throughout God's Word, why expect it to be used differently here? It is obvious that the concept of twelve tribes is deep-seated in God's scheme of things. Even when the number of tribes is greater than twelve, the special number twelve is used to represent both the fullness of Israel and of Christ's church. And we might say also, the fullness of free will.

Revelation 14:4–5 tells that: "These are the ones who were not defiled with women [pagan goddesses] for they are virgins [true believers in Christ]. These are the ones who follow the Lamb wherever He goes. These were redeemed from among men, being first fruits to God and to the Lamb.

And in their mouth was found no guile, for they are without fault before the throne of God." (The 144,000.)

Those above are Christians, Jew and Gentile, representing the full tribal spectrum of the Jewish olive tree. They, though being in the world, are separate from the world. These strong believers in Jesus are all represented by the church of Philadelphia, of which, Revelation 3:10 teaches this: "Because you have kept My [Jesus'] command to persevere, I also will keep you from the hour of trial [wrath] which shall come upon the whole world, to test [discipline] those who dwell on the earth." The Greek word for *keep* as in *keep you from*, is *tereo*. It means *to guard from loss or injury by keeping an eye on them*. In other words, protecting them through tribulation and wrath to Jesus' return. It does not indicate an early exit of the church before trouble starts, as many are taught to believe. These 144,000, representing the fullness of the twelve sons of Israel, and the projected fullness of the church, will experience tribulation and early wrath; protected from all by Jesus. They shall have three names inscribed upon their persons by the Holy Spirit Himself. Revelation 3:7–13 tell the complete story of the church of Philadelphia, while verse 12 provides the three holy names on these harvest workers for Christ that mark them as last days harvesters for the soon-to-come kingdom of God. The three names show who they belong to, where they are going, and who is protecting them. These very meaningful names are: *God, the New Jerusalem, and Christ's new name!* These names translate out to God's figurative seal on the foreheads of the 144,000 servants of God (Revelation 7:1–4).

The dynamics of the above depicted protection for these last days workers in the harvest fields for Christ are not new. All one need do is refer to Daniel 3:19–25 for how God saved Shadrach,

Meshach, and Abed-Nego in the superheated fiery furnace. A look at Daniel 6:16–23 will show another miraculous intervention by God in saving Daniel in the lion's den from certain death.

With the one hundred forty-four thousand being "redeemed from among men as first fruits to God" (Revelation 14:4), and with first fruits representing the tithe of the harvest, we are in need of a summary here. The fact is that *Israel is being biblically represented through all aspects of the last days harvest of souls for Christ by God's special number twelve*. This is accomplished by twelve's relationship to God's people, Israel, in its application to His last days harvest workers, seen symbolically as the one hundred forty-four thousand (12,000 12's).

The two witnesses will be specially equipped by God to serve the last days harvesters for Christ as a rallying point and a source of godly guidance. As a result of their immense Holy Spirit empowerment in dealing with demonic, worldly powers, the two witnesses will as well negotiate, intimidate, and rightfully influence the powers that be, subjecting them to the will of God, causing them to comply in providing the 144,000 with access to necessary logistics, approvals, etc., for furthering their various ministries.

It would now be good to know the biblical identities of these two witnesses. We will start first with Joshua the high priest. Haggai 1:1 reveals that Joshua is the son of Jehozadak the high priest. First Chronicles 6:15 reports that Jehozadak went into captivity by the hand of Nebuchadnezzar.

It is likely that Joshua was born in Babylon. He would have advanced to the office of high priest due to his being in the priestly line of Levi through his father.

Zechariah 2:10 sets the tone for this study and reads as follows: "Sing and rejoice, O daughter of Zion! [latter-day Israel] 'For behold, I am coming and I will dwell in your midst,' says the

Lord." So then, what we will read in Zechariah 3 is in reference to the end of the 6,000 years and the beginning of the millennial Sabbath. Verses 1 and 2 read as follows:

> Then he showed me Joshua the high priest standing before the Angel of the LORD, and Satan standing at his right hand to oppose him.
>
> And the LORD said to Satan, "The LORD rebuke you, Satan! The LORD who has chosen Jerusalem rebuke you! Is this not a brand plucked from the fire?"

We have just seen where the Lord has restrained Satan by command in regard to Satan bothering Joshua. We have also seen that the Lord calls Joshua a brand plucked from the fire. This would make Joshua a *fire brand*, which by dictionary authority is one who stirs up trouble or dissention.

What we read of the two witnesses in Revelation 11:3 is that God will give them power (the Holy Spirit) for them to prophesy for three-and-a-half years. Then in verses five and six, we learn that they would have power to be able to devour their enemies with fire that will proceed from their mouths. We are told also that they shall have power to shut heaven so no rain will fall, and they will be able to turn waters to blood, and to strike the earth with all plagues as often as they desire.

This is ample evidence that God's intent is for Joshua to function as a thorn in the side of Antichrist and those under his control; that is, as a "firebrand plucked from the fire." He and his companions, in pointing out salvation through Jesus to a lost and dying world, will become targets of retribution by the unrepentant which will be ineffective against them.

By the power of God endued to them, they will evangelize the unsaved in the midst of the most intimidating persecution that will rage against them by the followers of Antichrist. They will be immune as well to the ravages of famine, pestilence, warfare, and natural disasters to come upon the earth in that three-and-a-half years of tribulation and explosive initial wrath!

Zechariah provides more details of the coming together of Joshua and Satan standing before the Angel of the Lord (Jesus), in a meeting that lays the groundwork for the ministry of the two witnesses and the one hundred forty-four thousand. Zechariah 3:3–5 gives the following insight:

> Now Joshua was clothed with filthy garments, and was standing before the Angel.
>
> Then He [the angel] answered and spoke to those who stood before Him, saying, "Take away the filthy garments from him." And to him He said, "See, I have removed your iniquity from you, and I will clothe you with rich robes [the righteousness of Jesus]."
>
> And I said, "Let them put a clean turban on his head." So they put a clean turban on his head, and they put the clothes on him. And the Angel of the LORD stood by.

We have just seen Joshua the high priest, who came out of Babylon as a captive in that ungodly city, transformed from wearing the filthy clothing of sinfulness, to being clothed in rich robes of the righteousness of Christ.

Zechariah 3:6–9 continues:

> Then the Angel of the LORD admonished Joshua, saying,
>
> "Thus says the LORD of hosts: 'If you will walk in My ways, and if you will keep My command, then you shall also judge My house, and likewise have charge of My courts; I will give you places to walk among these who stand here [seven angels].

'Hear, O Joshua, the high priest, you and your companions [144,000] who sit [endure] before you, for they are a wondrous sign; for behold, I am bringing forth My Servant the BRANCH [Christ's second coming as a *branch* of God].

For behold, the stone [Jesus] that I have laid before Joshua: upon the stone are seven eyes [the omnipresence of God]. Behold, I will engrave its inscription,' [Lord of hosts] says the LORD of hosts, 'And I will remove the iniquity of that land [Israel] in one day.

The one day that the LORD is referring to here is the seventh, one thousand year day of the week of one thousand year days. This millennial Sabbath day, God's kingdom, will be the last and final day of this seven thousand year week. This should not be confused with the seventy weeks of Daniel 9:24. Daniel's weeks are seven year weeks, each having seven (one year long days). It was given specifically to Daniel's heritage, the Jews, but will affect all people. This one thousand year Sabbath, the last day of man's week, is God's earthly kingdom to be ruled by the Branch of God, Jesus Christ, and lies straight ahead. The millennial Sabbath will follow the first six millennial days of the week, Sunday through Friday. *We are now positioned at Friday evening, late in the final hour at twilight, just before sundown!* According to Jewish custom, sundown on the sixth day ends the work week and begins the Sabbath.

Following Zechariah 3:9, where the Lord of hosts states: "And I will remove the iniquity of that land in one day," Zechariah 3:10 continues with this:

'In that day,' says the LORD of hosts, 'everyone will invite his neighbor under his vine and under his fig tree.'

This is unquestionably the millennial Sabbath day.

We have now come to Zechariah 4, and the other member of the team, that God calls His two witnesses.

This witness also comes out of old Babylon. He was the leader of the tribe of Judah at the time the Persian King Cyrus released those Judean captives willing to return to Judea and Jerusalem with the primary objective of rebuilding the temple destroyed by Nebuchadnezzar. This man was a child of the captivity, being born in Babylon. His name means *begotten* in Babylon. He was appointed governor of Judea (a section of present-day Israel), by King Cyrus of Persia, who then ruled Babylon after its defeat by the Medes and Persians.

His name is Zerubbabel. He and Joshua the high priest, having been given permission by King Cyrus to return to Jerusalem to rebuild the temple, led the first group of captives back to Judea to accomplish this purpose. The book of Ezra gives many details concerning the scope of this endeavor.

Revelation 11:4 tells something quite important about the two witnesses. It informs as follows: "These are the two olive trees and the two lampstands standing before the God of the earth." On the surface, this description seems to defy logic. It is, however, a reasonable portrayal when we see that it is a reference to Zechariah 4. Here a vivid word picture is given of a golden lampstand holding seven lamps, with seven pipes feeding the lamps from a bowl of oil at the top of the lampstand. The golden bowl at the top has two pipes with flanged receptacles extending upward out of it; one at one side of the bowl and one at the other side. Standing at each side of the lampstand is an olive tree. A branch of each tree extends out and over the receptacle of one of the gold pipes. One tree is at the right, and the other is at the left of the lampstand. Golden oil flows from the two branches into the receptacles of the two gold pipes, and through the pipes into the bowl at the top of the lampstand.

Zechariah was shown this detailed vision by an angel after he was awakened from his sleep (Zechariah 4:1). He was then asked to describe what he had seen (Zechariah 4:2–3). After describing what he had seen, Zechariah asked the logical question: "What are these my Lord?" (Zechariah 4:4). So in verses six and seven, the angel answers:

> So he answered and said to me: "This is the word of the LORD to Zerubbabel: 'Not by might nor by power, but by My Spirit,' says the LORD of hosts.

> 'Who are you, O great mountain? [Antichrist] Before Zerubbabel you shall become a plain! And he shall bring forth the capstone with shouts of "Grace, grace to it!"'" (Zechariah 4:6–7)

So here, what the angel said in a few words, will require a few more to understand. With Zerubbabel being one of the two witnesses, we already know from Revelation 11 that both will be endowed with great power. The angel makes it clear this will not be Zerubbabel's power or might, but rather, the power will come from God's Holy Spirit.

The Holy Spirit, we will see, is central to learning the meaning of the golden lampstand and the two olive trees, as well as being the power to make the great mountain a plain.

With the power of the Holy Spirit, Zerubbabel shall bring forth the capstone with shouts of "Grace, grace to it!" The capstone, of course, is Jesus Christ at His second coming. The capstone of a building is at the top. In this case, it is a prominent, engraved, figurative stone at the top of a figurative temple. It seems quite certain that this symbolic temple is Christ's church since its inception up to the Lord's return, as well as being a physical millennial temple.

Zerubbabel will bring forth Jesus Christ at His second coming with shouts of "Grace, grace to it!" We see in Revelation 14:6 that the "angel flying in the midst of heaven, having the everlasting gospel to preach to those who dwell on the earth—to every nation, tribe, tongue, and people," portrays the gospel of Jesus Christ: *salvation by grace*. This grace marks the beginning and it defines the end of Christ's earthly church. Zerubbabel's message will be, *join up now for God's grace while you still can!* The angel we saw above, flying in the midst of heaven, now in Revelation 14:7 *emphasizes the extreme urgency of this last days message of grace*: saying with a loud voice, "Fear God and give glory to Him, for the hour of His judgment has come." The meaning is clear: *time is short!*

Now, Zechariah 4:8–10 continues with this:

Moreover the word of the LORD came to me, saying:

"The hands of Zerubbabel have laid the foundation of this temple; His hands shall also finish it. Then you will know that the LORD of hosts has sent Me to you.

For who has despised the day of small things? For these seven [lamps] rejoice to see the plumb line in the hand of Zerubbabel. They are the eyes of the LORD, which scan to and fro throughout the whole earth."

Zerubbabel and Joshua the high priest led the captives of Babylon, those willing to devote themselves to the task of rebuilding God's temple. These two once more (last days identities unkown), as God's two witnesses, will lead captives. This time captives of Christ, both Jew and Gentile, in a final harvest of souls in fields ripe for harvest; rebuilding Christ's figurative temple; His last days church while light yet lingers for a little while.

Now to summarize the symbolic vision that Zechariah saw of two olive trees; one at each side of a golden lampstand; we will do a review of the main points:

Each olive tree represents one of the two witnesses, Joshua the high priest and Zerubbabel, leader of the tribe of Judah at the time of rebuilding the temple permitted by King Cyrus. Each olive tree had a branch extending over the gold receptacle of one of the two gold pipes. These gold pipes extending up out of the gold bowl channel golden oil (Holy Spirit power) directly from the two witnesses to the gold bowl (Jesus Christ's true church). The two gold pipes represent the houses of Judah and Israel, which symbolically, through the number twelve, in turn represent the 144,000. The gold pipe under the olive tree representing Zerubbabel is sure to be the House of Judah, since Zerubbabel was the leader of that tribe at the time. For this reason, the other gold pipe would be the House of Israel, being under the olive tree representing Joshua the high priest. Joshua's capacity as high priest carries the connotation of completeness. Even though he represents the House of Israel, he is priest to both houses: all the children of Israel.

The two witnesses are endued with the Holy Spirit (Revelation 11:3). Holy Spirit power (golden oil), flows from them through the gold pipes (144,000) into the gold bowl (true church). The seven lamps on the lampstand (eyes of Christ), receiving input from the golden bowl through seven pipes, serve as guides in directing the ministry effort where needed.

As Christians, we find it difficult to give serious consideration to the concept of being reborn physically, because of the statement made in Hebrews 9:27 which says: "And as it is appointed for men to die once, but after this the judgment." This leaves little latitude for the idea of being reborn to another physical life, except in the case where an individual did not die, but was translated from life directly to heaven or hell without experiencing the effects of death. In this situation, that person could be reborn and still remain within the terms of Hebrews 9:27.

God's Word tells of two such occurrences: one with Enoch (Genesis 5:24; Hebrews 11:5) and the other with Elijah (2 Kings 2:11). We know from the historical record that Antiochus IV Epiphanes died a mad man in Persia. (*Illustrated Dictionary of the Bible*, 69) We don't know any more than this, other than that he would have gone directly to hell to await his rebirth as the antichrist. We shall find in Revelation 19:20 that he will not experience another physical death. The verse says:

> . . . These two [Antichrist and false prophet] were cast alive into the lake of fire burning with brimstone.

So at Armageddon, this pair shall embark upon their journey of eternal punishment without first experiencing physical death!

Although we do not know the circumstances of Zerubbabel's and Joshua's passing from this life, we do know what Revelation 11:4 tells us: "These are the two olive trees and the two lampstands standing before the God of the earth." Standing before God suggests being in heaven, prepared to return to do God's work.

Zechariah chapters 3 and 4 say much about the two witnesses. So a review here of chapter 4 could help to better understand Zerubbabel in his second life as one of the two witnesses. Verse 6 says that Zerubbabel will derive his great power, not from his own abilities, but from the Holy Spirit. Verse 7 tells that before Zerubbabel, the great mountain (Antichrist) will become a plain. This places his ministry in the end time rule of Antichrist.

Verse 7 also informs that Zerubbabel will bring forth the capstone, Jesus Christ, with shouts of "Grace, grace to it." This makes it clear that his ministry will be the last days preaching of the gospel of Jesus with salvation by *grace*!

Verse 9 states: Zerubbabel will finish the temple. A double meaning here; figuratively meaning the final days church of Christ, as well as a physical millennial temple to replace that which Antichrist will desecrate. This temple will last a thousand years—up to the time of the New Jerusalem, which is eternity. No temple will then be needed: "for the Lord God Almighty and the Lamb are its temple" (Revelation 21:22).

Verse 10 questions: "For who has despised the day of small things?" The Hebrew word for small is qatan. Its meaning is abbreviated, meaning shortened. This is a fitting word for Antichrist's brief reign; as Jesus will despise this dreadful time and will return to shorten it. Verse 10 also says: for these seven rejoice to see the plumb line in the hand of Zerubbabel." The plumb line is a tool used to build plumb walls; walls that are straight and true from top to bottom. These seven would refer to the seven lamps on the lampstand; and they rejoice to see Zerubbabel doing the work of the Lord. (Building up Christ's last days church!)

Verse 10 tells as well, referring to the seven: "They are the eyes of the Lord, which scan to and fro throughout the whole earth." The King James Version does not use the word *scan*, but rather, uses *run*, as in *run to and fro*. Outwardly they appear to have the same meaning. The fact is, as used here, their meanings are not the same. Eyes that "scan to and fro throughout the whole earth" are different than eyes that "run to and fro throughout the whole earth." The King James Version is considered to be the benchmark version by many when it comes to reliability, although more difficult to read and understand than some successor versions. It is therefore prudent to make comparisons of key words and phrases for clarification. The New King James Version used in this work needs a reliability check occasionally, and it seems that this is one of those times.

Eyes that scan to and fro throughout the whole earth would suggest the omnipresence of God. Eyes that run to and fro throughout the whole earth suggest angels, since eyes cannot run of their own accord. The Hebrew word *shuwt* as used in both the NKJV and the KJV means *to push forth, to travel to and fro*. Knowing this, it is obvious that the lamps, said to be "the eyes of the Lord" are meant here to be angels that travel to and fro throughout the whole earth. They would be seven angels, referred to as lamps on the lampstand. They will react to the Holy Spirit's desire coming down from the olive branches (two witnesses), through the two gold pipes (one hundred forty-four thousand), into the gold bowl (Jesus' church), and down through seven pipes to the seven lamps (angels).

We can see the seven angels that serve as the eyes of the Lord and travel throughout the whole earth, figuratively being eyes are, in fact, receiving godly impulses. And as eyes of the Lord, they send back images as with the retina of the eye. These images depict worldly conditions and circumstances for the final implementation of providing the gospel message where results will be most fruitful. So then, the one hundred forty-four thousand workers in the harvest fields, working under the guidance and patronage of Christ's church, and with the Holy Spirit in complete control, shall receive angelic direction for where the need for their efforts will be greatest and received most appreciably—all to the glory of God!

Now, moving ahead to finish up this symbolic picture:

Then I answered and said to him [angel], "What are these two olive trees; at the right of the lampstand and at its left?"

And I further answered and said to him, "What are these two olive branches that drip into the receptacles of the two gold pipes from which the golden oil drains?"

Then he answered me and said, "Do you not know what these are?" And I said, "No, my lord."

So he said, "These are the two anointed ones, who stand beside the Lord of the whole earth" (Zechariah 4:11–14).

So now, we see that this final verse, Zechariah 4:14, is the primary link of the lampstand and olive tree symbolism to Revelation 11:3–4, which bears repeating here:

And I will give power to my two witnesses, and they will prophesy one thousand two hundred and sixty days, clothed in sackcloth.

These are the two olive trees and the two lampstands standing before the God of the earth.

The prophesying of the two witnesses will, of course, focus on the gospel and the prophesied return of Jesus Christ. We can sum up their ministry by reviewing the angel's words intended for the end time evangelistic outreach of the one hundred forty-four thousand, which by association, will include the two witnesses as well. Revelation 14:6–7 reminds us:

Then I saw another angel flying in the midst of heaven, having the everlasting gospel to preach to those who dwell on the earth; to every nation, tribe, tongue, and people;

saying with a loud voice, "Fear God and give glory to Him, for the hour of His judgment has come; and worship Him who made heaven and earth, the sea and springs of water."

All the things we have been looking at concerning the two witnesses and the one hundred forty-four thousand will take place in the last one thousand two hundred sixty days; three-and-a-half years, just before Jesus will return. This period of ministry will occur in the Tribulation, and continue briefly into the explosive onslaught of initial wrath, with Jesus' saints kept safe through the upheaval to the moment of His return. Wrath will then intensify upon the earth, with God's Jewish remnant preserved through it all by Michael— a time of trouble "such as never was since there was a nation, even to that time" (Daniel 12:1).

For a perspective on final days occurrences, (See Table #1). Daniel 12:11 says: "And from the time that the daily sacrifice is taken away, and the abomination of desolation is set up, there shall be one thousand two hundred and ninety days." These 1,290 days are mostly congruent with the "time, times, and half a time" specified in Daniel 7:25, as being the length of time that the saints will be given into Antichrist's hand. They only partially overlap one another, however.

Saints will be in his hand 119 days, or about four months prior to Antichrist taking over the temple. This oppression will begin the Tribulation, which shall last 1,277 1/2 days (three-and-a-half years). It will commence 1,103 days after the now started peace treaty. And, it shall end at the Resurrection, with the return of Jesus Christ the King. This will be at the point where 176 1/2 days of wrath will yet remain. (See Table #1)

The 1,290 days mentioned above regarding taking away daily sacrifice in the temple, and the abomination of desolation being set up, represents the length of time that Antichrist will occupy the temple of God attempting to show the world that he is God. This abomination will end when Antichrist will see trouble brewing from the north, and will abandon the temple, heading for Egypt on a military mission of urgency. At this point, man's global Marxist empire, now in great disarray and about to explode in global civil war, will have yet, forty-five days left to live! Antichrist will take personal charge of military affairs and will have called in international community forces to meet anticipated force with force in Egypt.

As this writing interprets from Daniel's prophecy in Daniel 11:40, he will be assaulted from both the south and the north in a devastating two-pronged attack, which will require action on two fronts. God will draw the attackers off of the defeated; then turn the victors back to the north in a ground-and-sea-supported airborne raid on a tiny technological giant dwelling in the midst of madness.

At this terror-filled time, the world will be reeling from a string of natural and man-made disasters. The U.S.A, pictured in the Bible as a fallen woman, having abandoned Christian ethics for her pagan, humanistic, atheistic status in an orgy of global alliances, treaties, arrangements, and a variety of foreign dalliances (fornication), will be unavailable. The great natural disaster responsible for the darkening of the sun and moon that will herald Christ's return will have occurred, and all the multiple effects of its cataclysmic forces will have materialized. The need of oil and gas for electric generation and transportation will be great. It will be a desperate time; a time for desperate measures! But what about the 45 days added to the 1,290 that in Daniel 12:12 total 1,335?

These 45 days, extending beyond the 1,290, at which time Antichrist will leave the temple to deal with what he will see to be a serious Russian/Islamic axis threat to Egypt and Mid-East oil, will be an extremely traumatic and difficult time in the world. It seems conclusive, that this short forty-five day period of time is all that will be required for the battle of Egypt and the Armageddon disaster to be completed.

So then, Daniel 12:12, when it says: "Blessed is he who waits, and comes to the one thousand three hundred and thirty-five days," is indicating the survival of the Jewish remnant written in the book, to be miraculously removed to safety before the sacking of Jerusalem and the destruction of Israel. Zechariah 14:4–5 explain some key aspects of the event:

> And in that day His [Jesus'] feet will stand on the Mount of Olives, which faces Jerusalem on the east. And the Mount of Olives shall be split in two, from east to west, making a very large valley [This giant earthquake will occur the same hour as Christ's return and shall be triggered from above! Revelation 11:13]; half of the mountain shall move toward the north and half of it toward the south.

> Then you shall flee through My mountain valley, for the mountain valley shall reach to Azal. Yes, you shall flee as you fled from the earthquake in the days of Uzziah king of Judah. Thus the LORD my God will come, and all the saints with You.

The final sentence that states that the Lord shall come, and all the saints with Him, firmly ties this time of escape of the Jewish remnant to the time of God's wrath—the Day of the Lord. They will make their escape sometime soon after Jesus' return, and well before the Russian-led attack into the Mid-East oil fields. The saints, in spirit resurrection bodies, will be with Jesus. Revelation 19:13–14 confirms this in telling figuratively:

> He [Jesus] was clothed with a robe dipped in blood, and His name is called The Word of God.
>
> And the armies in heaven, clothed in fine linen, white and clean, followed Him on white horses.

So the Jewish remnant, to make a new start in the millennial kingdom of God under Jesus Christ, will escape from Jerusalem by way of the newly formed valley that was once the Mount of Olives. Then east into the country of Jordan, as we have now come to understand. After they are out of harm's way, the armies of the nations will attack Israel, and the Lord's army will destroy them. God's literal army, as we know, is not the army of the saints on white horses. This literal army is the figurative "sword which proceeded from the mouth of Him who sat on the horse" (Revelation 19:21) This army will be the Israeli Defense Force (IDF). Zechariah 12:6 says it very plainly:

> In that day [Day of the Lord] I will make the governors [generals] of Judah like a firepan in the woodpile, and like a fiery torch in the sheaves; they shall devour all the surrounding peoples on the right hand and on the left, but Jerusalem shall be inhabited again in her own place; Jerusalem.

Daniel was saved from death in the lion's den, and the three young men, Shadrach, Meshach, and Abed-Nego, saved out of Nebuchadnezzar's fiery furnace; (Daniel 3 and 6) are representative of salvation intended for the Jewish remnant. Against all odds, God will bring them through the winepress of His wrath.

# CHAPTER THIRTY

# THE WOMAN AND THE DRAGON

Revelation tells a story of a woman and a "great, fiery red dragon having seven heads and ten horns, and seven diadems on his heads" (Revelation 12:3). Revelation 12:1 describes the woman as being "clothed with the sun, with the moon under her feet, and on her head a garland of twelve stars."

The woman (Israel) and the dragon (Satan) are both modified in this chapter to their last days personalities. The woman becomes the Jewish remnant, and Satan becomes Antichrist. Revelation 12:2 informs that the woman was with child: "she cried out in labor and in pain to give birth."

Revelation 12:4 continues the symbolism; the dragon's tail drew a third of the stars (angels) of heaven and threw them to the earth: "And the dragon stood before the woman who was ready to give birth, to devour her Child as soon as it was born." Verse 5: "And she bore a male Child who was to rule all nations with a rod of iron. And her Child was caught up to God and to His throne."

After Christ's first earthly time (49 years, to be resolved in future pages), verse 6 leaps ahead almost 2,000 years to the seventieth week (Antichrist's time).

In Revelation 12:7–10, Satan the dragon and his angels are cast to earth, with no more access to heaven.

Revelation 12:13–17, the symbolism continues:

Now when the dragon saw that he had been cast to the earth, he persecuted the woman who gave birth to the male Child [Antichrist stops religious Jews sacrificing to God and he claims temple].

But the woman was given two wings of a great eagle, that she might fly into the wilderness to her place, where she is nourished for a time and times and half a time, from the presence of the serpent.

So the serpent spewed water out of his mouth like a flood after the woman, that he might cause her to be carried away by the flood.

But the earth helped the woman, and the earth opened its mouth and swallowed up the flood which the dragon had spewed out of his mouth. [Suggests Petra; extensive ancient tombs and underground city in southwestern Jordan].

And the dragon was enraged with the woman, and he went to make war with the rest of her offspring, who keep the commandments of God and have the testimony of Jesus Christ.

We have just read symbolic details of the Jewish remnant in preservation, through almost three years of severe tribulation and six months of wrath. Christians *will* see tribulation, Matthew 24:9. Daniel 7:25 says also: "Then the saints shall be given into his [Antichrist's] hand for a time and times and half a time [three-and-a-half years]." (Christians persevere in Jesus!)

First Corinthians 15:52 informs us that the Resurrection will occur at the last trumpet. These are the exact words:

in a moment, in the twinkling of an eye, at the last trumpet. For the trumpet will sound, and the dead will be raised incorruptible, and we shall be changed.

Keeping in mind what 1 Thessalonians 5:9 has to say about Christian saints not seeing wrath, and what 1 Corinthians 15:52 says about the Resurrection occurring at the last trumpet, how is it that the Resurrection will be at the fourth trumpet, rather than at the seventh? After all, isn't the seventh trumpet the last trumpet? As it turns out, not for Christians! The last trumpet for them will be the fourth. This exceptional trumpet call will make its indelible impact upon the planet in the immediate traumatic aftershock of three closely spaced cosmic collisions with earth. These, in concert, shall introduce the fourth trumpet at the point of one-third reduction of light from the heavenly bodies due to atmospheric contamination. One-third of the sea will be fouled, along with the loss of a third of the fish in it and of the ships on it. Then, too, one-third of fresh, open air water bodies will be fouled. At the exact point of this state of affairs, the fourth angel will sound his trumpet to announce *the return of Jesus Christ* and the accompanying resurrection and translation of the saints!

We obviously have a conflict to be resolved here. As mentioned, the Bible makes it very clear that Christians will not experience wrath and that they shall be taken to be with the Lord at the last trumpet. So with these thoughts in mind, we will seek resolutions to these perplexing questions.

# CHAPTER THIRTY-ONE

# CONFLICT RESOLUTION

Conflict resolution #1: Trumpet judgments are stages of wrath. The first four are *pure trumpets* and cause conditions of Jesus' prophesied return when there will be signs in the sun, moon, and stars: these orbs will be darkened. The fourth trumpet fulfills these requirements, with an important plus factor included. We shall observe this miraculous plus up close and in detail when we arrive at the immensely significant fourth trumpet; it will serve as proof of exoneration for some and indictment of others. The last three trumpets are *woe trumpets* or woes (Revelation 8:13). The fourth *pure trumpet* is last for Christians; the seventh trumpet *is a monumental woe!*

Conflict resolution #2: Even though Jesus will return in the Day of the Lord, at the fourth trumpet judgment soon after wrath will have begun, this early wrath has a large wide-open loophole through which saints who live at that time shall be kept safe from the great multiple destruction of the first three trumpets. These three shall share complicity equally in creating circumstances that will produce the loophole of the fourth trumpet. This heavenly conceived and ordained mechanism, designed to be applied to both of God's special groups (Christ's saints and God's Jewish remnant) will preserve the saints through the initial wrath for resurrection at Jesus' fourth trumpet return. It shall also ensure survival of the Jewish remnant to this very time as well for them to witness the glorious return of their Messiah: "and they shall see the Son of Man coming on the clouds of heaven with power and great glory" (Matthew 24:30).

God's holy Jewish remnant will then continue on under the protective care of the great archangel Michael, safely preserved through all terror of the aggravated assaults upon earth and aftermath, of several natural and manmade destructive events. These will be vividly observed in detail when we arrive at the seal, trumpet, and bowl judgments; further on down the road that the world is now treading in lock step with end time Bible prophecy!

The two witnesses and the one hundred forty-four thousand will project a powerful witness for the Lord Jesus Christ in the end time disorder of tribulation and early wrath. Reference the church of Philadelphia, with God's seal figuratively implanted on their foreheads, the power of which will be real. They will be protected in that time of severe testing, to accomplish the work that God has ordained that they do.

With the one hundred forty-four thousand being sealed against tribulation and initial wrath, it's sure that the Holy Spirit power of the two witnesses, with their ability to stalemate worldly power centers, shall be instrumental in the protection of these last days harvesters. Who will these 144,000 servants of Christ be, and how shall we recognize them? Many of these have ministries in our midst today; while others are quietly working in out-of-the-way places around the world. They will be recognized by their ability to persevere and continue their work for Jesus through severe persecution and difficult times.

Their ministries will include some, or all, of any number of existing Christian outreach services, such as one-on-one contact and follow-up, conducting crusades, TV, radio, feeding bodies and souls of the lost, hungry, and homeless; caring for the sick, diseased, and hopeless; rescuing women and girls trapped in the sex slave trade; providing Bibles and encouragement to struggling Christians whose worship of Jesus is against prevailing laws of tyrannical governments; and the teaching and training of indigenous workers to carry the gospel of Christ to their own people. Then there are such programs as providing misdirected governments with God's specific prophetic warnings for them if they do not repent and turn to the Lord, Christian theme parks, and museums; Christian media centers and showing of the Jesus film. These are some, but not all of last days ministries of the one hundred forty-four thousand's three-and-a-half years of evangelistic endeavors that will occupy their every waking moment in tribulation and into the jaws of early wrath.

Now, on the other side of the coin, we see what Luke 21:16–19 has to say in Jesus' own words:

> You will be betrayed even by parents and brothers, relatives and friends; and they will put some of you to death.
>
> And you will be hated by all for My name's sake.
>
> But not a hair of your head shall be lost.
>
> By your patience possess your souls.

For those who lose their lives because they follow Jesus in Antichrist's tribulation, not losing a single hair of their heads refers specifically to eternal life with Christ!

This time of upside-down values and principles that we now see all around us is but a preview of coming events. The mindset that causes this anomaly will continue to mature and harden in opposition to moral absolutes. Fear of having someone's moral values forced upon them will mutate to aggressive resentment against anyone who dares to disagree with the accepted morally corrupt positions that will be accepted as politically correct values. Abortion is a case in point!

# CHAPTER THIRTY-TWO

# THE POWER OF THE TWO WITNESSES

The great divide that can be seen so clearly in our present time, the gulf that separates those who defiantly cling to godly moral positions in opposition to generally accepted secular, humanist, and politically correct positions, will go on to widen. The two witnesses empowered by God will counterbalance the delusional will of the overwhelming majority. Revelation 11:5–6 tell John's understanding of the working of these powers:

> And if anyone wants to harm them, fire proceeds from their mouth and devours their enemies. And if anyone wants to harm them, he must be killed in this manner.

> These have power to shut heaven, so that no rain falls in the days of their prophecy; and they have power over waters to turn them to blood, and to strike the earth with all plagues, as often as they desire.

These potent abilities in the hands of two godly witnesses for Jesus provide for their achieving parity with their antagonists through the troubled waters for three-and-a-half years of tribulation. These abilities equal, or exceed, those of a high-tech government; and the implications of their use are awesome to contemplate!

When John viewed these visions of the Revelation, many were presented through the form of symbolism. One of the witnesses' powers provides a good example of this literary form. It is highly unlikely that these two witnesses of God would use the power to torch their enemies even if the enemies were trying to kill them. With the two having God's protection for three-and-a-half years, it would be unnecessary for them to kill those who would do them harm. It is far more likely that they will use the Holy Spirit's power much like Jesus used it; to avoid harm and capture, and to bring glory to God until the time for His atoning death on the cross. The two witnesses will share a number of common characteristics in their coming ministry with that of Jesus' earthly ministry.

After three-and-a-half years with the gospel message of salvation through faith in Jesus by grace and prophesying the soon return of Jesus Christ, they will be arrested. As with Jesus, no longer protected by God's Holy Spirit, they will be put to death. We have seen in Revelation 11:9–12 that those who dwell on the earth will celebrate; it would seem, prior to their dead bodies lying in a street in Jerusalem. They will refuse to allow the bodies to be properly laid to rest, because the two will have become such a torment to them. After three-and-one-half days, however, God will raise them to their feet for all to see, and shall call them to come up to Him. As seen before, this is a microcosm—a snapshot—a focal point—of the Resurrection that will be occurring all around them!

The two witnesses will be brought from death to life eternal after three-and-a-half days, as was the case with Jesus. (Jesus was likely crucified on Wednesday, not Friday.) The similarities don't end here. As with Jesus' earthly ministry of three-and-a-half years, so it will be with the two witnesses—that their ministry will last three-and-a-half years. As Jesus had supernatural powers from God by the Holy Spirit, so shall the two witnesses be granted supernatural powers by the Holy Spirit for their equivalent period of earthly service in bringing completion to Christ's church.

Now, a closer look at the powers to be granted to these two witnesses of Jesus will prove quite revealing!

In mental imagery we can see flames proceeding from the mouths of the two witnesses and engulfing their enemies whose intent it is to harm them. This is the scene as John viewed it in his vision of the Revelation. With the modern technical weaponry in the hands of governments today, if anyone were to attempt this manner of conflict resolution with their enemies, they would quickly be targeted and set upon unmercifully. They would be put under siege and pinned down. The time of their ministry would be consumed with self-defense to the detriment of Jesus' gospel. Here the question must be asked: Does anyone remember *Waco*?

It seems more fitting, with the objective of spreading the gospel message of Jesus Christ, that these witnesses for Christ will speak the Holy Spirit to those who wish to harm them. If this is true, then what John saw and took for literal fire was, in fact, a picture of the Holy Spirit proceeding from the mouths of the witnesses in a physical manifestation of tongues of spiritual fire.

There is a precedent in the Bible for the Holy Spirit taking the form of physical fire. It is found in Acts 2:1–4, which gives this account:

> When the Day of Pentecost had fully come, they were all with one accord in one place.

> And suddenly there came a sound from heaven, as of a rushing mighty wind, and it filled the whole house where they were sitting.

> Then there appeared to them divided tongues, as of fire, and one sat upon each of them.

> And they were all filled with the Holy Spirit and began to speak with other tongues, as the Spirit gave them utterance.

What we have just read is the account of the Holy Spirit having been sent by God to the followers of Jesus after His ascension to the right hand of the Father. The Holy Spirit was used mightily by these men and women in spreading the gospel of Jesus Christ. It is safe to say that the Holy Spirit will again be a major factor in the two witnesses final roundup of believers just before the door to life shall be slammed shut with the return of Jesus, signaling expansion of God's wrath.

If this conclusion is correct concerning tongues of fire from the mouths of the two witnesses, then those who wish to harm them shall, by the power of the Holy Spirit, experience a change of heart and will die to the world to experience rebirth from eternal death to eternal life with Christ. Imagine the distress these conversions will cause in the households and within groups of dedicated Christ-hating friends and relatives. Those to experience conversion will be considered *persona non grata* in their families and by these groups. With this happening on a regular basis over these three-and-a-half years, it shall become a great source of irritation in a world of politically correct values, actions, and non-Christian morals. It shall become a heavy burden for the world to bear.

Now add to this the ministries of the one hundred forty-four thousand servants of God, sealed against all that will come against them; and we can see one great movement for Jesus at the final hour!

A key Scripture that strongly supports the conclusion, that fire proceeding from the mouths of the two witnesses is in reality the Holy Spirit, is seen in Matthew 3:11. It concerns John the Baptist in his ministry to prepare the way for the first coming of the Messiah by preaching repentance and the act of water baptism. The two witnesses will provide the same service for Messiah's second coming, but this time with fire (Spiritual fire):

> I indeed baptize you with water unto repentance, but He who is coming after me is mightier than I, whose sandals I am not worthy to carry. He will baptize you with the Holy Spirit and fire.

These miracle rebirths in Christ will occur after a presentation of the gospel message, in some cases probably quite short and to the point and others might take more time, depending upon circumstances. The point is, that with the Holy Spirit manifested as a flame of fire, we are unquestionably seeing here baptism by fire! We are seeing a lost soul turning to Christ by a miraculous act of God—by the Spirit of God!

Jesus, in His earthly ministry, said some things about how we should act in situations where others would be trying to inflict harm or take advantage of us. These instructions today sound strange considering the way the world thinks; as they surely did at the time Jesus said them.

Here, in Matthew 5:39 is one of a number of instructions that Jesus gave, not only for the benefit of those in His audience, but also for the well-being of those to come later:

> But I tell you not to resist an evil person. But whoever slaps you on your right cheek, turn the other to him also.

Jesus, in Matthew 5:43–44, enlarged upon the above instruction with the following directions that are seemingly untenable by worldly standards:

> You have heard that it was said, 'You shall love your neighbor and hate your enemy.'

> But I say to you, love your enemies, bless those who curse you, do good to those who hate you, and pray for those who spitefully use you and persecute you.

In verse 45, Jesus gives us justification for acting in this apparently unnatural way:

> that you may be sons of your Father in heaven; for He makes His sun rise on the evil and on the good, and sends rain on the just and on the unjust.

So, we are to show love for our enemies, because God who created us all, loves them and has compassion for them. He sends rain on the unjust as well as on the just!

This takes us to the matter of the other powers entrusted to the two witnesses by God. These are given to the witnesses for their empowerment in dealing with the unsaved world. Based upon what we have just read of Jesus' commands to love our enemies and show compassion for them, we see an apparent conflict emerging here. With the witnesses able to withhold rain, contaminate waters, and to strike the earth with all plagues as often as they desire, they will be considered enemy number one by Antichrist and those who follow him.

These kinds of actions seem to conflict with the "love your enemy" principle so clearly expressed by Jesus. Actually, the power, when used wisely, will supplement love that the witnesses will have and show for their enemies. It will facilitate their ability to have a forum from which to proclaim the good news of Jesus Christ. By being able to retaliate on a large geographic scale with drought, heavy deposits of alkali, or some other contaminate in localized water sources, etc. President Theodore Roosevelt understood this wisdom and the power of "walk softly and carry a big stick"!

With Revelation 11:6 saying: "to strike the earth with all plagues as often as they desire," we are immediately curious as to what extent the witnesses will go in order to provoke those in power to obtain freedom for missionary outreach endeavors and other concessions in fulfillment of Holy Spirit urging.

Since the world does not always respond to a loving approach with a loving response, the witnesses will be able to fight fire with fire. The world only recognizes power; the greater the power, the greater the influence wielded by he, she, or it possessing the power. In the world, money is the greatest source of power as it can influence politicians, thus buy political power. In a showdown, however, money is no match for God. Money appeals primarily to base emotions. The emotions of greed, pleasure, and pride are all powerful motivational forces focused on personal gain and fulfillment. In competition with the most powerful of human emotions, love, however, they do not measure up. In Mark 12:30–31, Jesus relates the two greatest commandments. This is what He says:

> And you shall love the LORD your God with all your heart, with all your soul, with all your mind, and with all your strength. This is the first commandment.

> And the second, like it, is this: you shall love your neighbor as yourself. There is no other commandment greater than these.

Love conquers all. So locking up the heavens and striking the earth with any number of unnamed plagues will serve to provide the means for the witnesses to hold the world at bay while they fulfill their ministry. In so doing, they will be demonstrating great love, not only for God, but for all of mankind.

So, we see here that the positive soul-saving power of the witnesses' short, intensive three-and-a-half year ministry will be dependent upon the raw power of their various negative abilities. These great powers will impact the world scene on a grand scale. People will be brought to a saving relationship with Christ by *grace*, and all to the *glory of God!*

It is an understatement, to say the least, that this final three and half-year period prior to Christ's return will severely test Christians; and so it will. Nevertheless, we are seeing the means for a bright beacon of hope to shine forth.

The two witnesses, and the one hundred forty-four thousand will be spearheading a revival back to Jesus, as well as an ingathering of newly saved souls by the gospel of Christ. Jesus said in Matthew 24:14:

And this gospel of the kingdom will be preached in all the world as a witness to all the nations, and then the end will come.

The end Jesus referred to is actually a two-part ending. The first part, *grace*, will be ended at His return, when the door shall be shut at the Resurrection. The other referenced meaning of the word *end*, points to termination of *worldly government*, designed and stitched together by men, for men.

After the end of that which will fail, will be brought in the new that will endure. It will not be a democracy; nor will it be a communist dictatorship. It will not be a socialist government; nor will it be a constitutional republic. It will be a kingdom. It will be the kingdom of God on earth, under the authority of Jesus Christ. It will be a just and godly kingdom, reflecting the authority and power of God through the person of Jesus Christ. The saints will serve as representatives of Christ to the people of the earth. Authority for this is found in Revelation 20:6, which states:

Blessed and holy is he who has part in the first resurrection. Over such the second death has no power, but they shall be priests of God and of Christ, and shall reign with Him a thousand years.

The office of priest functions as the connecting link between God and man. The priest, in addition to ceremonial requirements, serves as teacher, mediator, and liaison in maintaining and/or furthering communication and unity in the populace as directed by God. So here we can see the connection between Jesus, who being God, will be King as well. The saints, serving as priests of God and of Christ, will have another title, and responsibility. This reference is made by the apostle Paul to the Corinthian church which, at the time, was having to deal with immorality within the church and with litigation between believers for all the world to see. He wanted them to settle their differences among themselves, and so in a chiding way, in 1 Corinthians 6:2, said the following:

Do you not know that the saints will judge the world? And if the world will be judged by you, are you unworthy to judge the smallest matters?

Here it is made known that another office awaits the millennial saints—that of judge. This is also, in the context of representing the King, Jesus Christ, to the nations and the people to the King. Samuel has two books in the Bible dedicated to him. He was both a priest to Israel and a judge over Israel. Both 1 and 2 Samuel make interesting reading for anyone wishing to view the ebb and flow of God's power in the daily life of ancient Israel administered by this godly servant of God. (This priest/judge status will occur again.)

Now for a closer look at one of the most intriguing and important prophecies in God's Holy Bible.

This prophecy, in conjunction with man's historical record, forms the basis for being able to read the timeline of some of the most provocative prophetic statements found in the Bible. God's contribution to end time revelation is completely accurate. Is man's equally so? Only time will tell. Israel is, as this is being written, agonizing in her ongoing push/pull, peace/war dealings with the Palestinians. Are the last few years of man's allotted 6,000 *being negotiated?*

# CHAPTER THIRTY-THREE

# THE SEVENTY WEEKS OF DANIEL 9:24–27

This seventy weeks prophecy is a major prophetic revelation in that it provides the means to read the Bible timeline involving an important segment of not only human history, but of mankind's very near future as well!

This veiled prophecy was given to Daniel while in prayer to God by the angel Gabriel, Daniel 9:20–23. It is given in four verses in Daniel 9:24–27. We will view them here, and begin with verse 24. This is what Gabriel told Daniel:

Seventy weeks are determined for your people and for your holy city, to finish the transgression, to make an end of sins, to make reconciliation for iniquity, to bring in everlasting righteousness, to seal up vision and prophecy, and to anoint the Most Holy.

The seventy weeks are seventy groups of seven years, or 490 years allotted by God: *to finish Israel's transgression.*

*To make an end of sins,* applies to the kingdom of God, to be established on earth by Jesus Christ. The Jewish remnant will recognize and worship their Messiah. Satan will be bound.

*To make reconciliation for iniquity* applies to the return of Christ and to bringing into the millennial kingdom of God the Jewish remnant that will be forgiven and cleansed of their prior iniquity (rejection of Christ). The Hebrew word for *reconciliation* is *kaphar*, which can mean any or all of the following: *forgive, pardon, purge away, cleanse*. So, their forgiveness as seen here, will be full and complete.

*To bring in everlasting righteousness* applies to the return of Jesus and the kingdom of God under the rule of Jesus Christ. Those of Daniel's people, the Jewish remnant, to enter the millennial kingdom of God, shall not enter because of their righteousness, as they will have none of their own. The righteousness of Christ will be ascribed to them. This priceless gift from Jesus shall be an everlasting righteousness!

*To seal up vision and prophecy* is letting the prescribed amount of time run its course; to bring into being prophesied events, predestined for a predetermined time and place, thus bringing prophecy to fruition.

*And to anoint the most holy* refers to recognizing Jesus as Lord of lords and King of kings at His return, repenting and worshipping Him as Messiah, King, and God!

The following verse provides enlightenment as to when the predetermined period of seventy weeks of years, or four hundred ninety years will begin. Daniel 9:25 has this to say concerning fulfillment of the stated objectives:

> Know therefore and understand, that from the going forth of the command to restore and build Jerusalem until Messiah the Prince, there shall be seven weeks and sixty-two weeks; the street shall be built again, and the wall, even in troublesome times.

The first decree issued, that allowed Jewish captives to return to Jerusalem and Judea, was by King Cyrus. At that time the decree stated the intent was to rebuild the temple. Joshua the high priest and Zerubbabel led the return and the efforts in this regard. See Ezra 1:1–2 and Ezra 2:1–2.

The second decree issued was by King Darius in 520 B.C. to allow the completion of the temple, started by Zerubbabel, but not completed. See Ezra 6:1–12.

The third decree was issued by King Artaxerxes in 458 B.C. This command provided for the return of the gold and silver articles of worship which had been taken by King Nebuchadnezzar when he defeated the kingdom of Judah, destroyed the temple, and carried the captives to Babylon. This decree also provided funds to purchase livestock and for restoring sacrifice and worship in the completed temple. See Ezra 7:1–26.

The fourth decree was issued again by King Artaxerxes, in 445 B.C (*Illustrated Dictionary of the Bible*, 106). This last decree by King Artaxerxes allowed for the rebuilding of Jerusalem with emphasis on the wall and gates. See Nehemiah 2:1–8.

This fourth decree or command is that which the seventy weeks of Daniel deals with; and so, starts the counting of years. The historical record tells us that this command was issued in the year 445 B.C. It not only allowed Jewish captives to return to Jerusalem and to rebuild portions of the city where needed, but in addition, provided lumber and funds to accomplish the work. Chapters 4 through 6 of Nehemiah describe the troublesome times through which the construction was accomplished, as prophesied in Daniel 9:25. These difficulties were inflicted by local people who felt enmity toward the Jews, fearing that if successful in rebuilding the city and the wall that Judah would become strong and pose a serious threat to them. The opposition that the Jewish builders faced was encountered through ridicule, threat of attack, discouragement, extortion, compromise, slander, and treachery. At one point, the builders had to divide in two groups, one stood guard with weapons while the other worked. These circumstances would constitute troublesome times without question.

All of this leaves little doubt that this is the decree spoken of in Daniel 9:25: "the street shall be built again, and the wall, even in troublesome times."

We next need to use 445 B.C. to establish the year of birth of Jesus Christ, the Messiah. Daniel 9:25 again states: ". . . know therefore and understand that from the going forth of the command to restore and build Jerusalem until [throughout] Messiah the Prince, there shall be seven weeks and sixty-two weeks."

If we multiply the sixty-two weeks by seven days per week, we get 434. We see that after the command given in 445 B.C., with each day of the prophecy representing one year, we arrive at 11 B.C. as the year of birth for the Messiah. This simply required that sixty-two weeks, 434 years until Messiah, be subtracted from 445 B.C., date of the command which reveals 11 B.C. as the year of the Messiah's birth.

This prophecy of the seventy weeks has three separate and distinct time periods. Even though the seven week period is first in the prophecy, *it is not the one to use first!*

Daniel 9:26 makes a clear statement regarding one of the groups of weeks. We read as follows: "And after the sixty-two-weeks Messiah shall be cut off, but not for Himself." This verse does not say after sixty-nine weeks Messiah shall be cut off. It says "after the sixty-two weeks Messiah shall be cut off." It does not say "immediately after the 62 weeks." It indicates that "some time thereafter, Messiah shall be cut off." This authenticates the period to follow, as being that within which Messiah shall be cut off. We will see that this period is the seven weeks that is given first in the prophecy!

There are two ways that we may be sure that the 7 weeks (49 years) segment is to be sequenced behind the 62 weeks (434 years) of the 70 weeks prophecy wherein Daniel 9:25 says: "that from the going forth of the command to restore and build Jerusalem until Messiah the Prince, there shall be seven weeks and sixty-two weeks."

For one thing, the word for *until*, as in *until Messiah* in the King James Version is *unto* Messiah. *Strong's Concordance* provides the source of this word *unto*, which is found to be the Greek word *eis*. It is complex in its generous quantity of grammatical applications. In addition to meaning *until*, it has several compound meanings, two of which relate to time. *To, into* indicate the point reached or entered of place—time; and also (*unto, throughout*). Both of these compound meanings have very similar applications and help to explain the working placement of the seven weeks segment behind the sixty-two weeks segment in the prophecy. This is an example of a Greek helper word being added in transcribing Hebrew Scripture to clarify the intent of the message, but which clarification was later overlooked.

It seems evident that there is more than meets the eye in the prophetic phrase until/unto Messiah. Since this phrase relates to time, it becomes obvious that the compound meanings are saying that, from the command to restore Jerusalem, *until and throughout Messiah's time,* there shall be seven weeks and sixty-two weeks! What is also obvious is that the seven weeks segment (forty-nine years) is Messiah's time, falling into place after the sixty-two weeks segment in correct placement for Messiah's forty-nine year time to reach the fullness for which it was intended!

What we have seen so far provides a basis from which to continue unlocking the hidden meanings of Daniel's intriguing prophecy for the nation of Israel. Given as 70 weeks (490 years), each of the three distinctive time segments has left, or will leave its footprint deeply embedded in human history. Time is the essence of the prophecy, and as such, must be segregated by time segment into its proper sequential order. The first two segments, as seen, apply in reverse contiguous order and are ancient history. The third segment is separated from the first two by a considerable span of years. And being representative of the last seven years of the six thousand free will years for mankind, is starting its progressively difficult seven-year journey across the landscape of Planet Earth.

With Jesus playing such a pivotal part in all that we are involved with here, and since we have previously, by different methodology, found the year of Christ's birth to be 11 B.C., we will now proceed to justify this date as being entirely reasonable and compatible with man's recorded history.

One other point: It is no secret that the Bible, in both Old and New Testaments, shouts from its pages that Jesus, the Messiah, the Lamb of God, the Christ, the Son of David, the Son of man, will return to earth near the very end of the last days. The year A.D. 2012, standing out as the biblically generated final year of the 6,000 years from Adam, the first man, to the return of Jesus Christ, the second Man (1 Corinthians 15:47), is irrefutably linked to the year of Jesus' birth.

An interesting sidelight regarding the year 11 B.C. and its relationship to Jesus' birth is noted in Carl Sagan's and Ann Druyan's book, "COMET", published in 1985 by Random House, Inc., pages 364–365. A list of thirty perihelion passages (closest point to the sun) is provided of Halley's comet in its elliptic, sun encompassing orbit, and at which time it is most visible from earth. These thirty passages were recorded by astronomers, twenty-nine of whom were "Chinese" and date all the way back to March 30, 239 B.C. They would be of little interest here except for the inclusion of one passage of the comet recorded for the date of October 5, 11 B.C.

For those who are familiar with the circumstances of Jesus' birth, as recorded in the gospel of Matthew, the star of Bethlehem is remembered as playing a prominent part in assisting the wise men from the East in locating the whereabouts of the Christ Child, whom they came to worship (Matthew 2:11). They had seen the star while in the East and followed it to Jerusalem, at which time they lost sight of it, possibly due to atmospheric conditions. They learned while in Jerusalem that the Christ Child was prophesied to be born in Bethlehem, and so, with Herod's encouragement, set out for that nearby town (Matthew 2:7–8). The star then reappeared: "and behold, the star which they had seen in the East went before them, till it came and stood over where the young Child was (Matthew 2:9)."

The solar wind, consisting of charged particles forcefully flowing outward from the entire surface of the sun, exert a stronger force on the comet's tail particles than does the sun's gravity. The solar wind then, pulls the comet's tail particles along with it, resulting in the tail always pointing away from the sun no matter which direction the comet is traveling while in perihelion passage. So, when the comet is in the correct position in its perihelion, fly-by passage around the sun, its tail will point downward. Even though a comet moves at extremely high speeds in perihelion, it is perceived from earth as standing still; and in this case, with its tail perpendicular to the sun and pointing down. Yes, comets too, can sometimes be seen in the daytime.

Now, God being God, can do creative things with perception, and so might have manipulated the atmosphere to create the illusion of the star moving in the wise men's short five mile journey from Jerusalem to Bethlehem. We don't know that it all happened this way, we just know that it all could have happened this way! So then, we will move ahead now and justify the Lord's year of birth as being 11 b.c. rather than a.d. 1

Anyone can see in their encyclopedia or Bible dictionary, by looking up Herod the Great, that he ruled as governor, and later as king of Judea from 37 b.c. to 4 b.c., in which year he died. This is the Herod, whose rule Jesus was born under. Herod the Great's son, Herod Archelaus, followed his father's rule with the title of governor and ruled this Roman province from 4 b.c. to a.d. 6.

We know from reading and hearing the account of Jesus' birth that Herod the Great, out of jealousy, wanted to kill Jesus shortly after He was born. Matthew 2:13 tells that an angel from God appeared to Joseph in a dream saying: "Arise, take the young child and His mother, flee to Egypt, and stay there until I bring you word; for Herod will seek the young Child to destroy Him."

Joseph did this (verses 14 and 15). Matthew 2:19–20 tell about Joseph receiving angelic notification of Herod's death. Verse 21 tells of Joseph, Mary, and Jesus making the journey back to Israel. Once there, Joseph took them to the somewhat isolated town of Nazareth in the southern foothills of the Lebanon mountain range. Nazareth is in Galilee, which was another Roman province in those days.

Matthew 2:22 makes an important statement relative to Jesus' age at His return. It tells us this: "But when Joseph heard that Archealous was reigning over Judea instead of his father Herod, he was afraid to go there. And being warned by God in a dream, he turned aside into the region of Galilee."

Since history states that Archealous ruled from 4 B.C. to A.D. 6, we know that Jesus returned within that period. It is reasonable to believe that Joseph would have been told to return with the child soon after Herod the Great had passed from the scene. We can then reasonably conclude that Jesus would have been returned within the same year, or no later than the following year after Herod the Great's death[19].

Coming back the same year would have had Jesus be seven at His return, being born in 11 B.C., minus 4 B.C. equals age seven. Should He have returned a year later in 3 B.C., He would have been age eight. Either age is compatible with Luke 2:40–50, where Jesus, at age twelve, accompanied His parents from Nazareth in Galilee to Jerusalem, for the celebration of the Feast of the Passover.

Within the book of Luke, the third gospel, there is yet more evidence in support of Jesus' birth as having occurred in 11 B.C. It is seen as providing a window of opportunity in combination with an archeological discovery in the form of an ancient coin. Luke 2:1–7 describes Jesus' birth in Bethlehem and the census that caused it to take place there in that particular town.

A census was called by Caesar Augustus requiring that all the world should be registered (Luke 2:1). Because Joseph was of the house and lineage of David, he, with Mary who was with child went from Nazareth, to the city of David, called Bethlehem to register (Luke 2:4–5).

Luke's contribution is seen here in Luke 2:2:

"This census first took place while Quirinius was governing Syria."

Although there is reference to more than one Quirinius in ancient history, this is the one who governed Syria at the time of Christ's birth in Bethlehem. The ancient archeological discovery i.e., a coin, shows Quirinius to have been porconsul (governor) of Syria from 11 B.C. until after 4 B.C., the year in which Herod died. Knowing that Jesus was born in Bethlehem in the days of Herod the king (Matthew 2:1) and that Quirinius governed Syria from 11 B.C. until after 4 B.C., we find this secular history to add yet, another layer of support for Jesus' birth having been in 11. B.C.[20]

The earlier exercise with Daniel's seventy weeks prophecy, which shows Jesus' birth as being in 11 B.C., is now again supported by the window seen above, and is in full agreement with the Bible record and Pharaoh Horemheb's reign resulting in the year of Jesus' birth being 11 B.C. With year 12 B.C. (one year prior) representing *THE TRUE ENDING POINT* of B.C. (before Christ) years, and with its corresponding number on the 6,000 years for man scale being year 3,988, we found our calender year 2012 to be the final year of the 6,000 years for man. (See Table #6). This was accomplished by subtracting 3,988 from 6,000, resulting in 2,012, or equivalent calendar year A.D. 2012. With the end so close, should we be worried? With a storm coming, should we take shelter? Now, for a look at our calendar problem . . .

# CHAPTER THIRTY-FOUR

# BLAME IT ON DIONYSIUS EXIGUUS ("DENNIS THE SHORT")

The following commentary is taken from a December 17, 1998 *Seattle Times* article by Hollis L. Engley of the Gannett News Service. We will use selected portions that give the facts and maintain continuity of the article:

"What happens when a calendar is based on a 500-year-old event only vaguely pinned down in time? Here's what happened.

"Though few scholars question the existence of the historical Jesus, no one knows for sure when he was born.

"The Bible's New Testament book of Matthew says, "Jesus was born in Bethlehem of Judea in the days of Herod the king." But historians know Herod died in the year now called 4 B.C. So today's scholars think Jesus was perhaps 4 or 5 years old or even older in the year 1 A.D.

"A sixth-century monk named Dionysius Exiguus ("Dennis the Short") didn't have access to 20th century scholarship when Pope John I asked him to determine a true date for Easter."

We now will pick up the story further on:

"Dionysius dumped the Diocletian calendar then in use, which established Year 1 as the year of the Roman Emperor Diocletian's ascent to the throne. He replaced it with a calendar dating from the birth of Jesus. He calculated, by means unknown today, that the birth happened 531 years before his current year. That became Year 1 A.D. for Dionysius, and eventually for the planet.

"Historians now know that the monk's calculations were off by at least a few years. That means Jesus' true 2000th birthday passed largely unnoticed in 1996 or 1997."

So it was the sixth-century monk "Dennis the Short," who established Anno Domini, "A.D.," the Year of our Lord, in relation to the dating of the current calendar. This designation is disturbing to some who would like to see it done away with. (A revealing sign of the times.)

Regarding the last line of the above article: we have reason to believe that Jesus' 2,000 birthday was in the year 1989; arrived at by subtracting the year of His birth in 11 B.C. from 2000 which equals A.D. 1989. What we have read above is an entirely secular article that strongly supports our biblical determination of Christ's birth being in 11 B.C. This date having been determined by using the Bible record in combination with the date of the untimely end of Pharaoh Horemheb's reign, resulted in calendar year A.D. 2012, revealed as the end of 6,000 years of man going his own way. This year 2012 then points to a slightly earlier marvelous return on dark, foreboding *clouds of glory!* The year, 2012, a milestone year for the Mayan people as previously seen, represents a shadow scenario to that which we are working with here. Revelation 12:12 has told us that Satan knows he has but a short time. Jesus, in Mark 13:32 said: "But of that day and hour no one knows, neither the angels in heaven, nor the Son, but only the Father."

It seems then, that Satan, though he did not know the year, day or the hour of Christ's return, may well have known the year ending the biblical 6,000! Now to return to the very important seven weeks segment (forty-nine years) of Daniel's pivotal prophecy.

# CHAPTER THIRTY-FIVE

# BACK TO THE SEVENTY WEEKS PROPHECY

The seven weeks, 49 years segment of the prophecy is unique in two ways. First, its time element emphasizes the number seven: 7 x 7 = 49. Since seven is God's number, it is not surprising that Jesus' time: His birth, ministry, death, resurrection, and birth of His church are all included in this 49-year working mid-segment. His number "squared," is God's perfect way of dedicating a time for His Son's first coming.

The second unique and unexpected aspect regarding the 49 years committed to the Messiah from His birth, through the birth-pangs of bringing forth His church as a testimony to His glory is this: have you noticed that these 49 years are a tenth (tithe) of the total of four hundred ninety years which make up the whole of the seventy weeks? (70 x 7 = 490)

Is it not fitting, that the prophecy segment given to the Lord Jesus which represents the *tithe*, or first fruits of the prophecy's essence, be stated first? The essence we know to be allotted time for Israel. Could this be the reason why the seven weeks segment was stated first rather than in the middle, even though its working relationship to the prophecy was in the mid-section? This would have been done to honor Him who is the Beginning and the End, and the First and the Last (Revelation 22:13). Jesus is seen here at the *beginning* and at the *end*!

Now to continue with the prophecy, we pick up where we left off in the middle of Daniel 9:26 where "Messiah shall be cut off, but not for Himself": "And the people of the prince who is to come shall destroy the city and the sanctuary. The end of it shall be with a flood, and till the end of the war desolations are determined."

As we know, this prince who is to come, whose people shall destroy the city and the sanctuary, was Antiochus IV Epiphanes. Yes, this occurred prior to Jesus' birth; so its being mentioned here makes it retroactive in the sequence of the prophecy. It happened, in fact, in 167 B.C. (*Illustrated Dictionary of the Bible*, 664). Now, we have seen within the seventy weeks of the prophecy, that a gulf of almost 2,000 years separates the seven weeks devoted to Jesus from the last one week given to Antichrist, wherein Jesus will return.

This prophecy makes no provision for activity within the almost 2,000 years of separation. Nevertheless, this is not to say that other Bible prophecy ignores these many years; it does not. But the transilient quality of this seventy weeks prophecy provides for it to do so.

Antiochus IV caused the temple to be corrupted with his sacrilegious statue of a Greek god and swine sacrifice. Strong renders the Hebrew word for *destroy* as *shachath*, which has several meanings, one of which is *destroy*, and another being *corrupt*. So, here we see a dual meaning. The city was physically destroyed in part, and the sanctuary (temple) spiritually corrupted. The *Reader's Digest Great Encyclopedic Dictionary* renders *corrupt* as, among other things, *unclean*. So here we see the prophecy fulfilled in detail by Antiochus IV Epiphanes.

In order to understand the reason why the reference to Antiochus IV is given where it is, we need to read Daniel 9:27, which foretells: "Then he shall confirm a covenant with many for one week; but in the middle of the week he shall bring an end to sacrifice and offering. And on the wing of abominations shall be one who makes desolate, even until the consummation, which is determined, is poured out on the desolate."

This verse, as we have seen, encompasses the final *one week* of the seventy weeks prophecy. You will recall, we have looked at these two verses, Daniel 9:26–27 before. We saw that the subtle transition from Antiochus IV Epiphanes to Antichrist was evident here. Verse 26 deals with Antiochus, while verse 27 refers to Antichrist who, in fact, will be or, more to the point, is the reborn Antiochus IV Epiphanes (God Manifest).

So now it becomes clear why the prophecy refers retroactively to Antiochus IV Epiphanes. Daniel 9:26 tells us: "After the sixty-two weeks Messiah shall be cut off, but not for himself." As we know, this refers to Messiah's seven weeks, devoted to providing a means of salvation from sin for future generations. This segment, behind the sixty-two weeks, places it properly to emphasize the monolithic character of the prophecy. It neutralizes the transition in time from Jesus' first coming to the last seven years, which introduces Antichrist and Jesus again at His second coming. Now we understand why Antiochus IV and his depredations in Daniel 9:26 were inserted just prior to Antichrist and his second opportunity for tyranny in Daniel 9:27: to smoothly make the transition from the seven weeks (all about Christ), to the seventieth week (much about Antichrist), to provide continuity, and to make the connection between Antiochus Epiphanes and Antichrist.

Little remains to be said about this time-sensitive prophecy other than: by the time you read this, those seven years will be underway. Jesus will despise this time of upside-down values and will return to end it!

The Bible tells a great deal about the seventieth week. Current trends will be maturing, and the complexity of the prophetic

Word tends to confuse much of the time rather than enlighten. The challenge here is to attempt to unravel some remaining mysteries of this brief time of extreme upheaval. Much of all that we have already looked into was prophesied to occur in the seventieth week. We will now continue to expand our understanding of these last seven years by examining at close hand, a group of prophesied chastening occurrences of earth-shaking magnitude. They are a stark portrayal of heretofore veiled and disguised trends, events, and yes—disasters!

# CHAPTER THIRTY-SIX

# THE SEAL, THE TRUMPET, AND THE BOWL JUDGMENTS

The seal, trumpet, and bowl judgments are real in their symbolic applications to the last seven years of the current six thousand—Daniel's seventieth week. Seals provide a brief outline of major trends to be encountered in this end time. The trumpets and the bowls both focus on a small number of cataclysmic events, destined to plague mankind in the last six months of that time period. Trumpet judgments generally depict the occurrence in its initial stage, while the bowl judgments show the *same events* in a later, more advanced final stage.

For a look at what these strange symbols want to tell us, we must start at the beginning with the seals.

The seals are mostly found in the sixth chapter of Revelation, while the preceding chapter, the fifth, sets the stage for the sixth.

The fifth chapter introduces us to the seals and to Him only who is worthy to open the scroll upon which the seals are fastened. The apostle John was very concerned when he saw the sealed scroll that no one could open. Revelation 5:4 explains: "So I wept much, because no one was found worthy to open and read the scroll, or to look at it."

Verse 5 continues: "But one of the elders said to me, 'Do not weep. Behold, the Lion of the tribe of Judah, the root of David, has prevailed to open the scroll and to loose its seven seals.

Verse 6 clarifies: "And I looked, and behold, in the midst of the throne and of the four living creatures, and in the midst of the elders, stood a Lamb as though it had been slain, having seven horns and seven eyes, which are the seven Spirits of God sent out into all the earth. (Recall the golden lampstand.)

Verse 7 proceeds: "Then He came and took the scroll out of the right hand of Him who sat on the throne."

With this much of chapter 5 behind us, we are now ready to move into chapter 6. So here we will look at the seals in detail, beginning with the mystery of Revelation 6:1–2:

> Now I saw when the Lamb opened one of the seals; and I heard one of the four living creatures saying with a voice like thunder, "Come and see."

> And I looked, and behold, a white horse. He who sat on it had a bow; and a crown was given to him, and he went out conquering and to conquer.

The white horse indicates that this person will be looked at as a hero, worthy of respect. The bow, as with the sword, represents military power. The bow was a sophisticated weapon. In combination with the arrow, it could reach out a considerable distance to bring down an enemy. So then, it seems that its use here hints at this rider on the white horse having a long reach with respect to his ability to intimidate and influence with military power. The crown given to him reveals that he acquires political power and authority. His going out conquering and to conquer, makes it clear that he will use his military strength to advance his agenda. Going out to conquer indicates an extended area of influence; in this case, it will be on a global scale using military power to intimidate, or otherwise force his will upon anyone reluctant to go along. There is a strong indication that the use of the bow in this instance refers to this person having the capability to launch long range missiles at will.

Who is this person? Why Antichrist, of course!

A look at the second seal takes us to Revelation 6:3–4:

When He opened the second seal, I heard the second living creature saying, "Come and see."

And another horse, fiery red, went out. And it was granted to the one who sat on it to take peace from the earth, and that people should kill one another; and there was given to him a great sword.

What was just read describes a period such as we are living in at present. Without trying to relate all the areas of ethnic hate, distrust, warfare, killing, and threatened warfare, we can, if we try, easily picture some of the major areas of discontent. The various ethnic nations of the former Yugoslavia, and practically the entire continent of Africa is in a blood-letting of one stage or another. The war in Iraq and its unsettled aftermath, Syria and Iran foment terrorism, North Korea threatens South Korea, China threatens Taiwan, India and Pakistan at the brink, Mid-East nations threaten Israel, Afghanistan purged, several South American nations with rebellions, Islamic terrorist cells freely roaming the planet, and so it goes. The U.S.A has troops stationed throughout this troubled world engaged in peace-keeping activities. It looks very much to-day that peace has been taken from the earth. Indications are that this trend will foster an overt act of global unification dedicated to world peace. We know, in fact, that the attempt is underway; and global unrest will be cited as one of the main areas of concern in justifying steps to bring nations of the world into a controlled forum for establishing perpetual, peaceful international relations. (*It will be called global governance.*)

Jesus, in Matthew 24:6 said this about our present time:

And you will hear of wars and rumors of wars. See that you are
not troubled; for all these things must come to pass, but the end
is not yet.

The third seal, Revelation 6:5–6:

When He opened the third seal, I heard the third living creature
say, "Come and see." So I looked, and behold, a black horse, and
he who sat on it had a pair of scales in his hand.

And I heard a voice in the midst of the four living creatures saying, "A quart of wheat for a denarius, and three quarts of barley
for a denarius; and do not harm the oil and the wine."

Famines are not new in the world; however, this third seal is
about serious, large scale famine. We shall later come upon compelling evidence indicating that this famine may well be caused
by lack of sunlight. Then, too, tampering with crop seeds through
gene splicing to improve yields is producing sterile seeds. He who
controls the food theoretically can control the world. Food will be
scarce and expensive.

"And do not harm the oil and the wine." This statement seems
out of place in the context of the prophecy. In a time of famine, the
last thing anyone would intentionally do would be to harm or as
the King James Version says, "hurt" any kind of foodstuffs. These
would all be in short supply. It seems, rather, that this statement
does not pertain to nutrition at all; but instead to two groups of
God's people to be unhurt by this scourge!

The question now becomes, which two groups of people? Not
a difficult question, since God really has but two special groups.
First, God's holy Jewish remnant. These will be protected through
tribulation and initial wrath. They shall see their Messiah at His
return, and will recognize Him. They will continue, protected
through all wrath and on into God's kingdom.

Next, Christian saints, both Christian Jews and Christian Gentiles are included here. These are saints, not because of their righteousness, but rather due to being born again in Jesus, they receive the righteousness which is through faith in Christ, the righteousness which is from God by faith, (See Phillippians 3:9). They follow Jesus regardless of circumstances or cost.

Since the Jewish remnant will not only go through the Tribulation, but the wrath as well to gain the Kingdom of God, it will be necessary for God to protect them through the time of upheaval. Reference to this is seen in Revelation 12:14–16. The children of Israel are shown by the apostle Paul as being the natural branches of the olive tree. Paul, in speaking to Gentile Christians in Romans 11:24, had this to say:

> For if you were cut out of the olive tree which is wild by nature [paganism], and were grafted contrary to nature into a cultivated olive tree [Judeo-based Christianity], how much more will these [Jews who accept Christ], who are natural branches, be grafted into their own olive tree?

Jews, being the natural branches of the cultivated olive tree have, however, been cut out by God because of unbelief. When they accept Christ as their true Messiah, they will be grafted back in. God knows those Jews who will accept Jesus at His coming. They will make up the holy remnant. They will therefore receive the archangel Michael's protection (Daniel 12:1). The olive tree holds the oil that drips into the golden pipes of the lampstand (Zechariah 4:12). Since the olive branches contain the oil, it seems clear and leaves little doubt that the Jewish remnant in this instance is the oil of the third seal!

Then the wine designation remains for Christians. Is this realistic based on Scripture? We will see that it is entirely scriptural by reading Jesus' own words in Mark 2:22:

And no one puts new wine into old wineskins; or else the new wine bursts the wineskins, the wine is spilled, and the wineskins are ruined. But new wine must be put into new wineskins.

In effect, what Jesus said here in this parable is that the new covenant (new wine) must be put in a new person; that is, a person who is born again in Jesus, (a new wineskin). Then Christians can easily be thought of as carrying the new covenant of Jesus' blood (new wine). So Christians, both Jew and Gentile, easily qualify as new wine or the wine of the third seal.

We will now look at the fourth seal, Revelation 6:7–8. These verses say something of the fourth horseman and read as follows:

When He opened the fourth seal, I heard the voice of the fourth living creature saying, "Come and see."

So I looked, and behold, a pale horse. And the name of him who sat on it was Death, and Hades followed with him. And power was given to them over a fourth of the earth, to kill with sword, with hunger, with death, and by the beasts of the earth.

Beasts do not have to be large. They may be small as well. It appears here that these will be tiny, microscopic, and represent bacteriological warfare. It will become clear later that the fourth seal represents God's wrath, including World War III, modern unrestrained warfare, where some of the world's multiple tons of stockpiled microscopic beasts of the earth will be unleashed to do what they were designed to do.

Now, there is some good news in all of this for the oil and the wine of the third seal. It confirms that they will not be harmed by this pair. With hades (hell) following along with death, we can derive from this that the death to occur of a fourth part of the earth is not the death of the saved. Saved souls do not go to hell. *The fourth seal references wrath to fall on the unsaved!* Paul, in 2 Corinthians 5:8 explains:

We are confident, yes, well pleased rather to be absent from the body and to be present with the Lord.

(Hell is reserved for the unsaved; not the saved; and not for the remnant.)

We shall see details of third and fourth seal wrath in the coming trumpet and bowl judgments. With the fifth seal about to disrupt our complacency, we will now learn that which God told Daniel 2,500 years ago was to take place in these last days, a direct Old Testament reference to a few years lying just ahead in our fast-approaching near future.

Daniel 7:25 tells of a far distant future (our time), with these challenging words for Christian saints:

He [Antichrist] shall speak pompous words against the Most High, shall persecute the saints of the Most High, and shall intend to change times and law. Then the saints shall be given into his hand for a time and times and half a time.

These three-and-a-half years mostly coincide with the ministries of the two witnesses and the one hundred forty-four thousand servants of God, just prior to Christ's return. (See Table #1)

Revelation 12:17 adds to Daniel's words concerning the same time period:

And the dragon [Satan working through Antichrist] was enraged with the woman [Jewish remnant], and he went to make war with the rest of her offspring, who keep the commandments of God and have the testimony of Jesus Christ.

The fifth seal provides a view of mistreatment of the saints spoken of in Daniel and Revelation above. The worst of the fifth seal maltreatment will occur in the three-and-a-half years prior to Jesus' return. This places the beginning of intense persecution 1,103 days after commencement of Mid-East peace (1,103 + 1,277.5 + 176.5 = 2,557 days—last 7 years. See Table #1). The Resurrection will occur in the middle of the seventh year (at the fourth trumpet).

The fifth seal, Revelation 6:9–11 shows the souls of Christians in heaven who had been martyred for the word of God and for the testimony which they held. They cried out to God to avenge their blood on the lost who dwell on the earth. They were given a white robe, and told that they should rest a little while longer, until both the number of their fellow servants and their brethren, who would be killed as they were, was completed.

This confirms that some Christians will be killed for their faith in Christ. Some will compromise their faith in order to survive a while longer on earth, but will forfeit their souls for eternity. Others will make it through to the return of Jesus Christ. The first group and the third group will both experience a resurrection to eternal life with Christ in incorruptible, resurrection bodies. The first group will experience the transformation from death, while the third group will partake of it from life (1 Thessalonians 4:16–17; 1 Corinthians 15:51–52).

The second group—compromised Christians, will wait for the second death at the end of the thousand year reign of Christ, reserved for those who miss the first (Revelation 20:4–6). The dreaded Great White Throne Judgment awaits those who will take part in the second death (Revelation 20:11–15).

The sixth seal is presented as follows:

I looked when He opened the sixth seal, and behold, there was a great earthquake; and the sun became black as sackcloth of hair, and the moon became like blood.

And the stars of heaven fell to the earth, as a fig tree drops its late figs when it is shaken by a mighty wind. [John is talking cosmic bombs here!]

Then the sky receded as a scroll when it is rolled up, and every mountain and island was moved out of its place.

And the kings of the earth, the great men, the rich men, the commanders, the mighty men, every slave and every free man, hid themselves in the caves and in the rocks of the mountains,

and said to the mountains and rocks, "Fall on us and hide us from the face of Him who sits on the throne and from the wrath of the Lamb!

"For the great day of His wrath has come, and who is able to stand?" (Revelation 6:12–17).

The sixth seal here provides a view of multiple-stage effects of a great compound natural disaster that will strike earth just before Jesus' return. These effects, are both initial and advanced stages of explosive activity from the plural event, which will announce the Lord's return. Then, after the Resurrection, destruction shall become fully developed and more clearly defined in the upcoming trumpet and bowl judgments.

Falling stars are the key to all the wrath of the lamb that the sixth seal reveals. This is, in fact, only a partial view of the total wrath that is predestined to erupt in multiple stages materializing directly from the wayward stars and to be observed in both initial and advanced stages straight ahead.

Jesus, provides a clear description of conditions as they shall exist at His return:

Immediately after the tribulation of those days the sun will be darkened, and the moon will not give its light; the stars will fall from heaven, and the powers of the heavens will be shaken.

Then the sign of the Son of Man will appear in heaven, and then all the tribes of the earth will mourn, and they will see the Son of Man coming on the clouds of heaven with power and great glory (Matthew 24:29–30).

In the account of the sixth seal—Revelation 6:12–17—after picturing the falling stars and the darkness, at which time Jesus will return, it describes, in verse 14, the sky receding as a scroll when it is rolled up, and islands and mountains being moved out of their places. These are direct results of events which we will see up close in the coming trumpet and bowl judgments. An interesting, but sad sidelight to this was seen in a ministry letter dated 1/17/05, from David Wilkerson, World Challenge, Inc., P.O. Box 260 Lindale, TX 75771, in which the earthquake caused tsunami of 12/26/04, affecting southern Asia, was reported to have caused an island in the Indian Ocean to move nearly one hundred feet. We will see biblical and scientific indications just ahead, that tsunamis referenced in the sixth seal judgment above may be considerably larger than this one. It can be said here one more time, because of its importance to be properly understood, that the falling stars are the cause of the conditions, spoken of by Jesus above that will exist at His return. We will find the solution to the mystery of the falling stars in the coming trumpet judgments.

The sixth seal talks about wrath, which will begin immediately following tribulation, and just before the return of the Lord Jesus Christ. We will now expand upon this term *wrath*, since it is sometimes referred to in Bible prophecy by another name.

The apostle Paul says that the Day of the Lord, God's wrath, will come upon the unsaved as a thief in the night, and they will see sudden destruction. He explains also that Christians will not be included in this destruction because they are destined for salvation through Jesus Christ. Here are his words from 1 Thessalonians 5:2–4:

> For you yourselves know perfectly that the day of the Lord so comes as a thief in the night.

> For when they say, "Peace and safety!" then sudden destruction comes upon them, as labor pains upon a pregnant woman. And they shall not escape.

> But you, brethren, are not in darkness, so that this Day should overtake you as a thief.

Then, verse 9 provides relief for a troubled soul:

For God did not appoint us to wrath, but to obtain salvation through our Lord Jesus Christ (1 Thessalonians 5:9).

Destruction coming upon the unsaved as a thief in the night and described as labor pains coming upon a pregnant woman, is a perfectly precise means of describing the multiple cosmic event that will overtake earth and unexpectedly bring the commencement of God's wrath. We shall see it unmasked with all its various details and phases in the pages just ahead.

Christians in the early days of Jesus' church knew the signs leading to the dreadful Day of the Lord; they knew that it was not meant for them. They were aware, also, that those to be adversely affected by it would be caught by surprise. How did they know? They were told, and they believed.

Now, to the seventh seal, Revelation 8:1–5. The seventh seal is dedicated solely to introducing the seven trumpet judgments. In John's vision, he saw seven angels standing before God, and they were given seven trumpets. We see God's number seven again, indicating an inherent importance of this number in God's organizational plan. Revelation 8:3 pictures another angel with a golden censer approaching the throne of God, and to whom much incense was given, that he should offer it with the prayers of the saints upon the golden altar that was before the throne.

Revelation 8:4: "And the smoke of the incense, with the prayers of the saints, ascended before God from the angel's hand." This is a symbolic picture of God receiving and hearing the prayers of His people. In the next verse, we see His response: "Then the angel took the censer, filled it with fire from the altar, and threw it to the earth. And there were noises, thunderings, lightnings, and an earthquake." This is God's answer to the souls pictured in the fifth seal; that is, of those who had been "slain for the word of God and for the testimony which they held." They had cried out to God to avenge their deaths on the misdirected who dwell on the earth (Revelation 6:9–11).

We will soon see that the angel's censer, filled with fire and thrown to earth, will turn out to be a concise interpretation of the natural disaster (act of God) destined to begin the Day of the Lord; thereby declaring the impending return of Jesus Christ!

# CHAPTER THIRTY-SEVEN

# THE SEVEN TRUMPETS

The trumpets, as with the seals and bowls, represent variations of God's judgment (punishment) upon unrepentant mankind, but with unique characteristics. To begin with, the first three trumpets represent initial wrath, setting the stage for Christ's return at the fourth. Then come the other three called woes. Here, the fifth trumpet announces the initial stage of the fourth and last cosmic intruder. It is succeeded by the sixth trumpet which details advanced-stage wrath to be caused by a related set of problems. Then, the seventh trumpet concludes the string of wrathful events and stages with a look back at several past happenings in the Day of the Lord, most of which were seen in the sixth seal.

While the trumpet judgments are seen as mostly initial stages of several wrathful events, bowl judgments represent mostly advanced stages of these very same events. Trumpets and bowls, both fully submerged in the six-month-long Day of the Lord, are joined there by the second, third, fourth and sixth seals, all depicting their parts in this terrible day.

# CHAPTER THIRTY-EIGHT

# THE FIRST TRUMPET

So the seven angels who had the seven trumpets prepared themselves to sound.

The first angel sounded: And hail and fire followed, mingled with blood, and they were thrown to the earth; and a third of the trees were burned up, and all green grass was burned up (Revelation 8:6–7).

In its abbreviated way, this fully describes a comet. The materials that the apostle John saw in his vision—hail (ice); blood (rocky dust particles mixed in the ice, appearing as flecks of blood); and fire (sun's reflection off the coma and tail). These were gathered together to form a comet and hurled to earth.

The encyclopedic description of a comet describes three separate parts. The first part; the nucleus is a solid, icy core consisting of ice and various kinds of rocky dust particles. Using Halley's comet as an example; eighty percent of the ice is formed from water, fifteen percent from carbon monoxide and the remainder is frozen carbon dioxide, methane, and ammonia.

The comet travels around the sun in an elongated oval orbit that may be less than one hundred percent fixed in its path due to possible perturbation by other heavenly bodies. The fact that planets travel in almost circular orbits, brings comets periodically across orbits of planets and their satellites. These infrequent incursions of comets into the orbits of planets will upon occasion result in a collision with a planet or its satellite—witness the pockmarks on the moon. Of course, asteroids and meteorites must bear their responsibility in all of this as well.

The second part of the comet, the coma, a cloudy atmosphere encasing the nucleus, is generated as the comet approaches the sun. Radiation pressure from the sun causes the frozen nucleus to give off gases and grit, forming the coma and the third part of the comet structure, the tail.

This third part, the tail, consists of gases and dust particles coming from the coma, which in turn originate from the frozen, dirty, gas and grit generating, ice nucleus. Particles coming from the coma are caught in the solar wind, consisting of charged particles ejected from the sun. The force of these solar wind particles acting on the particles coming from the coma is considerably stronger than the gravitational force of the sun; thus the solar wind pulls these coma particles along, forming the tail of the comet which for this reason, always points away from the sun. Neither the nucleus nor the coma and tail are on fire as the comet travels its orbit. It is seen because of sunlight reflecting off these coma/tail particles; and so, at times, appears to be a ball of fire streaking through the sky.

The diameter of the comet nucleus varies greatly one from another, but are commonly less than 10 miles (16 kilometers) across. The comas of some comets reach diameters of nearly 1 million miles (1.6 million kilometers). Some tails extend to distances of 100 million miles (160 million kilometers), with something solid and of the considerable size referenced above, should it enter earth's atmosphere very bad things would happen.[21]

But why go into all of this? It seems quite certain, considering all aspects of Bible-provided details, that the first five trumpets are all about a comet striking earth. This action would set up the conditions that Jesus, in Matthew 24:29, said would exist at His second coming: "Immediately after the tribulation of those days the sun will be darkened, and the moon will not give its light; the stars will fall from heaven, and the powers of the heavens will be shaken." Question: how can one comet be seen as multiple falling stars? Answer ahead!

It is obvious that fire plays a large part in these trumpet judgments from what we read in Revelation 8:5. Here, an angel with a censer "filled it with fire from the altar, and threw it to the earth. And there were noises, thunderings, lightnings, and an earthquake." Since the event just described immediately precedes the trumpet judgments in the Revelation account, in this instance, it unquestionably sets the stage for the trumpets.

Fire being hurled to earth and causing an earthquake, noises, lightnings, and thunderings, is John's description for what he observed which adds detail to the first trumpet. So then, we shall look closely at this first trumpet blast. Revelation 8:7 says that after the first trumpet sounded: "Hail and fire followed, mingled with blood, and they were thrown to earth." Here we see the symbolic formation of a comet.

A comet supplies each ingredient: *hail*, frozen icy nucleus formed by ice crystals; *fire*, outer space sunlight reflecting off of coma and tail particles. *Mingled with blood* equates with dust and grit in combination with gases emitted from the solid, frozen nucleus causing formation of the coma and tail.

John, in the vision, was shown individual parts of a forming comet. He then described what he had seen by relating the unfamiliar to things that he was familiar with. Yes, saved Christians and the Jewish remnant will be very much present when the comet strikes.

But God has provided a loophole in this prophesied destruction to preserve them! (It is one-third!)

Considering the aftermath: "a third of the trees were burned up, and all green grass was burned up" (Revelation 8:7). There is no mention of human loss leading to the conclusion that this impact will occur in an uninhabited area of forest and grassland. Speculation could focus on Siberia or a similar area as a likely ground zero location for this event mainly due to it being sparsely populated. Then, too, its topography consists mostly of forests and grass covered plains. As we shall see, real fires will result with devastating effects.

Now, to continue with what John saw being formed and hurled to earth. As the account of the second trumpet blast is read below, we will find it to be problematic in relation to a single comet strike; so read on for the solution.

# CHAPTER THIRTY-NINE

# THE SECOND TRUMPET

Then the second angel sounded: and something like a great mountain burning with fire was thrown into the sea, and a third of the sea became blood.

And a third of the living creatures in the sea died, and a third of the ships were destroyed (Revelation 8:8–9).

The above object could be thought of as an asteroid. Even another comet, except that close or simultaneous strikes of multiple comets or asteroids and comets is too far fetched to contemplate. There is a simple answer to the puzzle; however, *a comet breaking up as it slams into earth's heavy atmosphere!* This second trumpet obviously describes another fragment of the broken comet. The sequence of trumpet events starting with the first on through to the fifth strongly suggest a close succession of impacts with a pause contained within. The first through the third, then skipping the fourth, and hitting again in the fifth.

A comet breaking up in a planet's atmosphere is not unusual. We have a good example of this happening with the planet Jupiter. The encyclopedic description of the event boiled down to minimum facts unfolds as follows:

A comet, later named Shoemaker-Levy 9, having been drawn from its orbit around the sun into an orbit around Jupiter by the gravitational force of the planet, was spotted from Earth. At the time it was found, it had already broken into twenty-one pieces, undoubtedly because of its close proximity to the large planet.

Scientific calculations made on Earth, showed that the orbiting fragments would crash into Jupiter in July 1994.

These fragments had been first photographed by astronomer David H. Levy in March 1993 while filming an area of space near Jupiter. The image of the fragmented comet was discovered by associate Carolyn Shoemaker while reviewing the films; thus accounting for the names Shoemaker-Levy being associated with the naming of the comet. (David H. Levy, article titled "Was Chicken Little Right?" *Parade Magazine*, May 10, 1998, 14.) In this article, Mr. Levy also presents a hypothetical example of a large comet striking earth; a chilling exercise in extrapolation. It drives home, as with a sledgehammer, the awesome power, not only of God's universe, but of His prophetic word! We will look at this hypothetical example a bit further on.

Now, back to the Shoemaker-Levy 9 fragmented comet, encyclopedic account:

The Hubble Space Telescope was in orbit around Earth, and the Galileo space probe was on its way to Jupiter. Scientists on Earth were ready. When the crash came, it occurred on the back side of Jupiter. Galileo was in position to observe and photograph, but equipment malfunction prevented this. Jupiter's rotation, however, brought the crash site around in less than half an hour, to where Hubble could photograph it. Scientists estimate that the larger fragments were from one-third to two-and-a-half miles in diameter.

The impacts caused large explosions. The explosions scattered comet debris over large areas, some larger than the diameter of the earth. Jupiter has the volume of a thousand Earths, so these areas did not cover a great percentage of Jupiter's surface. The debris gradually spread into a dark haze of fine material that remained suspended for several months in Jupiter's upper atmosphere.

There is another important difference between earth and Jupiter besides size regarding a comet hit. Earth has a solid crust; where Jupiter has rather a gaseous surface of hydrogen and helium under its atmosphere. This gas surface condition extends into Jupiter, gradually making the transition to liquid about a quarter of the way into the planet toward its solid rocky core.[22] In Levy's article, the speed of a large comet fragment, as it hit Jupiter was 140,000 miles per hour. This would explain why they exploded, and why it was the comet debris only that was scattered over large areas, and why the haze of fine particles didn't darken Jupiter's atmosphere any more than they did. There was no rock-laden earth thrown up, as would be the case with Planet Earth.

The following statements are taken from an article that appeared in the *Seattle Times*, February 12, 1998, page A-11. It is titled, *Asteroid Hurtling to Earth Could Cause Huge Tsunami* written by Glennda Chui of Knight Ridder Newspapers. Selected portions are reviewed here:

As if months of darkness, global crop failures and large-scale wildfires set by a rain of molten debris were not enough reasons to worry about a large asteroid hitting Earth, scientists have simulated one more scary consequence: a gigantic tsunami that could kill millions and even erase small costal nations in just a few hours. (Then every island fled away, and the mountains were not found; seventh bowl, Revelation 16:20.)

The article goes on to tell about the work of an astrophysicist regarding a killer asteroid, that in hitting earth in the past, was responsible, according to the scientific view, of blocking sunlight causing loss of vegetation and ultimately the demise of the dinosaurs. (The Christian view is at odds with the dating of this dinosaur conclusion.) The quote continues:

His computer models [the astrophysicist's] of an asteroid half that size [that doomed the dinosaurs]—about three miles across—show if it fell in the Pacific Ocean between California and Hawaii, the resulting tsunami would tower up to 1,000 feet high when it crashed to shore.

Comment: It is thought, given like size, that there is little destructive difference between the strike of an asteroid or a comet to earth.

Here, we will pick up the article again:

The odds of an asteroid that big [three miles across] hitting Earth are estimated at 1 in 10 million. If it did happen, tsunamis would be only part of a pattern of destruction unprecedented in human history. The impact would kick up enough dust to darken Earth for months, said a director of space at NASA's Ames Research Center in Mountain View, California. This would lead to global crop failures and starvation, as well as devastate natural ecosystems. [Famine of the third seal?]

But other calculations indicate a much smaller asteroid—one that would cause only local damage if it hit land—would set off a series of tsunamis that would wash over thousands of miles of coastline, should the asteroid land in deep ocean.

And there will be signs in the sun, in the moon, and in the stars; and on the earth distress of nations, with perplexity, the sea and the waves roaring (Luke 21:25).

The David H. Levy article mentioned above, of a hypothetical comet strike to earth, will be reviewed here. Since it is quite long, selected portions will be used which present the data that we have an interest in. It starts with the following:

It is an evening in May 1999. The sky is clear, and there is no moon. High in the north, just below the Big Dipper, a comet blazes. Found only a few weeks earlier by an amateur astronomer through her small telescope, it has been getting brighter until, tonight, it far outshines everything else in the sky.

The end comes swiftly. The comet breaks through the upper atmosphere destroying the Earth's protective ozone layer. There is a deafening sonic boom. Seconds later, with the force of 100 million hydrogen bombs, the comet slams into the Pacific Ocean just off the coast of Los Angeles. Virtually every rock within 5 miles of ground zero is instantly vaporized. The Earth trembles as a force 12 quake topples any animal trying to stand up. In less than a minute, a mighty shockwave gouges out a crater 100 miles wide and 25 miles deep. Another shockwave tears the comet apart and its remnants vaporize as they plow into Earth.

"For the great day of His wrath has come, and who is able to stand?" (Revelation 6:17).

Mile-high tsunamis rush upward from the point of impact and speed across the Pacific, flooding costal cities from Los Angeles to Tokyo. The force of impact generates enormous heat, and a fireball of hot gas, visible for thousands of miles, rises high into the atmosphere. Millions of tons of rocky debris and dust billow upward in a gigantic cloud. All over the Earth, storms of heavy rocks—the debris dredged up by the impact—strike the ground with enough violence to tear it up. Anyone outdoors feels temperatures as high as an oven set to broiling. Ground fires ignite and quickly spread around the world.

That's just the overture. As the worldwide fires burn for months, fine dust thickens high in the Earth's atmosphere. The sky becomes black as a darkroom, and for more than six months there is no sunlight anywhere on Earth. Cooling rains fall, but they are poisoned with sulfuric acid. After more than a year of darkness, the sky finally clears, and temperatures begin a slow rise as the Earth turns into a giant greenhouse.

There was a great earthquake; and the sun became black as sackcloth of hair, and the moon became like blood; sixth seal (Revelation 6:12).

The strikingly similar effects in Levy's scenario to certain Bible prophesied events of the seal, trumpet, and bowl judgments, will come to be seen as having prophetic implications of their own.

It seems that Levy's scenario, though a single impact, fully reflects the first, second, third, and fifth trumpets. It would also fulfill part of the seventh trumpet, the first four bowls, part of the fifth and seventh bowls, as well as all of the sixth seal. His single comet appears to be larger than the Bible's multiple fragments as they strike earth; however, we shall see amazing similarities between Levy's scientific postulation, and God's prophetic Word!

We can now return to the second trumpet, and deal with it on the basis of what we have seen written by astronomers who study these things.

We saw in the second trumpet, as a result of something like a great mountain burning with fire being thrown into the sea "that a third of the sea became blood: and a third of the living creatures in the sea died, and a third of the ships were destroyed."

This second trumpet, along with the first and third, define a period of time immediately after the Tribulation, that will loudly proclaim the beginning of wrath. A perilous time, with earth reeling from initial impacts and resulting mayhem characteristic of great disruptive, traumatic disasters, multiplied several times over; and darkness will begin to envelop earth. These three fragments, including the sea strike, will blast large craters in earth's crust. Red-hot rocks and debris will cause fires far and wide as they fall back to earth.

The limited effect of the first trumpet fragment to one-third of the trees, and second trumpet fragment to one-third of the sea, the creatures in the sea, and the ships on the sea, specifies initial, immature, wrath effects, to begin shortly before Jesus' return. This one-third loophole provides the means of escape from wrath for God's people. As we know, bowl judgments depict advanced stages of the same wrathful event as pictured in the like numbered initial stage trumpet judgments. (The sixth trumpet and sixth bowl are reversed.) The second bowl judgment provides a view of the advanced stage of a wrath event which began with the initial stage depicted in the second trumpet judgment. All trumpet and bowl activity is a part of God's wrath, which defines the six-month-long Day of the Lord. The second bowl then provides the reader of Bible prophecy with a glimpse of the remaining two-thirds of the second fragment's effect to achieve total havoc. In the bowl verse, the sea became blood as of a dead man; and all living creatures in the sea died. Soil from the second fragment crater at the bottom of the sea has by this time fully contaminated the water to cause it to appear as blood, and now all sea creatures are dead.

We shall now surmise the frequency of fragment crashes to earth. In the David Levy article referred to earlier, he tells of the crash frequency of the Shoemaker-Levy 9 comet fragments to the surface of Jupiter:

> The crashes, which took place in July 1994, were the most incredible explosions ever seen on another world. With each few hours came more fireworks.

"With each few hours came more fireworks": this may preview things to come on earth; thus providing a solution to the mysteries of the first, second, third, and fifth trumpet judgments. The alternative to spaced fragment strikes is as given below:

With earth, when the comet strikes and breaks up, unless they will be pulled into orbit by earth's gravitational field beforehand, as was the case with Shoemaker-Levy 9 around Jupiter, these fragments will hit earth simultaneously. They would, however, take different paths to our planet's surface.

The apostle John, in Revelation 6:13, in the context of the sixth seal, gives his impression of the falling stars:

And the stars of heaven fell to the earth, as a fig tree drops its late figs when it is shaken by a mighty wind.

Since figs do not all drop at the same time, this verse seems to favor spaced crashes to earth, as does 1 Thessalonians 5:2–3:

For you yourselves know perfectly that the day of the Lord so comes as a thief in the night.

For when they say, "Peace and safety!" then sudden destruction comes upon them, as labor pains upon a pregnant woman. And they shall not escape.

Anyone familiar with labor pains knows right away that this verse is talking about spaced events.

So now we may want to consider that this comet will break into four pieces as it plows into earth's heavy atmosphere; with the fragments being pulled into earth orbit and crashing periodically to the planet's surface a short time after the initial breakup. God's prophetic Word on this subject also strongly indicates considerable surprise on the part of earth's inhabitants, as it says: "For when they say, 'Peace and safety!' then sudden destruction comes upon them as labor pains upon a pregnant woman." This speaks of an undetected approach to earth of the comet with little or no advanced warning before the collision.

In this regard, Mr. David H. Levy has a companion article to the one in which he described a hypothetical comet strike to earth. This one on the same page, titled "Let's Take It Seriously," among other things, reveals the existence of a vast number of both known and unknown asteroids and comets. It explains also, that one of the unknowns could strike earth: "with only a few second's warning."[23]

Here, once more, man's science fully supports God's Word in its reference to end time prophesied occurrences. A few seconds warning sufficiently fulfills 1 Thessalonians 5:2, wherein it says:

For you yourselves know perfectly that the day of the Lord so comes as a thief in the night.

Now, back to the "orbiting fragments understanding regarding frequency of crashes."

To add support to the orbiting fragment understanding, we shall soon see Bible evidence that indicates a separation between the first three fragment crashes and the devastation of the fourth fragment crash to earth at the fifth trumpet. But, now the third angel is about to sound!

# CHAPTER FORTY

# THE THIRD TRUMPET

Then the third angel sounded: and a great star fell from heaven, burning like a torch, and it fell on a third of the rivers and on the springs of water.

The name of the star is Wormwood. A third of the waters became wormwood, and many men died from the water, because it was made bitter (Revelation 8:10–11).

Progression to one-third binds this third trumpet fragment to the first two crashes in establishing the three as partners in announcing the onset of God's wrath. After a brief, majestic interlude to be framed by the boundaries of the fourth trumpet, and triggered by the cumulative aggregate of one-third reduction in light transmission from the heavenly bodies, the relentless progression through the remaining two-thirds of wrathful duration will continue. We shall see the glorious interlude up close and in detail when we arrive at the fourth trumpet.

The first three fragments, as they crash to earth, work in concert to produce the one-third water and atmospheric contamination which plays such an important part in the forthcoming return of Jesus Christ, and the resurrection of the saints.

With the buildup to the grandeur of the fourth trumpet now in place, we shall continue with the muddy details of the third trumpet.

Environmental impact of these three dirt, rock, and miscellaneous debris throwing explosions will all contribute to contamination of open bodies of water. This condition, as it progresses, will more than likely involve sulfuric-acid-laced rain as well. Even though John, as he viewed the vision, gave the third fragment, the great star (burning like a torch) and named Wormwood, full credit for fouling the fresh water bodies, the other two fragments will bear some responsibility for it as well.

We are now in need of relief from this vicious outer space bombardment. We shall see later biblical evidence of how long it may take, measured in days to reach the grace period of the fourth trumpet. Results of these attacks will be specific in what and whom they affect. This is the one-third loophole; wrath avoidance for God's people in the handful of days until Jesus' return. Wrath shall bypass the Jewish remnant and saints who will experience resurrection from life rather than from death.

The next trumpet proclaims the arrival of Jesus Christ at His second coming. It establishes conditions called for in the first three gospels. So that there will be no misunderstanding as to conditions that will prevail at the Lord's return, please read the following verses: Matthew 24:29–30; Mark 13:24–26; Luke 21:25–27.

This next trumpet, the fourth, is the last trumpet of 1 Corinthians 15:52, which discusses the Resurrection:

in a moment, in the twinkling of an eye, at the last trumpet. For the trumpet will sound, and the dead will be raised incorruptible, and we shall be changed.

Here, Paul is talking of that which was discussed above; resurrection of the saints when Christ returns at the blast of the trumpet that will be for them, *the last trumpet!*

In 1 Thessalonians 4:16–17, Paul refers to the trumpet of God in reference to the same occurrence, but does not modify *trumpet* with *last* in respect to its position in the sequence. Here it says:

> For the Lord Himself will descend from heaven with a shout, with the voice of an archangel, and with the trumpet of God. And the dead in Christ will rise first.

> Then we who are alive and remain shall be caught up together with them in the clouds to meet the Lord in the air. And thus we shall always be with the Lord.

# CHAPTER FORTY-ONE

# THE FOURTH TRUMPET

Then the fourth angel sounded: and a third of the sun was struck, a third of the moon, and a third of the stars, so that a third of them were darkened. A third of the day did not shine, and likewise the night.

And I looked, and I heard an angel flying through the midst of heaven, saying with a loud voice, "Woe, woe, woe to the inhabitants of the earth, because of the remaining blasts of the trumpet of the three angels who are about to sound!" (Revelation 8:12–13).

This trumpet does not represent a comet fragment; instead, it represents the culmination of the one-third effect of the first three closely spaced fragment crashes. The fourth trumpet expresses this one-third effect in resultant atmospheric contamination with one-third reduction in illumination from the sun, moon, and stars. The fourth trumpet does something else also with its emphasis on one-third natural light reduction. It announces the return of Jesus Christ, Son of God! This one-third point, represents a hair trigger alignment with the majestic splendor of the absolutely most magnificent occurrence to grace this lost and searching planet in what will be, at that time, the last 1,979 years since His resurrection, said by some to have occurred in A.D. 32! This stellar manifestation will fulfill all prophetic Scripture foretelling of this magnificent event. In the twinkling of an eye, saints will be changed from corruptible to incorruptible, and death shall be swallowed up in victory (1 Corinthians 15:51–54).

We are now aware of the one-third mathematic representation which provides physical escape for the then-living saints to be brought through the initial cataclysmic labor pains of the first three comet fragment crashes to earth. How will the escape come about? With God in control, the method is clear. God's people will be kept out of the way of the first three encounters with offspring of a wayward solar traveler by Holy Spirit manipulation of the elements of time and space. They will be in the right place at the right time! The one-third loophole shall be for God's people, the saints, and the Jewish remnant, as was the Passover for God's chosen people, the children of Israel when they were kept from the angel of death in preparation for their exodus from bondage in Egypt. Though the death angel in one night destroyed all the first-born of Egypt, both man and beast, the homes of the Israelites were passed over because they had followed God's instructions in how to prepare for this selective protection, while at the same time, death was taking a heavy toll all around them.

God's Word makes it very clear that Christians can not earn their salvation. It is a gift, and Christians believe by faith that Jesus paid our penalty for sin in our lives. We know, therefore that we are free from the penalty of sin as we live our lives in repentance and humility in accordance with direction from God's Holy Spirit.

In respect to the Jewish remnant whose names God has written in the Book, it seems that they will be following His commandments and His ordinances of which, observing the Passover on an ongoing annual basis is one. They, as with the saints, will have met God's requirements; and so for saints, a brief immunity to wrath until Jesus' return. For the remnant, protection from tribulation and all the wrathful Day of the Lord!

The kingdom of God lies directly ahead in which God's two people groups, the oil and the wine of the third seal, shall both play important, but vastly different roles. We are on a landing approach to this most desired destination. The passage will not be without turbulence; so pray to God through Jesus Christ, His Son that you will persevere. We will see glimpses of the seventh day in pages ahead. The thousand-year Sabbath will be as the name suggests, a day of rest, but will serve also to prepare mankind for the eternal future. This eternity as we know, will be a time of duration (endless), and is available in two forms; one really good and the other really bad. And, yes, as you probably already know, the choice is ours! So then, the mission here is to let the Holy Bible tell what God's Word wants us to know regarding His plans for adjustments to His creation. The first phase is almost over, and the second phase is about to begin. The question then must be asked: will we be ready? If we are not yet sure, we can read on and while doing so, a conclusion will certainly begin to form in our minds.

The Bible holds the secrets of earth's near-term traumatic encounter with fragments of our solar system. We could say, "There is a bumpy ride ahead!" So for reassurance, we will return to the greatest of Trumpets, the Fourth, and continue with the solution to all the trouble. (TIME IS STILL ON OUR SIDE!)

Now, we have uncovered another priceless asset of the mathematical percentage of one-third. This point of radiant light restriction from the sun, moon, and stars represents a glaring sign. It signifies the return of the Son of Man: "Then the sign of the Son of Man will appear in heaven, and then all the tribes of the earth will mourn, and they will see the Son of Man coming on the clouds of heaven with power and great glory." Matthew 24:30.

To Christians, this shall be a sign of His imminent return and the beginning of their eternal relationship with the real Master of the universe. To the others, it will be a frightening time. And when the Lord is seen coming on these clouds; to some, clouds of glory—to others, fearful clouds of dread and uncertainty—grief, mourning, and lamenting will follow, for the loss of such an irreplaceable gift! These are the circumstances; and this is the occurrence: the magnificent return of the Lord Jesus Christ on the foreboding clouds of heaven with power and great glory.

Now, with the very important fourth trumpet behind us, it is time to visit the trumpet that could be described as *"The mother of all trumpet mysteries."* Within its boundaries we will find the answers to perplexing questions concerning the veiled, approximately six-month-long Day of the Lord. This fifth trumpet continues a series of initial wrath events that were interrupted by the power and glory of the fourth trumpet.

# CHAPTER FORTY-TWO

# THE FIFTH TRUMPET

Then the fifth angel sounded: And I saw a star fallen from heaven to the earth. To him was given the key to the bottomless pit.

And he opened the bottomless pit, and smoke arose out of the pit like the smoke of a great furnace. So the sun and the air were darkened because of the smoke of the pit.

Then out of the smoke locusts came upon the earth. And to them was given power, as the scorpions of the earth have power.

They were commanded not to harm the grass of the earth, or any green thing, or any tree, but only those men who do not have the seal of God on their foreheads.

And they were not given authority to kill them, but to torment them for five months. Their torment was like the torment of a scorpion when it strikes a man.

In those days men will seek death and will not find it; they will desire to die, and death will flee from them.

The shape of the locusts was like horses prepared for battle. On their heads were crowns of something like gold, and their faces were like the faces of men.

They had hair like women's hair, and their teeth were like lions' teeth.

And they had breastplates like breastplates of iron, and the sound of their wings was like the sound of chariots with many horses running into battle.

They had tails like scorpions, and there were stings in their tails. Their power was to hurt men five months.

And they had as king over them the angel of the bottomless pit, whose name in Hebrew is Abaddon, but in Greek he has the name Apollyon.

One woe is past. Behold, still two more woes are coming after these things (Revelation 9:1–12).

This fifth trumpet is very revealing in details pertaining to the Holy Land, which expands our knowledge of the end time and the numerous difficulties with which mankind will be struggling.

The best way to deal with the several important points given in this chapter is to itemize them as we will do here:

1. The first point made is that a star was fallen from heaven, given the key to the bottomless pit, and opened it releasing a great amount of smoke; and locusts came upon the earth. These prey upon humans not having the seal of God on their foreheads.

   a. This star is not an angel as some believe, but rather, another comet fragment that plunged to earth, sending high into the atmosphere, dust and debris, which John describes as smoke from the bottomless pit. The worsening condition of the atmosphere will be contributed to by all of the four fragments, and smoke may very well be part of the light-restricting elements that John saw and described as arising out of the bottomless pit.

b. This fragment impact will produce a huge, open wound in the earth. Comet, rock, and earth will vaporize instantly, as mighty shockwaves gouge out this large volcano-like crater. A great fireball of hot gases, earth, rock, and comet debris will belch forth, further darkening an already-expanding darkness that will, now, be growing well in advance of the one-third effect of the fourth trumpet. Pandemonium on earth will rule entirely as the explosive fragments begin their attack on the planet. The unquestioned power of the force holding the heavenly bodies in place will appear to have been shaken. Luke 21:26 makes this point: ". . . men's hearts failing them from fear and the expectation of those things which are coming on the earth, for the powers of heaven will be shaken."

2. This wrath will not touch the Jewish remnant, having God's seal of protection on their foreheads (Revelation 9:4).

3. Now about the locusts. John described them as shaped "like horses prepared for battle," having lion's teeth, the faces of men, and hair like women's hair. He pictured them also as having crowns of something like gold on their heads and breastplates like breastplates of iron. He described the sound of their wings as like the sound of chariots with many horses running into battle and their tails as having stings like scorpion's tails. He makes an important disclosure next, in that he says in verses 5 and 10, that their power was to hurt men for five months. He explains as well who their king was: "The angel of the bottomless pit," who, in either Hebrew or Greek, is the same entity: Satan.

a.  Satan, to be sure, will indwell Antichrist, the reborn tyrant, Antiochus IV Epiphanes; so then, outwardly, it shall be Antichrist who will be seen as controlling these objects.

b.  They are, in fact, objects instead of insects. John viewed this scene almost two thousand years ago. The only way he could describe them was to compare them to things he was familiar with. These futuristic objects had features that resembled, but did not duplicate, things that were well known to him. So, when he compared their shape to horses prepared for battle, he was giving his best selection of what was familiar, to represent something out of his world. Horses would be considered large in relation to other members of the animal kingdom. It then seems certain that these were quite large flying objects. Had they been smaller, he would have compared them to sheep, dogs, or rodents.

c.  John, being constrained by lack of foreknowledge of end time technology, when he was suddenly confronted with it in the vision, had to search for answers. His logical mind created comparisons of the characteristics of these creatures, as he considered them to be, to what in his mind they resembled most—locusts. He then used feature similarities such as horses prepared for battle, having lion's teeth, crowns of gold on their heads, faces of men, women's hair, breastplates of iron, and their wings producing the sound of chariots with many horses running into battle. All these feature likenesses point toward much larger size than would be expected in a locust-size creature. With these thoughts in mind, we can then safely conclude that what John actually saw were helicopters.

d.  We need to clear up one point before we go on, that point being: the helicopters did not come out of the bottomless

288

pit. It is easy to see why John may have thought that they had, as the darkening material that John called smoke was spewing from a hole in the ground. Call it a crater. This, the fourth comet fragment collision with earth at say, 140,000 miles an hour with all accompanying fireworks, could appear as nothing less than the *mouth of hell!*

No, the helicopters didn't come out of the crater, they came out of the smoke. John said in Revelation 9:3–5:

> Then out of the smoke locusts came upon the earth. And to them was given power, as the scorpions of the earth have power.
>
> They were commanded not to harm the grass of the earth, or any green thing, or any tree, but only those men who do not have the seal of God on their foreheads.
>
> And they were not given authority to kill them, but to torment them for five months. And their torment was like the torment of a scorpion when it strikes a man.
>
> The question is: if these choppers are under the control of Antichrist, why are they attacking those very people who follow and worship him? The key to the answer can be summed up in one word: *"chemtrails."* Most everyone is familiar with the condensation trails caused by high-flying jet aircraft, shortened to *contrails* for convenience in describing the fluffy white vapor trails. They can be seen from time to time stretching across the sky, marking the recent path of a jet aircraft.
>
> In recent years a phenomenon has developed in the skies that is not being reported by the dominant media, but which portends ill for mankind. The activity in question is the mass production of *chemtrails* by relatively

low-flying aircraft of various descriptions. The word *chemtrail* is a spin-off of *contrail*, referring to chemical trails rather than condensation trails. The reason for this cynical interpretation of these harmless looking cloud trails that sometimes crisscross and fill the skies is that at times a sticky spider web-like material falls out of them. To make matters worse, this material has been blamed for making those people sick who have come in physical contact with it, causing a severe flu-like condition. It has been reported that after laboratory analysis of samples that the material consisted of aircraft fuel as carrier, with several strains of bacteria and yeasts piggybacking on it.

So, what is going on? No one is talking. Would our government know about it? *It most certainly would!*

The fact is, it is being handled as a non-event, which is common procedure for situations not meant for public disclosure. It has been concluded by some, being in the dark as to what is really going on, that it is an attempt to restore the ozone layer. Whether or not this is accurate is not publicly known, but it makes the point.[24]

It appears to be an attempt to accomplish some perceived good, at the cost of an acceptable level of risk to the human population. This is nothing new. Consider the early atom bomb testing, with inadequate safety procedures in place: the use of agent orange in Vietnam, the Gulf War inoculations, now blamed for the Gulf War illness among veterans of that conflict. An acceptable level of risk is what Revelation 9:3–5 is all about!

The objects called locusts were "commanded not to harm the grass of the earth, or any green thing, or any tree, but only those men who do not have the seal of God on their foreheads" (Revelation 9:4).

The Bible, two thousand years ago, foretold the ecological movement that would grip the world in the last days, which places the welfare of plants and animals over that of human beings.

e. The international community of nations (global government), now in the process of forming, is in no uncertain terms, rushing into and fully embracing worship of mother earth. The enshrining of earth through establishment of ecological standards, taking of large tracts of natural areas from human use, and reducing human involvement on public lands and on private property as well, is all in an advanced stage.

The ecological movement is strong and getting stronger. It is the wave of the future, and Antichrist will ride it right up to his throne in the temple of God. When this ecological disaster strikes earth, he will be under strong pressure to do something; as prolonged darkening of the sun would bring worldwide famine. Antichrist will, therefore, carry out what he will deem appropriate action to deal effectively with the problem. He will introduce into the atmosphere, chemical or biological agents, or a combination thereof by means of a fleet of helicopters in an attempt to neutralize contamination and clear the air. Since he will be part of and beholden to the ecological movement, he will choose to place the welfare of plant life over that of the human population; an acceptable level of risk, with so much at stake!

f. The fallout, according to Revelation 9:5, will affect those without the seal of God on their foreheads [those other than the Jewish remnant]: "like the torment of a scorpion when it strikes a man." Revelation 9:6 continues:

> In those days men will seek death and will not find it; they will desire to die, and death will flee from them.

g. The fifth trumpet gives a time reference that can be useful in making several determinations. Revelation 9:5 says this:

> And they were not given authority to kill them, but to torment them for five months.

Since this torment of five months is a part of God's wrath upon unrepentant mankind, it now becomes known that the end of the wrath will not be for at least five more months. It appears that the aerial spraying may have some beneficial effect in clearing the air, since Mid-East warfare will break out approximately three-and-a-half months later and culminate in the terrible Battle of Armageddon. We shall see biblical evidence for this timing as we continue to peel away layers of Bible prophecy.

John says in Revelation 6:12 that "the sun became black as sackcloth of hair, and the moon became like blood." This large battle may be affected in its course by night vision equipment in the possession of some, and/or Antichrist's air-clearing activities. Then, too, Revelation 16:10 indicates that the Mid-East, the location of Antichrist's throne, may experience the heaviest pollution. More on this is coming up!

Now, to address the issue of the timing of the Lord's return. It is very difficult, based upon all that the Bible tells about circumstances at the time of His coming not to know, if not precisely, at least the general time period of His foretold return. He will return as a thief—unexpectedly, only to the unsaved in the form of wrath.

Matthew 24:37–39 compares the Lord's second coming with Noah's ark and the great Flood. These verses are critical to the truth of the Resurrection. Jesus Himself provides this comparison:

> But as the days of Noah were, so also will the coming of the Son of Man be.

> For as in the days before the flood, they were eating and drinking, marrying and giving in marriage, until the day that Noah entered the ark, and did not know until the flood came and took them all away, so also will the coming of the Son of Man be.

Noah and his family being carried in the ark to safety represents the Resurrection. They knew almost precisely when the flood would begin to manifest, and were ready when it swept the unsaved away.

This explanation from the mouth of the Lord Himself clearly defines His intent to preserve all His people together at one time through the initial stage of His wrath. This judgment will be directed at the unrepentant of the earth. There is no mention of God having divided Noah's family into two groups. One to rapture out early while keeping the other for the most difficult work of completing and filling the ark through what would become intensifying persecution by the unsaved as they became increasingly fearful of and hostile to the beliefs and commitment of this gentle family of believers.

What we have seen so far regarding six thousand years from Adam to the end of that span, resulting in man being cut off in his attempt to magnify himself to perfection in his own power, is in and of itself quite dramatic. But the question becomes: how accurate is the presumption that man is limited to six thousand years of free will tenure prior to God's one thousand year kingdom on earth?

This work is not about prophesying a date for the Lord's return. It is rather an attempt to allow the pages of the Bible to speak for themselves. Do they, in fact, give a close approximation of the time of His return? Faith is the answer! We cannot see air, nevertheless, we know it is all around us. How do we know? By faith! We have faith in the finite amount of knowledge that we possess concerning air; so we know it exists without ever seeing it. Believing God's Word is no different!

Abundant evidence, seen with clarity all around us, shows that man, in his own power, has just about run his course. From pristine purity and undeveloped human potential, to high-tech moral debasement and out-of-control creative development with exponential potential for evil to overcome good. Almost anyone can see that man, given a little more time, is going to blow himself up! Would God step in and salvage His creation for the *good* that He had originally intended for it prior to the advent of sin? He has intervened twice before: the Flood, and with the tower of Babel, man's first attempt to attain God status. Why not again? To prevent the inevitable, God *will* intervene two more times! See Matthew 24:21–22 and Revelation 20:7–9.

CHAPTER FORTY-THREE

# EVALUATING "SIX THOUSAND YEARS FOR MANKIND"

In considering reasons to believe that 6,000 years represent the fullness of mankind's unrestricted term on God's Planet Earth, we can see that man himself, left to his own devices, is busily chipping away at his own longevity. This fact alone strongly supports the conclusion being expressed here for a forced ending by God before man finally, in pushing the envelope, inevitably goes over the edge.

But there are biblical reasons as well, which all in some way relate to the point made above. Man is not inherently good as some like to believe, but inherently bad. Consequently, we can expect the worst from him. Witness legal abortion, legal pornography, legal sexual perversions, and legal dumbing down of coming generations by our public schools. Then there is the legal lying carried out by government, and those wishing to attain to or retain political office. Spin has become a legal art form in perverting facts to fit a desired outcome. But enough of this; the point is made! Where will it all end? That is the subject at hand!

We know that 2 Peter 3:8 tells us that: "With the Lord one day is as a thousand years, and a thousand years as one day." Genesis

2:2 says this: "And on the seventh day God ended His work which He had done, and He rested on the seventh day from all His work which He had done." Genesis 2:3 follows with: "Then God blessed the seventh day and sanctified it, because on it He rested from all His work which God had created and made." God's work of creation was accomplished in twenty-four-hour days; however, Peter explained that God attaches varying values to days as we have seen and will continue to see.

Keeping 2 Peter 3:8 in mind, the one thousand year kingdom of God (Sabbath) argues strongly for the first six one thousand year days to precede it. Then, too, as we have seen, we are at our present time, in relation to those six days, right at the door to the seventh millennial day, Saturday! We recall that man's number is six. When his number six is multiplied by days of one thousand years duration, we arrive at 6,000 years for man. When we consider which direction we are headed in man's headlong plunge into self-inflicted extinction, we can figuratively see the hand of God reaching down and *saving man from himself!*

A major signpost that cries out for God's intervention into man's attempt to create God status for himself again is his recently acquired proficiency in manipulating the genetic code of human, animal, and plant life. If we have learned anything at all about God from His previous two interventions into the affairs of men, reference the Flood and the Tower of Babel, this should be a bright, flashing red light indicating that God is about to act again! Then, too, we must consider that in His Bible, He has given considerable detail as to just what He intends to do, and how and when He intends to do it!

Letting reason prevail then points to God allowing the first phase of human tenancy of His Planet Earth to remain in a gray area, not precisely defined, for a specific reason. That reason would relate to the human quality of faith. This trait—faith is very important in God's relationship to man, as we well know. Strong faith, little faith, and no faith are areas that separate individuals in every category of human endeavor, relationships, and beliefs.

So then, this is where the answer lies to the question of 6,000 years. God's Word does not make a clear statement, but requires that if we are to know beforehand when to expect our free will, wheeling and dealing days to reach critical mass, it will require faith in what we have learned from His written Word as applied to the times in which we live. An attempt has been made here to bring God's Word together with the current state of world affairs to provide a medium from which anyone, the faithful, or the faithless may judge based on evidence. The absence of conclusiveness requires faith in what the evidential inclinations signify. The evidence supporting 6,000 years is strong, broad, and believable. And so now be warned; in the pages just ahead, *it is about to be put on steroids!*

Because of the weight of the implications surrounding the number six in its relationship to man throughout God's Word, Christians have believed for a long time that six combined with the apostle Peter's assertion that: "with God one day is as a thousand years, and a thousand years as one day" pointed directly to six thousand years. Yes, six one thousand year days for man's free will, to do what seems right in his own eyes—then the Sabbath.

Culminating events of the age we are living in completely support this position, as man's global government, spoken of so vividly in Revelation, built upon world trade, forms before our eyes. Until now, the projected end of the sixth day was not known, but the assumption was that it must be soon. We may now wish to modify that consideration to *very soon!*

# CHAPTER FORTY-FOUR

# PROPHECY BY THE NUMBERS

Our journey into Bible prophecy has up to now been littered with numbers—all kinds of numbers. God's number 7, man's number 6, and a variety of other very meaningful figures as well. A short list will reveal: 12–144,000–666–70–2,669–1,319–3,988–6,000–2012–11–1877—and 1947. We are now about to encounter connotations attributable to two of the above numbers that, to say the least, are awesome to behold!

A fact known by most is that there are universal laws that affect us all. Several can be named here that we each encounter every day of our lives on Planet Earth. The law of gravity, the passing of time, the speed of sound, the speed of light, and a reaction for every action; these make the point. Since God created the universe in the first place, these could be said to be God's laws. It seems that God has a certain numerical law, or perhaps it should be called a factor of evidence. Since it is of somewhat less significance than those laws given above, we will here then call it a factor. And since it involves the number 9, we will call it the "Factor of 9."

This Factor of 9 has an intimate relationship with Tyre/U.S.A/Babylon the Great/the Great Harlot, and the one the Bible says will take center stage in world events through most of the last seven years of the current six thousand. This factor has been widely demonstrated and described in detail publicly by the mathematical genius who discovered it as he explains "quite by accident." Nevertheless, there may still be many who are not aware of it, and they are sure to be impressed; if for no other reason than its unique value as a conversation piece. It is said that the early Mayan people had a strong affection for the number nine, which likely relates to their having been highly superstitious. It may well be that they knew and used this factor in ongoing superstitious applications involving their daily lives and in their pagan religious practices.

In the samples of the Factor of 9 that we will look at, some will take the position that one would need to be superstitious to believe that the results had any relevance. Others will argue that the results are just good examples of coincidence. Then there are some others of us who will believe that the God who spoke the universe into being could and did implant the seeds of end time prophecy into the biblically derived numbers that we will subject to the power of this awesome Factor of 9.

Now, for the benefit of all who may not be familiar with this mathematical mystery, an explanation is in order. This factor applies to all numbers larger than nine. It is applied in three simple steps. The result of its application is always a whole number quotient produced by dividing a modified number larger than nine by nine. Just to demonstrate that this is not as complex as it may sound, we will take the number 90 as an example. It is easy to see that 90 can be divided by 9 to produce a whole number quotient: 10. But what about 91? How can this number be divided evenly by 9? This is where we apply the three steps of the Factor of 9:

Step A. Add the digits in 91: $9 + 1 = 10$
Step B. Subtract the total of the digits from the original number: $91 - 10 = 81$
Step C. Divide the modified number by 9: $81 \div 9 = 9$

"But," you may protest, "you changed the number!" Yes, of course, that is the way the Factor of 9 works. Any number larger than nine, when modified by the three steps, will be evenly divisible by nine. So the resulting quotient, if it had any special meaning or relationship to something else, would be attained because the Factor of 9 had been applied to the original number. The resulting condensation of the original number then, if it had any recognizable relationship to the original number, might be viewed with interest. And with considerable interest, in fact, if circumstances warranted.

There is a pair of sensitive numbers, both generated by the Bible in combination with historical dates. We have seen them both in the setting of end time Bible prophecy. If they are, in fact, numbers to be taken seriously, we might then expect that they would provide some corroborative evidence of their relevance when acted upon by God's Factor of 9.

That then is the challenge. We have seen how the factor works; so we will apply it to the first number, which in this case is the 6,000 free will years for mankind. This is a difficult one for many to warm up to. The Bible spends considerable time detailing what will happen at the end of this period of time, and focuses on a specific high-profile individual, who will be much in evidence in the last seven years. God's Word even provides a means to numerically identify this person; a triple series of man's number, which if he has his way, many will be carrying around with them!

What happens when this little-known factor is applied to our controversial number 6,000?

Step A. Add the digits in 6,000: $6 + 0 + 0 + 0 = 6$
Step B. Subtract the total of the digits from the original number:
$6,000 - 6 = 5,994$
Step C. Divide the modified number by 9: $5,994 \div 9 = 666$

Is anyone surprised after that introduction? Point made, nevertheless. It is now somewhat more difficult for doubters to doubt the truth of what we have seen in God's book, the Bible, correlated with man's historical record, bluntly stating that man's self-determination is programmed for six thousand years. The unerring accuracy of this numerically determined number, biblically stated as being the number of the beast (Antichrist), who represents the end of the end time, and which being derived from the number marking the end, is hard to ignore. (See Revelation 13:18)

While the reader ponders the relevance of the above disclosure, we will evaluate the other Bible-generated number of interest. That being A.D. 2012, purported to be the year that will see the end of the six thousand years; and by association, the end of Tyre/U.S.A/Mystery Babylon the Great as well.

With mass communications, electronically and satellite enhanced, and the written word, all in such an advanced state of penetration and acceptance by world populations, and with mass media entirely agenda-driven as it is, the planet is like a sponge in a septic tank. Receiving little unbiased truth, and with slanted, twisted information pouring forth daily, the world is saturated with toxicity. God's Word is shunned for more, assumed to be, enlightening paths to greater understanding. Now, for truth-seekers and all others—stay where you are—greater understanding can be in your future!

If the above example of God's omnipotence, though very impressive, is not sufficient to sway the more intractable of those engaged in evaluating this work, the next one should, by reason of being completely accurate, precise, and exact, not only unite the quotient with the date, 2012, but should also strengthen one's faith in the depth of Bible truth!

How does the factor contribute to any greater appreciation for the already-stand-out date of A.D. 2012?

Step A. Add the digits in 2012: 2 + 0 + 1 + 2 = 5
Step B. Subtract the total of the digits from the original number:
2,012 - 5 = 2,007
Step C. Divide the modified number by 9: 2,007 ÷ 9 = 223

Did something go wrong here? No! We just have one more question to answer. In the first example we knew beforehand the relationship of the quotient, 666, to the antichrist that the 6,000 years pointed to. In this second example, the relationship of this quotient, 223, to the year 2012 must yet be established. So what does it mean? It was stated above that the Factor of 9 has an intimate relationship with Tyre/U.S.A/Babylon the Great/the Great Harlot, so we will start there.

With this Great Harlot, according to God's Word, condemned to destruction in the Day of the Lord, the last six months of the current six thousand years, we could make an educated guess that this number, 223, could quite possibly apply to her. When we subtract 223 years from the year 2012, we find the result to be the year 1789. Still not on board? This is the very year that the federal government of the United States of America was born! Contrary to common belief, the U.S.A did not come into being in the year 1776. Even though the Declaration of Independence was adopted by the Continental Congress on July 4, 1776, much remained undone which required completion before the United States federal government could come into existence.

The colonies fought and won the war-with a peace treaty being signed in Paris on November 30, 1782. Now, with victory in the Revolutionary War and at last free from the yoke of England, they existed as a collection of independent states, managing their own affairs; and distrusting any semblance of a strong central authority. The strength of their mutually cooperative effort was drawn from a collection of agreed upon articles called the *Articles of Confederation*. This resulted in very little central authority, no executive head, no power to impose taxes, to control trade, or settle quarrels among or between individual colony/states.

It soon became apparent that a central government having more authority was needed to solve numerous and mounting problems being encountered on a national, as well as an international level. After a certain amount of turmoil involving opposition, suspicion, and bargaining, finally agreement was reached on a governing document called The Constitution. (It was framed and adopted in 1787, subsequently ratified by each state, and put into effect March 4th, 1789).[25] The independent states accepted unified control, and a new federal government was formed. The United States of America was born, and the new nation began her activities with the appointment of George Washington as president in the spring of 1789.[26]

So what is the significance of all of this? The number 223, being derived from the year 2012 by the Factor of 9 *represents America's age in the year 2012*. It appears that God may have seen fit to provide this additional supporting evidence, call it circumstantial; nevertheless, it fully supports His centuries-old written documentation describing in detail, the end of the 6,000 years and coinciding end of the Great Harlot. This revelation of her lifespan as being 223 years could only be a final plea by God for His people (those who will listen to Him) to stand apart from her sinful ways!

Our effort in this work is about searching for the truth of Bible prophecy; so with that goal in mind, just one final thought before moving on with that search.

With truth as elusive as it has proven to be, it could be likened to the fragile scent of a fine perfume thinly wafting through the air. Some in the room will be inhaling at just the precise moment that their olfactory sense is about to make contact with the essence, thus receiving fulfillment of the scent's promise. Others will be exhaling at the precise moment, effectively preventing contact, and missing all value of the rare and exquisite fragrance.

So, with the Factor of 9 etched in our memories, we can continue to mentally debate its relevance regarding the two examples just witnessed. Faith, again is the answer. If we believe in the all-powerful God of the Bible (Father, Son, and Holy Spirit), then the debate is over before it can begin! Otherwise, since we are judging the relevance of God's Word, the Book of Truth in its prophetic projections of an end time, and that time's relationship to mankind, we may wish to add the above work of the Factor of 9 to the evidence already obtained.

Now we come again to the 6,000 years. The millennial Sabbath (kingdom of God) clearly spelled out as lasting one thousand years in Revelation 20:4, argues strongly for the prior 6,000 years (6 one thousand year days) to suffice for the fullness of man's self-determination. Add to that the current eruption of man's worldly travel, and his exponentially expanding knowledge, just as the prophet Daniel said would occur (Daniel 12:4), where he is told: "But you Daniel, shut up the words, and seal the book until the time of the end; many shall run to and fro, and knowledge shall increase."

Then there is the damning evidence of man's current out-of-control, lustful, prideful, hedonistic moral freefall, as referenced earlier and which the apostle Paul so vividly identified with the last days in 2 Timothy 3:1–5. It is worth reading again for its uncanny portrayal of humanistic attitudes and behaviors that we see all around us today.

There it is: some will see the evidence and believe its relevance for today. Others will see the signs and believe they have no relevance whatsoever. To the second group, a word of caution: as you begin to see more dramatic, prophetic occurrences taking place, you may still change your mind; however, *if you die tomorrow, or you wait too long, it will be too late!*

This time in which we live requires strong ties to Christ. It is critical for Christians to face the reality of the future, protected by the whole armor of God as explained by the apostle Paul in Ephesians 6:11–17.

Now, more woe wrath to come. The first woe, fifth trumpet was a picture of initial stage woe wrath. The second woe, sixth trumpet is advanced stage of the sixth bowl of initial wrath, a reversal of normal order.

# CHAPTER FORTY-FIVE

# THE SIXTH TRUMPET-ADVANCED STAGE WRATH

Then the sixth angel sounded: and I heard a voice from the four horns of the golden altar which is before God,

saying to the sixth angel who had the trumpet, "Release the four angels who are bound at the great river Euphrates."

So the four angels, who had been prepared for the hour and day and month and year, were released to kill a third of mankind.

Now the number of the army of the horsemen was two hundred million; I heard the number of them.

And thus I saw the horses in the vision: those who sat on them had breastplates of fiery red, hyacinth blue, and sulfur yellow; and the heads of the horses were like the heads of lions; and out of their mouths came fire, smoke, and brimstone.

By these three plagues a third of mankind was killed; by the fire and the smoke and the brimstone which came out of their mouths.

For their power is in their mouth and in their tails; for their tails are like serpents, having heads; and with them they do harm.

But the rest of mankind, who were not killed by these plagues, did not repent of the works of their hands, that they should not worship demons, and idols of gold, silver, brass, stone, and wood, which can neither see nor hear nor walk [Materialism.]

And they did not repent of their murders [abortion] or their sorceries or their sexual immorality or their thefts (Revelation 9:13–21).

We have looked at some parts of this trumpet judgment earlier, as they applied to the men of the east and Armageddon. There are several points that stand out in this very terrible judgment. One is that such a large number of lives will be lost. One-third of mankind is a huge number of people; two billion by today's count. The large number of lost lives will be due to the fire and the smoke and the brimstone which comes out of the horses' mouths. The horses, of course, would be a variety of military vehicles; tanks, armored personnel carriers, self-propelled mortars, artillery, missile launchers, etc. These will be in the hands of the diverse military forces representing their various nations and blocs to be involved in this coming Mid-East conflict (Also complicit, will be missile silos and nuclear armed submarines).

As noted, one-third of mankind lost in this war is a terrible loss of life. World population by this time, however, will be reduced; possibly a great deal. First, by comet fragments striking earth and by the resurrection of the saints (Translation of those alive from mortal to immortal). These extraordinary events—the fragment attack ending with the fifth trumpet in the same hour as the Resurrection at Jesus' return will take a toll. Human loss due to advancing stages of destruction from the comet incursion will continue to multiply. Some second phase losses will result from famine due to lack of sunlight from atmospheric contamination as seen in the third seal. Then fires caused far and wide by returning red-hot rocks and burning debris; reflected by foul and loathsome sores, that we shall see up close in the first bowl judgment. We can add to that, more loss from fouled water bodies and the effect of peace being taken from the earth as expressed by the second seal, and in which time we may now be living. All these things and others will contribute their part in reducing human population before the war even begins (The south Asian tsunami could be one also)!

This disastrous war will accent the effectiveness of unrestrained proliferation of war materials being produced and sold all over the world by a few technically advanced nations; with Russia and the United States doing their part. To add to the arming of the world, we can add the reported outright theft of United States' national defense secrets by unfriendly nations, and gifts of missile and computer technology presented to questionable nations by United States corporations and the government itself.

There is no question; the world is being armed to the teeth. Where will it end? The answer is obvious! But one question remains about this great gathering of military forces briefly described in the sixth trumpet (Revelation 9:17). This mentions the breastplates of different colors. Since Bible prophecies do not as a rule divulge unimportant detail, we can assume then that these colors are of some importance. The pages of the Bible point to three hostile military powers being represented there in the great battle near Jerusalem. These being the axis formed by the Russian/Islamic alliance, the men of the east, and the international community under Antichrist.

With two hundred million military personnel gathered together in a geographically restricted area of reduced visibility, how will they be able to tell with certainty who is who? There has never in the history of the world ever been a military gathering approaching this number. Would the three forces identify their personnel in some way to prevent loss of life from friendly fire, say with red, blue, and yellow?

Zechariah 14:10 tells that in the Day of the Lord: "Jerusalem shall be raised up," but with only the temple mount to later be inhabited in its exact place. Verses 11 through 13 tell more:

The people shall dwell in it; and no longer shall there be utter destruction, but Jerusalem shall be safely inhabited.

And this shall be the plague with which the LORD will strike all the people who fought against Jerusalem: Their flesh shall dissolve while they stand on their feet, their eyes shall dissolve in their sockets, and their tongues shall dissolve in their mouths.

It shall come to pass in that day that a great panic from the LORD will be among them. Everyone will seize the hand of his neighbor, and raise his hand against his neighbor's hand.

Here we see again what is going to happen. From the description of the plague on the people who will come against Jerusalem in verse 12, we can derive that God knew very well that Israel would possess neutron weapons, which destroy flesh, but are harmless against buildings and land. There will, of course, be physical damage to structures in Jerusalem from conventional weapons and a very large earthquake. However, if nuclear weapons were to be used, the site would be sufficiently radioactive to prevent rebuilding and resettlement of the whole area for a very long time. The fact is, Jerusalem will be rebuilt, down sized, and relocated just inside the southern perimeter of a mountain top that shortly before its elevation was the city of Jerusalem. (See Tables #3 and #4)

Another key point is: "a great panic from the Lord will be among them." (Invading armies.) At times, the Lord conveniently uses man and his inventions to carry out His intent. This seems very likely not to be an exception; but how would man be used here to carry out God's will in this instance?

With a large number of people confined to such a restricted area, when the neutron weapons begin to explode, there will be panic. If for this, or any reason, color identifiers, whether colored body armor, colored cloth worn on the torso, or something else, were discarded to prevent correct identification, it would be a simple matter for confusion to gain the upper hand, especially since it is God's will that it be so.

One more possibility for mass confusion as to who is who would exist if troops in large numbers would change their colors in order to be able to approach an enemy position, but then be fired upon by their own forces. Thus, role changing may play an important part in ensuing confusion, and ultimate annihilation of all hostile forces. Panic and bewilderment will dominate in the madness and terror of friendly fire; in which, neighbor strikes down neighbor and friend executes friend!

With the horror of the sixth trumpet (second woe) duly noted, we will go on to the seventh and final trumpet, the third woe.

# CHAPTER FORTY-SIX

# THE SEVENTH TRUMPET

Then the seventh angel sounded: and there were loud voices in heaven, saying, "The kingdoms of this world have become the kingdoms of our Lord and of His Christ, and He shall reign forever and ever!"

And the twenty-four elders who sat before God on their thrones fell on their faces and worshiped God,

saying: "We give You thanks, O Lord God Almighty, the One who is and who was and who is to come, because You have taken Your great power and reigned.

The nations were angry, and Your wrath has come, and the time of the dead, that they should be judged, and that You should reward Your servants the prophets and the saints, and those who fear your name, small and great, and should destroy those who destroy the earth."

Then the temple of God was opened in heaven, and the ark of His covenant was seen in His temple. And there were lightnings, noises, thunderings, an earthquake, and great hail (Revelation 11:15–19).

As becomes obvious after reading these verses, the seventh trumpet is basically a review of what has already occurred. For example:

A.  Verses 17-18 disclose four circumstances that at the beginning of Christ's reign have already happened:

1.  You have taken Your great power and reigned.

2.  The nations were angry, and Your wrath has come,

3.  And the time of the dead, that they should be judged, has come.

    And that You should reward Your servants the prophets and the saints, and those who fear Your name, small and great.

4.  And should destroy those who destroy the earth.

    We see that all these things have come to pass at, or prior to the time Christ begins His reign. Having returned at the fourth trumpet, He will begin His reign in the seventh, after the Day of the Lord has ended.

This shows evidence that verse 19, the last verse of the seventh trumpet, is also speaking of things past. Wrathful occurrences which will have begun just prior to Jesus' return, and that will have ended before His reign. These things are:

1.  lightnings—streaking comet fragments.

2.  noises—great explosions at points of impact.

3.  thunderings—ear-splitting eruptions.

4. earthquake—mighty earthquakes upon impact.

5. great hail—red-hot rocks returning to earth?

Recall that the seventh seal was simply an introduction to the Seven Trumpets. Here we have found that the seventh trumpet is a history lesson corresponding with wrath events of the sixth seal and the first, second, third, and fifth trumpets. We will now go to the bowl judgments, and observe the finality of these episodes of powerful advanced wrath.

Revelation 15:1 provides insight as to the meaning of the bowl judgments. It says this:

> Then I saw another sign in heaven, great and marvelous: seven angels having the seven last plagues, for in them the wrath of God is complete.

These bowls finish the wrath of God, which shall begin shortly before Jesus will return at the one-third point of water and atmospheric contamination resulting from the first three fragments, and which will reach maximum density in the bowls.

CHAPTER FORTY-SEVEN

# THE FIRST BOWL

Then I heard a loud voice from the temple saying to the seven angels, "Go and pour out the bowls of the wrath of God on the earth."

So the first went and poured out his bowl upon the earth, and a foul and loathsome sore came upon the men who had the mark of the beast and those who worshiped his image (Revelation 16:1–2).

The first bowl adds detail to, and rounds out the destructive effects of the first trumpet comet fragment, where: hail (ice), fire (comet coma glow), mixed with blood (gas and dirty, rocky dust particles) "were thrown to earth; and a third of the trees were burned up, and all green grass was burned up."

Now we are being made aware that "a foul and loathsome sore came upon the men who had the mark of the beast and those who worship his image."

It is being clarified that God's people will be either absent, or protected from these sores; then too, what will be their cause? It seems quite certain that these sores, being foul and loathsome, will be caused by burns. An immediate result of such an awesome, and powerful impact with Planet Earth will be millions of tons of rock, earth, and burning debris thrown high into the atmosphere. As the heavier smoldering material and rocks begin returning to earth, they will be hot—very hot, and will ignite fires as they crash back to the ground. These fires will not be selective in affecting trees and grass specifically, as were fires caused by the first fragment's initial impact in a low population area. These secondary bowl fires will claim all that lies in their paths including human populations.

Here we have seen an example of subtle transition from initial effects of the first trumpet judgment to a later, fully developed stage of the same event in its like-numbered bowl.

CHAPTER FORTY-EIGHT

# THE SECOND BOWL

Then the second angel poured out his bowl on the sea, and it became blood as of a dead man; and every living creature in the sea died (Revelation 16:3).

The second bowl was previously included with discussion of the second trumpet to show correlation between trumpets and bowls. There are, nevertheless, other foreseen effects of the great mountain burning with fire that was thrown into the sea at the second trumpet. We can look at these others here as recorded in the sixth seal. This account includes the initial explosion of the sea impact with resulting tsunamis washing over adjacent land areas.

We do not know which sea or ocean, this second fragment will strike. We do know, however, that islands and mountains will be affected by it. The mountains may be on the islands themselves, or inland from the shoreline of the land mass surrounding the impacted body of water or both.

The rearrangement of the landscape, seascape, and the sky was shown to John, and his impressions are recorded here in the sixth seal, Revelation 6:14. This verse tells what to expect:

Then the sky receded as a scroll when it is rolled up, and every mountain and island was moved out of its place.

Luke, in his gospel, refers to yet another view of other specific effects of the devastating water impact of the second trumpet: "the sea and waves roaring," in connection with the return of Jesus at a time when there will be signs in the sun, moon, and stars (Luke 21:25–27).

We will now look again at the secular newspaper article by Glennda Chui that appeared in *The Seattle Times* of February 12, 1998, titled: "Asteroid hurtling to Earth could cause huge tsunami." Beginning with this statement of comfort, it says:

Scientists don't think the crash will happen in our lifetime, but want to be prepared.

The article then continues by launching into several alarming potential concerns:

As if months of darkness, global crop failures and large-scale wildfires set by a rain of molten debris were not enough reasons to worry about a large asteroid hitting earth, scientists have simulated one more scary consequence: a gigantic tsunami that could kill millions and even erase small costal nations in just a few hours.

Though the chance of that happening in our lifetime is slim, it's been a topic of serious scientific concern for more than two decades—a concern made more vivid when a string of comet fragments slammed into Jupiter in 1994.

Now, it seems relevant to believe that the Bible and its much-misunderstood prophecies aimed at our very time in modern history is a book to take seriously—*very seriously!*

With that frightening end to our consideration of the second bowl, we will now go on to bowl number three.

# CHAPTER FORTY-NINE

# THE THIRD BOWL

Then the third angel poured out his bowl on the rivers and springs of water, and they became blood (Revelation 16:4).

This is a later stage of the third trumpet fragment blast; where rivers, and springs of water had become fallout contaminated by one-third from that and the previous two impacts. With this third bowl, open-air fresh water supplies are now fully contaminated, having progressed to a high saturation. This will cause the water to appear as blood. Revelation 16:5–6 continues:

And I heard the angel of the waters saying: "You are righteous, O Lord, the One who is and who was and who is to be, because You have judged these things.

For they have shed the blood of saints and prophets, and You have given them blood to drink. For it is their just due." (For a laser like view of the penalty for harming a fetus, see Exodus 21:22-24. We are, however, still under grace through Christ for the repentant!)

Here again, reference is given to this plague being directed only at the unsaved. God's people are in one instance protected, and in the other, no longer here. Reference to the water as blood seems to be an exercise in poetic justice, showing the water to be as undrinkable as the blood they so freely shed!

# CHAPTER FIFTY

# THE FOURTH BOWL

Then the fourth angel poured out his bowl on the sun, and power was given to him to scorch men with fire.

And men were scorched with great heat, and they blasphemed the name of God who has power over these plagues; and they did not repent and give Him glory (Revelation 16:8–9).

Another reference to these being the lost; as they blasphemed God, and did not repent and give Him glory. More markings of the Day of the Lord.

This is a later stage of the fourth trumpet, where:

Then the fourth angel sounded: and a third of the sun was struck, a third of the moon, and a third of the stars, so that a third of them were darkened. A third of the day did not shine, and likewise the night (Revelation 8:12).

What we derive from this fourth bowl is this: after the one-third darkening at the fourth trumpet (when Jesus will return), the darkness will progress to the deep darkening of the sixth seal (Revelation 6:12). The damaging effects of airborne debris—dust, dirt, smoke, soot, etc., will take their toll on what is left of the ozone layer. The abrasive action on this delicate shield will, when the sun reappears, have rendered it less than completely effective in screening out ultraviolet rays from the sun. Yes, Antichrist's efforts to clear atmospheric contamination may have some benefit also; and perhaps may even intensify the caustic effects of the airborne ozone destroying contaminates thrown up by the cosmic intrusion. When the sun reemerges, while being insufficiently filtered through ozone, it will become an enemy of mankind, being extremely harmful to the eyes and causing severe burns. This, on top of aerial spray reactions, and foul and loathsome sores from worldwide fires. This trial for man lies just over the horizon. In Joel 2:2, the prophet called it a day of clouds and thick darkness; God calls it Day of the Lord, but lost man will call it *hell on earth!*

We know it will be a very long day consisting of many days of great difficulty and suffering for unrepentant humanity. A day to avoid at all costs. Unfortunately for many, there is but one way to avoid it or its eternal aftermath. That way is: "By the narrow gate, and the difficult way that leads to life, and there are few who find it" (Matthew 7:14).

What is the narrow gate and the difficult way? The narrow gate clearly shows that there is only one way. That one way is Jesus Christ! This has something to do with it being a difficult way for some. Satan has successfully established the big lie that man can be God and that God is in everything. This is but one aspect of multiple delusions that Satan has injected into human minds in this end time. He, Satan, has also established the belief among many that members of all religions worship the same God. Nothing could be further from the truth! So we see that with those being afflicted with these delusions, truth is what they want it to be; and the source of all truth, Jesus Christ, becomes a stumbling block and foolishness; just as the apostle Paul confirmed in 1 Corinthians 1:23:

> but we preach Christ crucified [salvation through Christ's shed blood], to the Jews a stumbling block and to the Greeks [Gentiles] foolishness.

Paul went on to explain in verse 24 that to those who are called (hear the gospel, and accept Jesus as Lord), that Christ is "the power of God and the wisdom of God." These are not idle words. They form the foundation of the wall that separates true believers in Christ from non-believers. Jesus, the essence of God, is a stumbling block to all who would be God, would denigrate God, or worship another god!

So the pages of the Bible say it again and again, *Jesus Christ is the only way to eternal salvation!* The alternative: *the tragic loss of this gift—translated* wrath!

The purpose and hope for this writing is that it will demonstrate clearly the absolute power and authority of the Holy Bible. We are only scratching the surface of its relevance for today, tomorrow, and forever. Its pages relating to our time are being unlocked. They offer hope for all who will accept their truth. There are alternatives of all descriptions being put forward in our day that require more faith to believe by far, than the proven validity of God's Holy Word. Each must decide which path he/she shall follow in establishing their eternal reward—*it's a savings account, not a lottery!*

Jesus explained this principle in Matthew 6:19–21:

Do not lay up for yourselves treasures on earth, where moth and rust destroy and where thieves break in and steal;

but lay up for yourselves treasures in heaven, where neither moth nor rust destroys and where thieves do not break in and steal.

For where your treasure is, there your heart will be also.

*No religion*, including Christianity, has the power to bring anyone to the *saving grace of God* without one being born again in Jesus Christ! Jesus, in John 3:3 made it clear:

Jesus answered and said to him, "Most assuredly, I say to you, unless one is born again, he cannot see the kingdom of God."

321

John 3:16 carries on:

For God so loved the world that He gave His only begotten Son, that whoever believes in Him should not perish but have everlasting life.

John 3:17–18 explains God's reasoning:

For God did not send His Son into the world to condemn the world, but that the world through Him might be saved.

He who believes in Him is not condemned; but he who does not believe is condemned already, because he has not believed in the name of the only begotten Son of God.

*There is the answer* for those who may have considered God too harsh in His intended treatment of non-believers, with promised infliction of wrath upon them. *All are already condemned who do not/will not believe in the Son of God!*

If, however, by this writing or any other means, we can see the truth of God's Word and how it relates to us, and while we still have time, want to avail ourselves of the *saving grace* of God by the shed blood of Jesus Christ, we can pray this prayer:

Father God Almighty, I know that I am a sinner, and I repent of my sins. I accept Your Son Jesus Christ as my Lord and Savior. I know that I am now a new creation, and will turn my life around through the power of your Holy Spirit to bring glory to You. In Your name Lord Jesus I pray, Amen.

If you prayed this prayer in truth and sincerity, you have just been *born again*! But like any newborn babe, you need colostrum milk. The mother's milk of a follower of Christ (a true Christian) is the *Bible*. The New Testament will acquaint you quickly with Jesus and His life, death, and resurrection. Start here, and then become familiar with the Old Testament, starting in Genesis and go on through. Don't speed read, but rather, go slowly and carefully. To be certain that you understand the meaning of the content as you proceed, ask the Lord Jesus to show you His truth!

In addition to Bible reading, you will need to associate with other believers in Christ for fellowship and support. You will now have become number one on Satan's most wanted list. Do not expect this to be easy. However, never forget: "He [Jesus] who is in you is greater than he [Satan] who is in the world" (1 John 4:4) The power of Jesus Christ is much greater than that which Satan possesses. You, therefore, must avail yourself of His power through prayer. His power is *real*! You may tap into it whenever the need arises by praying to God in the name of Jesus, knowing that you will receive what you need—not necessarily want. As a believer in Christ, you will come to know pure joy as you abide in His powerful presence.

*The Holy Spirit will change your outlook, your life, and your destiny!*

As we have biblically seen, Jesus will return just after the wrath begins, when atmospheric contamination has reduced light from the heavenly bodies by one-third. Born again Christians need fear nothing from this awesome spectacle!

# CHAPTER FIFTY-ONE

# THE FIFTH BOWL

Then the fifth angel poured out his bowl on the throne of the beast, and his kingdom became full of darkness; and they gnawed their tongues because of the pain.

They blasphemed the God of heaven because of their pains and their sores, and did not repent of their deeds (Revelation 16:10–11).

This account provides a precise view of advanced effects of festering sores inflicted on man by aerial spraying as encountered in the fifth trumpet episode of initial wrath.

A. This bowl, poured out on the throne of the beast, clearly tells that the intensity of this judgment will be centered in the Mid-East, specifically, the vicinity of Israel. This is, after all, where Antichrist's throne will be; and contamination will then encircle the earth! This disclosure is in agreement with our earlier conclusion in studying the fifth trumpet, that Antichrist would concentrate his efforts to clear the atmosphere with chemical/bacterial spraying of his own immediate domain. This will be Israel, the place of his throne, the site of Armageddon, and it seems the target area of the fourth fragment as well. Antichrist will not, however, completely ignore other important agricultural areas of the world, with resulting mayhem inflicted on his followers, who unfortunately are not plants, trees, or any green thing, nor have they ever been!

B. True to the message of the fifth trumpet, Antichrist's kingdom (the whole earth) became full of darkness.

C. The fifth bowl focuses also on the advanced stage of pain and suffering from effects of the fifth trumpet's aerial spraying, which caused the painful sores like scorpion stings on those without God's seal. (The Jewish remnant will be sealed against all wrath.) This aerial spraying will certainly be carried out in other parts of the world also (Antichrist's kingdom); however, Israel (location of his throne) will be heavily polluted and in great need. Then, too, it seems reasonable to believe that condition of the atmosphere there will be cleared sufficiently for the great battle (Armageddon) to proceed. Within the fifth trumpet, and by association the fifth bowl, it appears that the fourth comet fragment of the fifth trumpet is almost certainly to be the cause of the mighty and great earthquake, the greatest earthquake of all time, and which shall result in (Jerusalem) later being divided into three parts (Revelation 16:18–19). (See Table #4) And almost certainly the same great earthquake that will strike Jerusalem the same hour as the resurrection of the two witnesses takes place; Revelation 11:13 (a microcosm of the Resurrection at Christ's return). And almost certainly the same earthquake prophesied to be responsible in the end time for raising up (elevating) Jerusalem; Zechariah 14:10, taking the temple and Antichrist up with it; but then to later in the millennial kingdom, become the mountain of the LORD'S house (Isaiah 2:2).

# CHAPTER FIFTY-TWO

# THE SIXTH BOWL

Since we have looked at this bowl earlier, a summary will do here:

> Then the sixth angel poured out his bowl on the great river Euphrates, and its water was dried up, so that the way of the kings from the east might be prepared.
>
> And I saw three unclean spirits like frogs coming out of the mouth of the dragon, out of the mouth of the beast, and out of the mouth of the false prophet.
>
> For they are spirits of demons, performing signs, which go out to the kings of the earth and of the whole world, to gather them to the battle of that great day of God Almighty (Revelation 16:12–14).
>
> And they gathered them together to the place called in Hebrew, Armageddon (Revelation 16:12–16).

This fully supports the sixth trumpet judgment, which told about the four angels being released at the River Euphrates, to kill a third of mankind. The sixth trumpet, and the sixth bowl judgments, are *an exception to the rule that gives direction to the first five* trumpets and bowls—where trumpets deal with the initial effects, and the bowls depict completion. With these two, the sixth trumpet gives final details involving the size of the armies, characteristics of the weapons, and reference to the total loss of life from the conflict. These details tend to form a picture of completion in the reader's mind.

The sixth bowl then, to complete the reversal of roles in this instance, gives initial information pertaining to how the armies came to be there in the first place, having been called there by demon messengers of Satan.

The relevant point is that we, the readers of this book, are aware of the reversal, and will observe its impact as it unfolds ahead.

# CHAPTER FIFTY-THREE

# JESUS' RETURN AS A THIEF!

The sixth bowl has its beginning with the sending out of spirits (like frogs), before the wrath begins. These spirits shall sow the seeds of discontent that will germinate below the surface, to reach full bloom after the outer space bombardment of earth will create a new reality; a new paradigm: the desperate need for a dependable source of energy—OIL!

> Behold, I am coming as a thief. Blessed is he who watches, and keeps his garments, lest he walk naked and they see his shame (Revelation 16:15).

In trying to understand placement of this verse in the sixth bowl of initial wrath, we must keep in mind that this bowl is actually a precursor to the beginning of all of God's wrath not necessarily to just that which will manifest in the sixth trumpet—in that instance—of advanced wrath!

With Jesus saying that He will come as a thief (Revelation 16:15) immediately following verse 14, in which the demon spirits are said to go out to the kings of the earth to gather them to the Battle of Armageddon, we can conclude that Jesus is foretelling His intent to harvest the grapes of wrath. This will be the culmination of God's wrath on unrepentant mankind, and will of necessity, occur upon completion of the great gathering of the kings of the earth and their military forces there in God's glorious land.

Now, a look at the Bible's symbolic account of this most terrible harvest of lost souls. Revelation 14:19–20 provides this view, written almost two thousand years in advance as a warning to the final generation to quit running away from Jesus Christ. Jesus, the only way out of an otherwise lost and deplorable human condition with eternal, like-kind consequences. The verses say this:

> So the angel thrust his sickle into the earth and gathered the vine of the earth, and threw it into the great winepress of the wrath of God [Armageddon].

> And the winepress was trampled outside the city [Jerusalem], and blood came out of the winepress, up to the horses' bridles, for one thousand six hundred furlongs [Symbolic devastation].

Interestingly, in Revelation 16:15, where Jesus says He is coming as a thief, His statement continues with "Blessed is he who watches, and keeps his garments, lest he walk naked and they see his shame."

So what does it mean?

Since the coming as a thief statement is qualified as to circumstances by the previous verse (Revelation 16:14), that is, the demonic calling of the nations to Israel, it is clear that this statement is Jesus' last warning, given in that same time period. This is the final warning to the wayward; carried to the world through exceedingly difficult times by the two witnesses and the 144,000 servants of God—to prepare the way for the impending return of Jesus Christ the King—to occur just after the time of trouble like no other will have begun with *shock and awe!*

The second, cautionary part ("blessed is he who watches, and keeps his garments, lest he walk naked and they see his shame"), is also a product of the same three-and-a-half years of last days warning by those mentioned above. This is a warning also! This time to Christians, and its setting is the same short period of remaining grace just before the resurrection to eternal life with Christ. This entire two-part cautioning is seen here as God's last good-faith effort to prevent as many as possible, both Christians and non-Christians, from blindly marching headlong into His awful winepress of wrath in a face-to-face confrontation with a determined and angry God!

In reference to the second part of the two-part reminder, addressed specifically to Christians—how can we clarify its intent so that we may relate to it in a meaningful way? That is, how can we see its serious reality sufficiently, so that we will not be caught in the trap (the winepress of God's wrath) that it symbolically pictures? The challenge: watching, and keeping our garments, lest we walk naked and they see our shame.

This warning/reminder refers to the resurrection of the saved and them not missing it, because they didn't keep their garments (imputed righteousness of Christ—translated *grace*) in good condition. Jesus' parable in Matthew 22:8–14, compared salvation at the Resurrection with a wedding being attended by properly attired wedding guests. In order to fully appreciate the meaning of Jesus' words (Blessed is he who watches, and keeps his garments, lest he walk naked and they see his shame) we need to identify the key words. There are two: watches and keeps; so being English interpretations, we must now look at the original Greek. The Greek word for *watches* is *gregoreuo*, meaning, *be vigilant, be watchful, keep awake*. The Greek word for *keeps* is *tereo*, meaning, *to guard from loss or injury*.

With this understanding in mind, we will look at the basis for Jesus' remarks, which is summed up in His parable, highlighted in

Matthew 22:1–14. It deals with a king who had arranged a wedding for his son, and the invited guests refused to come to the wedding despite the fact dinner (grace) was ready and waiting. So the king sent servants out again to the guests, telling them that the dinner was ready, but they again refused to come. The king then had his servants go out to the highways and byways, and invite as many as would come, both good and bad, and in time the wedding hall was filled (mostly with Gentiles).

Here, we see a wedding hall filled with substitute guests, both good and bad. The good being those committed to Christ. The bad, lacking that commitment, having instead, a superficial attraction based more on appearance than substance. All were invited, but some (the bad) came without making any attempt to clean themselves up in preparation for this special occasion (Resurrection). So now, we will view the climax to this critically important and symbolically presented scene described in Matthew 22:11–14:

> But when the king came in to see the guests, he saw a man there who did not have on a wedding garment.
>
> So he said to him, "Friend, how did you come in here without a wedding garment?" And he was speechless.
>
> Then the king said to the servants, "Bind him hand and foot, take him away, and cast him into outer darkness; there will be weeping and gnashing of teeth."
>
> For many are called, but few are chosen.

Here, in this parable, is shown the importance of first having on wedding-quality garments, and second, for those who have them, of not letting the garments deteriorate or become soiled.

This parable, as we know, pertains to salvation. The wedding garments are, in fact, the imputed righteousness of Christ. In the parable, those in attendance were expected to have clean garments of wedding quality. This then, is what Jesus means when He says, "Blessed is he who watches, and keeps his garments, lest he walk naked and they see his shame." One who professes to be a Christian is expected to have and maintain the righteousness imputed to him by the Son, Jesus Christ. Since we, who are unrighteous ourselves, once having received this righteousness from Jesus, are expected not to lose it!

The placement of the underlying passage, that is, Jesus' statement in Revelation 16:15 of "coming as a thief," in one instance, and: "Blessed is he who watches, and keeps his garments," in the other instance, is now seen as a consequence. A reference to previous final and last minute warnings that His judgment is about to fall and will affect all people, *either in a positive way or a negative way!* This warning, placed in the precursor, demonic calling of sixth bowl initial wrath preceding the wrath itself, defines Jesus' special three-and-a-half year final ministry by His two witnesses and His one hundred forty-four thousand godly servants. It spans the same length of time, as did His first earthly ministry. It gives the same message. It will progress with the use of supernatural miracles as did Christ's first ministry, and it will end as with Christ's, in the death and resurrection of these two witnesses of Jesus!

The departure from similarities with Jesus' first earthly ministry shows itself in the very next verse:

And they gathered them together to the place called in Hebrew, Armageddon (Revelation 16:16).

So here then is the physical portion of the penalty to those who will not heed the final call to *salvation,* the harvest of the *grapes of wrath!* There is more—much more—the out of sight, unseen, supernatural reality of eternal punishment; the human soul (emotions, will, and intellect)—the real you—coupled to and energized by the human spirit, forming a living, thinking, feeling, calculating spiritual being. One having enormous potential not being restricted by a physical body, yet prevented from free expression and movement, because of the penal restrictions levied at judgment by a just and righteous God! This place was referred to by Jesus in His parable of the wedding dinner as outer darkness. It is described in an even less desirable way in Revelation 20:11–15.

Now, having traversed the minefield of the sixth bowl, we will take our chances in the seventh. Actually, we have little to fear from the seventh bowl, as it is—well, better wait and let the seventh bowl tell its own story!

CHAPTER FIFTY-FOUR

# THE SEVENTH BOWL

Then the seventh angel poured out his bowl into the air, and a loud voice came out of the temple of heaven, from the throne, saying, "It is done!" (Revelation 16:17).

This tells us that, with the consummation of the Third World War, highlighted by the great Battle of Armageddon, expanded by nuclear exchanges between nuclear nations and aggravated by natural disasters, the wrath of God on unrepentant mankind is complete!

The seventh bowl then, true to the form of the seventh trumpet, is also concerned with history. It is a review of that which has already taken place. Verse 18 begins the retro view:

And there were noises and thunderings and lightnings; and there was a great earthquake, such a mighty and great earthquake as had not occurred since men were on the earth (Revelation 16:18).

Verse 19 continues with the historical review:

Now the great city was divided into three parts, and the cities of the nations fell. And great Babylon was remembered before God, to give her the cup of the wine of the fierceness of His wrath.

The great city, of course, is Jerusalem. This great earthquake fits the description of the one that in Zechariah 14:4–5, was prophesied to split the Mount of Olives in two parts, forming an escape route for God's holy remnant to flee to safety in Jordan. Great Babylon (America), is shown here in this simplified version of God's wrathful Day of the Lord as receiving the cup of the fierceness of His wrath. This confirms her judgment as a fact in the approximately six-month long Day of the Lord. God's wrath, to occur in the gathering darkness of crisis-dominated days, beginning just prior to Jesus' return, when, as foretold in Luke 21:26:

> men's hearts failing them from fear and the expectation of those things which are coming on the earth, for the powers of heaven will be shaken.

The ten still-coherent global trading blocs with exponentially increasing need, or perceived need for oil and fresh water, will hate the harlot, make her desolate and naked, eat her flesh and burn her with fire (Revelation 17:16). She will have become an abomination in their sight, a risk, a threat, a liability, a target of opportunity. Justification will be plentiful, the stakes high, and the circumstances desperate. Mid-East oil, the prize, will escape the harlot's grasp! Soon thereafter, renegade forces within the neophyte ten-member union will exert their will in a reckless act of greed and naked aggression, directed at their own, one-time co-conspirators. This act will set up circumstances for God's intervention in protecting His holy remnant, His glorious land, and His glorious holy mountain (Jerusalem)!

The fact of the matter is, God is telling us His intentions in advance. He knows the beginning and the end. By His prophets and through the Bible, He is taking us into His confidence; telling us what is about to come upon the earth. Some will pay attention; some will not. The unbeliever's delusion, notwithstanding, we will continue to open as many remaining doors to prophetic awareness as the Lord provides the ability to accomplish.

Regarding the seventh bowl statements given after the fact of noises, thunderings, lightnings, a great earthquake at Jerusalem, and Great Babylon receiving the cup of the wine of the fierceness of God's wrath, Revelation 16:19 records this as well: ". . . and the cities of the nations fell."

# CHAPTER FIFTY-FIVE

# NO SPECULATION—JUST CERTAINTY!

With God's Word foretelling that the cities of the nations will fall, we should pay attention! This word is not from Nostradamus, a remote viewer, or a well-known psychic limited by the bonds of physical existence and spiritual misguidance. This is the mighty God of the Bible, the Creator of the universe, the source of all knowledge and power! When God speaks, the prudent listen. So we can be sure that cities of the nations are going to fall. The question now arises—which cities?

In ancient times, and as often found biblically, cities were frequently used to reference particular nations, because the city was the dominant force within the nation. City-states were not uncommon, either, with Tyre being a good example. When, in the Bible, cities are specified in relation to end times, we can be quite sure that with political power today residing largely with the nation rather than its cities, that these references to a city certainly include modern-day nations as well.

Which cities? Zechariah, in chapter 9, specifies several of Israel's neighbors. These are Damascus and Hamath in Syria, and Tyre in Lebanon. The Gaza Strip, an area on the west coast of Israel settled heavily by Palestinians and which has been transferred to the Palestinian authority has the cities of Gaza, Ekron, and nearby Ashkelon singled out for destruction.

As for certain nations destined for the same end, Ezekiel speaks of this in the context of end times, again in reference to Israel's neighbors. Jordan, as a nation, has existed only since 1946. It is, nevertheless, identified by several small ancient nations that occupied the western portion of what is now modern Jordan. We have seen prior reference to these early enemies of Israel: Ammon, Moab, and Edom.

We will briefly indulge here in recalling several other nations, previously seen as being specified by Ezekiel for destruction in the last days: Egypt, Ethiopia, Libya, Turkey (called Lydia), Iraq (called Assyria), and Iran (called Elam and Persia). These cities and nations, listed by God for destruction, have one thing in common; they are all in the same general area. The great crash to earth of the fourth comet fragment at the fifth trumpet will likely be the cause of the "great earthquake, such a mighty and great earthquake as had not occurred since men were on the earth" (Revelation 16:18). It will destroy a tenth of Jerusalem (Revelation 11:13). Being in that regional vicinity, it may topple cities in surrounding nations as well. However, as God's Word has already spoken, each on the list, thrown down by the earthquake or not, will have its fate sealed in the ensuing tragedy of World War III, as will Magog and those who live in security in the coastlands (Ezekiel 39:6).

This ends our biblical prophetic journey through the Tribulation and wrath of the seals, trumpets, and bowls. How far ahead do these things lurk? As difficult as it is to come to grips with, that question has already been answered. To say it another way: the future is not now; but it exists, not as a vague product of chance, but as a known reality!

We have looked at man's failing attempt to achieve God status for himself, while at the same time being exposed to unmerciful satanic/demonic influence. Man is not, therefore, the unchallenged master of his own destiny. Unfortunately, many people are unaware of the spirit dimension that exists around them, or of its increasing influence on humans.

In the age in which we live, this accelerated demonic activity, spoken of by Bible prophets and apostles of Jesus Christ, as well as Jesus Himself in the gospels, is referred to in a general way as the quickening. Those giving this term to "the working of Satan, with all power," as told by the apostle Paul in 2 Thessalonians 2:9 regarding the spiritual aspects, and by Jesus in Matthew 24:7 regarding the physical aspects of this quickening, accelerated end time activity, are quite correct. Jesus, in Matthew 24:4-8, called it "the beginning of sorrows." Modern man has sort of figured it out for himself without benefit of God's blueprint found within the pages of the greatest book ever written, God's Word. Think of what this generation might accomplish if it were to remove the old Book from the dresser drawer, open it up and read it. *The results could very well change the course of history!*

Before we move beyond Daniel's seventieth week, the last seven years of the current six thousand, we will review one more set of prophetic circumstances that relate directly to these seven years. They, in fact, represent the godly aspect of this final week of years, which we need to understand before advancing to encounter the mysteries of God's earthly kingdom!

# CHAPTER FIFTY-SIX

# ANOTHER BODY OF EVIDENCE

Within the old Book is found yet a third body of evidence fully supporting our two earlier episodes into discovering a biblically generated general time period dedicated to the Lord's return. This disclosure has lain dormant in the book of Revelation. The evidence exists as a period of time given as a number of days dedicated to an end time occurrence. It is found in Revelation 11:3 and specifies "one thousand two hundred and sixty days" for God's two witnesses to prophesy concerning the imminent return of Christ the King. Then, at the end of this 1,260 days, we have seen in vivid and symbolic word pictures what God's Bible says is to happen. We will see below something of how Christ's return will relate to the end of the witnesses' ministry.

The heretofore-unrealized implications of this specific number of days as they apply to Daniel's seventieth week now appear to be unsealed. We shall see their realization here.

The starting point for these last seven years is the treaty of peace between Israel and the Palestinians. It is biblically found, with Mayan enhancement, to have commenced on June 19, 2005, and so this is our starting place. In order to let this time segment, measured in days, reveal its specific part in the last seven years, we will attempt to place it in its proper position within the 2,557 days of the last week of years. This seven-year period will contain two leap years—2008 and 2012—years evenly divisible by four.

First, the peace treaty starts the counting of seven years that began in 2005, plus 2,557 days (seven years) takes us to the year 2012. We have full agreement with earlier work so far! Question: How accurate is the assumption throughout this writing that God's wrath will last six months? To start with, we will remember that man's number is six; so what could be more fitting than that man's number be the controlling influence in establishing the boundaries of this time of great human trial? We shall then let six months represent our estimation of what it will turn out to be. We shall prove this length of time to be realistic from Scripture.

The second point that bears on this time as reasonably being six months is that we know that five months of wrath will remain after the aerial spraying of atmospheric contamination, which will be expanded by the fourth fragment at the fifth trumpet. Pain and suffering inflicted upon followers of Antichrist resulting from aerial spraying will continue for five months (Revelation 9:10).

Third point: when God mentions periods of time given in months, He uses 30-day months; so then, the five months given in the fifth trumpet as representing remaining months of wrath will total 150 days. We can then add one more 30-day month, to total 180 days, which will stand for our, as yet assumed six-month long Day of the Lord; God's wrath upon the unrepentant.

Fourth point: here we have followed God's method of allocating thirty days to His referenced months, as well as having His referred to periods of days divisible by 30-day months. Yet, we are still constrained by having to deal with 365-day years, with each fourth year having 366 days. So then, here below is the method of choice in arriving at an estimated time period for our Lord's imminent return using what God Himself has given us in His Holy Word.

Point number five: these six months can start on any day of any month, but working with 30-day months while dealing with our calendar is not entirely feasible. We can therefore conclude that we must use the average days per month figure when allocating time to years and year portions relative to remaining within constraints of a 365-day calendar year. So then, the average number of days in a month using our calendar is found by dividing 365 days by 12 months, which yields 30.42 average number of days in an average month. Now, when we apply this formula to the estimated six months of wrath, we find it to be 182.5 days. There are several things that we can do with these additional 2.5 days, but we shall set them aside for now and look for more possible additional days to add to these 2.5 that we already have.

Yes, there are more days unaccounted for—the 3.5 days that the two witnesses will lie dead in a street of Jerusalem. These are additional to the 1,260 days of their ministry, and at the end of which, it seems certain, lies the time of Jesus Christ's return to rule the world with a rod of iron. We will add these 3.5 days to the 2.5 days, for a total of six wild card days. Here, man's number six has popped up again!

Now a comment about the rod of iron. This does not represent a hateful, vengeful spirit of retribution. It represents rather a willingness to show mercy to those who have given evidence through a broad range of actions, attitudes, and beliefs that they are not for Him, or with Him, but instead are dead-set against Him. Jesus' attitude when He returns will be no different than when He came to earth the first time. He came in love then, and He will come in love again! His first sojourn among us resulted in salvation for all who will avail themselves of this gift. His coming a second time will provide the same result, salvation for all survivors who will avail themselves of it. The only difference in the acquiring of this salvation will exist in conditions of the Lord's second advent, the reason for it, and the terms associated with it. The grace that we now enjoy will be gone, and a new kind of grace will be in effect. We shall see this new form of grace in detail as it relates to Israel and, in fact, in its relationship to the entire world as we progress to, and into dealing with God's millennial earthly kingdom.

So, the rod of iron will be used in a manner similar to that wielded by the two witnesses in their Holy Spirit empowered ministry lasting 1,260 days and leading directly to the return of the King of kings!

Now, we are in need of a summary in order to merge the various parts of the seventieth week of Daniel that we have been dissecting segment by segment, and which now deserve to be reconstructed. The hope is to provide a better understanding of its content, which will contain much of all that so many would prefer to have just go away!

| | | | |
|---|---|---|---|
| a. | Treaty to the start of two witnesses' ministry (An arbitrary figure expanded by two leap year days which accrue to this time segment) | + | 1,117.0 days |
| b. | Length of two witnesses' ministry (Includes 2.5 days of wrath) | + | 1,260.0 days |
| c. | The Two Witnesses lie dead in the street | + | 3.5 days |
| d. | 182.5 days of wrath less 6 wild card days | = | 176.5 days |

|  |  |  |
|---|---|---|
| Total days in Daniel's Seventieth Week (See Table #1) | = | 2,557.0 days |

We have here, accounted for the 6 additional wild card days by placing them within and at the beginning of the 182.5 calendar days of wrath. These 6 days, as we know, include the 2.5 days required for working with 365 day years and the 3.5 days that the two witnesses will lie dead in the street. We have also accounted for the 2 additional leap year days for the years 2008 and 2012.

Keeping in mind Matthew 24:29, which says: "Immediately after the tribulation of those days [difficult days for Christians], the sun will be darkened, and the moon will not give its light; the stars will fall from heaven, and the powers of the heavens will be shaken."

The next two verses, 30 and 31, continue the description of the Lord's return by saying that at this time of a darkened sun, moon, and stars, that the sign of the Son of Man will be seen in heaven. He will then send His angels with a great sound of a trumpet, and they will gather together His elect from the four winds (the earth) and from one end of heaven to the other.

No question at all that this is the Resurrection at Christ's return. God's wrath follows immediately after the Tribulation, which will likely end with pronouncement of the death sentence for the two witnesses. They will likely be tried in the UN International Criminal court, which in and of itself speaks much for how guilt and the death sentence will be arrived at. Now, with the reading of the death penalty for the witnesses, the Day of the Lord will come on the unsaved as a thief in the night. The comet will strike that very day, and will fragment into four chunks of violent ice, loudly announcing the beginning of the end!

Public sentiment will be running so strongly against these two godly witnesses for Jesus (i.e., rejoicing and merry making in celebration of their conviction for high crimes against the common good), that justice will be fast tracked in this case (possibly influenced by four large comet fragments freely orbiting the earth). And a public execution will be carried out in a community square in the Holy City two-and-one-half days later. Upon the point of their death, wrath will be two-and-a-half days into its duration. Its force will be felt in the form of great fear, escalating into raw panic among those who were not expecting it; as the first, then the second, and the third streaking fragments strike earth and begin to generate atmospheric contamination, which will quickly commence to encircle the earth.

Shock and fear, more than a dislike of these two witnesses for Jesus will manifest to prevent authorities from providing burial for the dead. Their bodies, left lying in public view for three-and-a-half days will provide intermittent TV news-bite coverage dispersed plentifully throughout broader documentation of a cataclysmic attack by cosmic forces on mother Gaia (Planet Earth).

It will now be day six after the sentence of death shall have been read; with then simultaneous assault upon earth's atmosphere by a solar traveler; and three of its offspring will have come calling. Atmospheric pollution will have now darkened all of the earth. The Old Testament prophet Joel, in chapter 2:1–2, gives a warning for this time: "For the day of the Lord is coming, for it is at hand: a day of darkness and gloominess, a day of clouds and thick darkness." (These are our six wild card days; the first six terror-filled days of God's wrath!) (See Table #7)

As we have seen earlier, God will maintain tight control over all that will be happening in this near future time. On the sixth day, darkening will have reached the point of one-third of total darkness, and God will send His Son to rescue His witnesses, both dead and alive! 1 Thessalonians 4:15–17 tells just how it will be:

> For this we say to you by the word of the Lord, that we who are alive and remain until the coming of the Lord will by no means precede those who are asleep.

> For the Lord Himself will descend from heaven with a shout, with the voice of an archangel, and with the trumpet of God. And the dead in Christ will rise first.

> Then we who are alive and remain shall be caught up together with them in the clouds to meet the Lord in the air. And thus we shall always be with the Lord.

So, we have here arrived at the fourth trumpet, with one-third reduction in light from the sun, moon, and stars; and the case has just been made, that this is the sixth day in the six-month long Day of the Lord!

This sixth day is not over yet, however, as we will see another aspect of it that will play an important part in the lives of God's Jewish remnant; those who will live through it all to take their rightful inheritance; the land of Israel!

The Resurrection will be history. And as if this will not be enough to hold the attention of those remaining, it will be the time—within the very hour of Jesus' triumphant return—that the fourth fragment of the broken comet as seen in the fifth trumpet judgment will crash to earth in fulfillment of Bible prophecy. Among other things, this explosive encounter with earth will set off a great and mighty earthquake, the greatest since men have been on the earth (Revelation 16:18). The Mount of Olives will be split in two parts, forming a great valley, which will serve as an escape route for God's Jewish remnant to make their way through in reaching safety in the country of Jordan. Here they will be watched over by the great archangel Michael until all invading forces have been extinguished in the land.

Another result of this greatest of all earthquakes will be the violent upheaval of Jerusalem, so that the affected area will become a mountain top upon which the rebuilt Jerusalem shall later, rest and exist throughout the millennial kingdom of Jesus Christ (Zechariah 14:10–11; Ezekiel 40:2).

Now, a comment concerning the location of the fourth comet fragment crash to earth; seen so vividly in the fifth trumpet judgment. The Bible tells that the fifth bowl of advanced wrath will be poured on Antichrist's throne. Since his throne will be in Israel, the fourth crash site must be in close proximity or within that nation. But where? There is a part of present day Israel that is, in fact, quite close to Jerusalem that will not be included in millennial Israel. This is the area of interest as a potential crash site location. We shall see it identified later as we deal with millennial Israel in detail.

We have been looking at a completely scriptural composite of time segments that, like pieces of a jigsaw puzzle, produce a picture of something when placed into and locked in their proper places.

If, in fact, this is a reasonable representation of the timing of that which is headed our way, possibly we should be able to find some evidence, or sign, that would point to God's hand in it all. We have seen in God's working so far, *six* thousand years for man's free will with, it seems, *six* months of wrath, and His Son's return *six* days into its duration. This fully implicates this composite picture of (666) in its numerical reference to man as stemming directly from the mind of God!

It is with some relief that we will now leave the tribulation and wrath of Daniel's seventieth week. A final aspect of the carnage yet remains, however. We could ignore it, but it prepares the Holy Land for the central part that it is destined to play; so we will look at it here.

# CHAPTER FIFTY-SEVEN

# CLEANSING THE LAND

"It will come to pass in that day that I will give Gog a burial place there in Israel, the valley of those who pass by east of the sea; and it will obstruct travelers, because there they will bury Gog and all his multitude. Therefore they will call it the Valley of Hamon Gog [multitude of Gog].

"For seven months the House of Israel will be burying them, in order to cleanse the land.

"Indeed all the people of the land will be burying, and they will gain renown for it on the day that I am glorified," says the Lord GOD.

"They will set apart men regularly employed, with the help of a search party, to pass through the land and bury those bodies remaining on the ground, in order to cleanse it. At the end of seven months they will make a search.

"The search party will pass through the land; and when anyone sees a man's bone, he shall set up a marker by it, till the buriers have buried it in the Valley of Hamon Gog" (Ezekiel 39:11–15).

Just as it was necessary to purify and cleanse the temple of God after Antiochus IV Epiphanes desecrated it, thereby establishing at that time the celebration of Hanukkah, it will be necessary to cleanse the land so that God's purpose may proceed. (The millennial Sabbath—kingdom of God).

God's number *seven* is in use in the above verses, in that the time for burial of the dead is said to require Israel's effort for *one week* of months. The number seven, regarding the aftermath of this great conflict is used also in Ezekiel 39:9. Here its use is to specify time required for disposal of all the equipment brought into Israel by the armies gathered there, but used largely for their own destruction. In this instance, the length of time is to be *seven* years. Then, in Ezekiel 39:10, within this same week of seven years, as well as disposal of all of the invaders' war materiel, is mentioned the plundering by Israel of all having value, brought in by those who will have come to pillage her.

So, we see that God's number seven, being used twice in the cleansing effort, limits the time expended for this work to one week of years. It will be a great undertaking for a decimated Israel, one that will require a plan and someone in charge who will not only know the plan, but will have full support from the remnant and the authority to make it happen. Is anyone asking who this person will be? There is, of course, only one nominee to fill this job position. His nomination was made in heaven, and He is highly qualified for the job!

# CHAPTER FIFTY-EIGHT

# PRELUDE TO THE KINGDOM
# OF
# GOD ON EARTH

God's Servant, the *Branch*, Second Person of the Godhead, Jesus Christ, will head up the operation. It was, after all, His plan in the first place. Zechariah 6:12–13 provide a brief synopsis of how Christ's reign will begin:

> "Then speak to him, saying, 'Thus says the LORD of hosts, saying: "Behold, the Man whose name is the BRANCH! From His place He shall branch out, and He shall build the temple of the LORD;
>
> Yes, He shall build the temple of the LORD. He shall bear the glory, and shall sit and rule on His throne; so He shall be a priest on His throne, and the counsel of peace shall be between them both.'"

Being austere in style, these verses include more than meets the eye. They, in fact, tell a great deal in a few words, as only God seems to be able to do. They show that Jesus Christ will build the temple and will sit and rule on His throne. But where is His throne? And where is His place? Answers to these questions will be found in future pages, but to clarify the point somewhat, neither will be in the temple. In addition to Jesus ruling Israel from His throne and bearing the glory, we are told that He will do something else, which in effect involves supervision of His entire earthly kingdom. The phrase repeated here is "From His place He shall branch out," a simple statement, yet with global consequences. The dictionary meaning of *branch out* is *to extend*. The New King James Version then is saying that Jesus, the Branch, will extend His rule out. The older version, the King James Bible, says: "and he shall grow up out of his place." The dictionary gives a meaning for *grow up* as *to reach maturity or full growth*. The following verse, Zechariah 6:13, provides the reason for the branching out or the growing up. It says: "He shall bear the glory, and shall sit and rule on His throne" (from Israel, His rule will encompass the entire earth!).

Another of the things that we are told He shall do is to build the temple of the Lord. With the temple being in Israel, He will not need to branch out or reach full capacity in global rule to accomplish this. Nevertheless, He will branch out/grow His rule worldwide while He shall be sitting and ruling from His throne. Something is missing here! The missing element is, of course, His saints. He will have need for representatives, for lack of a better word. In the Bible, we find that the saints will fill this need. The saints are scripturally described as being judges, and in Revelation 20:6, it says "they shall be priests of God and of Christ, and shall reign with Him a thousand years." (They will globally represent Jesus, the King, in His new *one world government!*)

Chaos will be in great evidence at the transition from the ashes of a failed world dictatorship, to the budding of a new kind of world government under the rule of God Himself in the person of Jesus Christ. The need for Jesus' global representatives will be real. A new way of living will begin, and the remaining world population will need guidance and redirection. New rules will be put in place, and authority established. In spite of extensive hardship, humanity will finally be able to breath a sigh of relief and know that *all is right with the world!* (See Table #7)

# CHAPTER FIFTY-NINE

# THE LORD JESUS CHRIST REIGNS

In reference to the Lord's return, we find in Zechariah 14:5:

> Then you shall flee through My mountain valley, for the mountain valley shall reach to Azal. Yes, you shall flee as you fled from the earthquake in the days of Uzziah king of Judah. Thus the LORD my God will come, and all the saints with You. [Then the abomination of desolation is seen continuing in the holy place.]

Verses 6 and 7 continue:

> It shall come to pass in that day that there will be no light; the lights will diminish.

> It shall be one day which is known to the LORD; neither day nor night. But at evening time it shall happen that it will be light.

The day of diminished light is the Day of the Lord. At evening (day's end), it shall be *light*. The Hebrew word for *light* used here is *owr*, meaning: *illumination, luminary, happiness, bright, clear, day, light, morning,* and *sun.* Judging from the selection and considering the verses, it seems that light which is to manifest at the Day of the Lord's end, speaks of a new morning, a clear, bright and happy day. The millennial Sabbath, a day of rest and preparation for the eternal future. Here stands the *dawning of the seventh millennial day!*

Zechariah 14:8 provides evidence that Jesus will have begun to reign:

> And in that day it shall be that living waters shall flow from Jerusalem, half of them toward the eastern sea and half of them toward the western sea; in both summer and winter it shall occur.

These living waters will be chemical. The Hebrew word for *water* here is *chay*, with a number of meanings tending to the physical. Some of these are: *keep alive, raw, fresh, water, strong, appetite, maintenance, life.* We will see later in greater detail the waters that will flow east. They, though being in the physical realm, will have some Holy Spirit empowered qualities.

In John 4:13–14, Jesus compares chemical water with His living water:

> Jesus answered and said to her, "Whoever drinks of this water will thirst again,

> "but whoever drinks of the water that I shall give him will never thirst. But the water that I shall give him will become in him a fountain of water springing up into everlasting life."

This is reference to receiving the Holy Spirit in a repentant rebirth with belief in Jesus Christ, at which time sin is forgiven by God's *grace.* This grace will end at the Resurrection. A new dynamic will exist in the millennial Sabbath; Satan and his demons will be removed; and *mankind will outgrow sin!*

The prophet Joel talks about the thousand year millennial Sabbath Day in Joel 3:18:

And it will come to pass in that day that the mountains shall drip with new wine, The hills shall flow with milk, and all the brooks of Judah shall be flooded with water; a fountain shall flow from the House of the LORD and water the Valley of Acacias. [A dry valley supporting only the acacia tree.]

This Valley of Acacias will be supplied with chemical living water as we will see described fully in Ezekiel 47 ahead. The fountain to originate from under the millennial temple will become a mighty river with miraculous powers: a wonder to behold and will have special meaning for all. The land of Israel will be reclaimed for God's holy Jewish remnant. (*Peace at last!*)

We know God's millennial kingdom has been a subject of interest for Old Testament prophets well over two thousand years before the fact. Israel received some word from God on the subject recorded in Isaiah 2:2–4, which we see here:

Now it shall come to pass in the latter days that the mountain of the Lord's house shall be established on the top of the mountains, and shall be exalted above the hills; and all nations shall flow to it.

Many people shall come and say, "Come, and let us go up to the mountain of the LORD, to the House of the God of Jacob; He will teach us His ways, and we shall walk in His paths." For out of Zion shall go forth the law, and the word of the LORD from Jerusalem.

He shall judge between the nations, and rebuke many people; they shall beat their swords into plowshares, and their spears into pruning hooks; nation shall not lift up sword against nation, neither shall they learn war anymore.

Here, from this early writing of God's intent for His earthly kingdom, it is clear that He will be worshipped as God by all the earth. It is also made known that He will rebuke when necessary, and that He will teach His ways as the law of the land. The location of His throne is given, and He leaves no doubt at all that war is of the past and shall not be tolerated.

After the defeat of the final divided world empire; divided at first into the apostate religious and political/economic halves, but then later divided again by the treachery of three of the ten-member blocs; a dazed and frightened remnant of humanity will be like lost sheep in need of a shepherd. The void will be filled immediately by the Lion of Judah and His field workers, the saints, in imperishable resurrection bodies!

The prophet Zechariah, in Zechariah 14:9–10 reveals important topographical changes to affect Jerusalem and surrounding area, presumably as a result of the great earthquake to strike Jerusalem and split the Mount of Olives apart at the Lord's return:

> And the LORD shall be King over all the earth. In that day it shall be; "The LORD is one," and His name one.

> All the land shall be turned into a plain from Geba to Rimmon south of Jerusalem. Jerusalem shall be raised up and inhabited in her place from Benjamin's Gate to the place of the First Gate and the Corner Gate, and from the Tower of Hananeel to the king's winepresses. [This, the temple mount will live again!]

*The Mountain top shall be as flat as the plain around it.*

Zechariah has foretold here that all the land surrounding Jerusalem from Geba, about six miles northeast of Jerusalem, to Rimmon, about forty miles south, will be turned into a plain. And, in addition to this topographical correction, Jerusalem shall be raised up, downsized, and relocated on the south portion of the mountain top, with only the temple mount being inhabited in its current place. (See Table #4) The picture that emerges depicts a level, tillable plain surrounding a mountain top, crowned by the new city, which will be known by a new name. More about this future hub of the universe as we observe the landscape of the soon-to-come kingdom of God in pages ahead.

It is likely that this earthquake will be triggered by the fourth comet fragment, the one that is seen in the fifth trumpet. This would be one and the same "great earthquake that will strike Jerusalem in the same hour that the Lord will return and call up the two witnesses in the Resurrection; and in which a tenth of the city is said to fall with loss of seven thousand lives" (Revelation 11:13). This, then, will require that the fourth fragment of the fifth trumpet strike in the vicinity of Israel. This is scriptural, since Antichrist's throne will be in the temple of God at Jerusalem, and Revelation 16:10 says of the fifth bowl (advanced wrath): "Then the fifth angel poured out his bowl on the throne of the beast, and his kingdom became full of darkness." With Antichrist's throne being in Jerusalem at that time, the appearance is that Israel will be the site of the fourth fragment's plunge to earth! But where in Israel?

Millennial Israel will have need for all the land of its foretold inheritance. And it is unlikely as well, that God would send a comet fragment into this area, which at the time of the cosmic attack will hold all, or most of Israel's remnant being protected through tribulation and then all wrath. For these reasons, it seems more likely that the fifth trumpet fragment, responsible for creating the large gaping hole in the ground that John described as the bottomless pit, will crash in an adjoining area. The lower portion of the Negev Desert of southern modern day Israel will not be included in the tribal portions of millennial Israel. This area, being part of Israel today, then makes it a site of interest. Using the Levy scenario as an example, could the reason that it will not be included in millennial Israel be that perhaps it will have a gigantic hole in it, say the width of the Negev, and anywhere from five to ten miles deep?

So the pieces fit together in placing Jesus' return just after the wrath of God will commence; with protection provided for the remnant of Israel and the saints of the Most High, right through the appearance in the heavens of the dark and cloudy sign of the second advent, to the conspicuous coming of the Son of Man on clouds of glory!

# CHAPTER SIXTY

# THE NEW JERUSALEM

Now I saw a new heaven and a new earth, for the first heaven and the first earth had passed away. Also there was no more sea (Revelation 21:1).

Then, Revelation 21:16 provides some specific physical information concerning the New Jerusalem (the new heaven) that will replace God's earthly kingdom at the end of the thousand years. The verse says this:

The city is laid out as a square; its length is as great as its breadth. And he measured the city with the reed: twelve thousand furlongs [1,500 miles]. Its length, breadth, and height are equal.

Earth, during the millennial kingdom, will be much as it is today physically, but with a new system of government. After that, however, it will be a different story. To help us better understand something of the unusual successor to God's millennial kingdom on earth that the Bible calls New Jerusalem, we must look at the Greek word for *heaven, ouranos.* This can mean *heaven, God's abode or heaven as sky or air.* With this understanding in mind, we can now proceed and attempt to peel away the layers clouding this issue in search of the facts! The subject here is the new heaven—Revelation 21:2:

> Then I, John, saw the holy city, New Jerusalem, coming down out of heaven from God, prepared as a bride adorned for her husband.

Here, after the thousand year kingdom of God on earth is ended, John saw the new heaven (abode of God) coming down out of heaven (the sky). The word *ouranos* is used for both.

How do we know the New Jerusalem, a cube 1,500 miles square and 1,500 miles high, will be the abode of God? Revelation 21:22–23 gives the answer:

> But I saw no temple in it, for the Lord God Almighty and the Lamb are its temple.

> The city had no need of the sun or of the moon to shine in it, for the glory of God illuminated it. The Lamb is its light.

After the angel measured the city, he measured the wall. Revelation 21:17–18 describes the wall:

> Then he measured its wall: one hundred and forty-four cubits, according to the measure of a man, that is, of an angel.

> The construction of its wall was of jasper; and the city was pure gold, like clear glass.

When we consider the wall, with one cubit being equal to eighteen inches, we find the wall to be 216 feet. But John doesn't say if that is thickness or height, possibly because he may have felt he had already made it clear that it was thickness, when he gave the city's height as being 1,500 miles high. Speculation suggests that it was measured through one of the wall's gated openings which would readily provide the walls' thickness; so then, it would seem reasonable to believe that the city's wall will be 216 feet thick. Of course, nothing we could build today of that thickness would reach anywhere near 1,500 miles high. But with God, we know that all things are possible!

With the New Jerusalem being 1,500 miles square, and we can be sure that it will come down over the location of the old Jerusalem; there could then no longer be a Dead Sea. It will extend well into the area of the Mediterranean Sea as well as that of the Red Sea. But as we have already seen in Revelation 21:1, there will be a new heaven and a new earth, for the first heaven and the first earth will have passed away, and there will be *no more sea.*

We have read in Revelation 21:23 that the city would have no need of the sun or of the moon to shine, for the glory of God will illuminate it, and the Lamb will be its light. We can only guess as to the cause of the lack of sunshine. Will the sun provide light, which will be ineffective due to the wall extending up 1,500 miles or will there no longer be a sun or moon or anything else in space (heaven)?

The variable radiance of God's glory, of course, is more than sufficient to light the city. Exodus 24:17 tells something of God's glory at the time Moses was going up on Mount Sinai to receive God's law directly from Him. The verse provides this view:

The sight of the glory of the LORD was like a consuming fire on the top of the mountain in the eyes of the children of Israel.

Also, in the same vein, Exodus 34:34–35 tell of Moses wearing a veil over his face when going before the children of Israel after having been in the presence of the Lord because of brightness of the Lord's glory lingering on his face.

We will see God's glory exposed and in operational mode in the millennial kingdom. And, then in the final eternal kingdom of God, the saved will again be exposed to God's splendid glory, which will light up all of the new heaven!

A point of interest here is the interaction of the number *twelve* in the structural integrity of the city's (New Jerusalem's) wall. The thickness of which, in Revelation 21:17, is given as 144 cubits. This exhibits yet another use of the number *twelve* in honoring the concept of the original twelve sons of Jacob (Israel). Case in point: the wall of the heavenly city mathematically fulfills God's promise to bless mankind through Abraham's seed—through the twelve sons down to the Messiah, and freedom from the penalty of sin by His shed blood!

The number *twelve* is the golden thread connecting the nation of Israel, through the twelve sons of Jacob, to the fact of salvation by *grace* through Jesus. This is emphasized by the 144,000 servants of God (12,000 twelves) "being firstfruits to God and to the Lamb." The New Jerusalem itself exemplifies the number *twelve*; having a base area of 12,000 x 12,000 furlongs, enclosed by its wall of 12 x 12 cubits in thickness, and a height of 12,000 furlongs. This huge wall, resting upon twelve foundations, has twelve openings, using twelve great oversized pearl gates!

It seems obvious that this use of twelve's in the New Jerusalem is a concept of rhythmic creativity stemming from the complex mind of God. Its purpose: to provide saved mankind with an eternal/external reminder of the position of honor held by His chosen people—Israel—the cultivated olive tree!

What will it be like in New Jerusalem? Revelation 21:4 tells us "And God will wipe away every tear from their eyes; there shall be no more death, nor sorrow, nor crying; and there shall be no more pain, for the former things have passed away." So now, knowing some of what there will *not be*—we can then know as well some of what there *will be*.

There will be no death. This tells us that there will be eternal life; no more sorrow—this implies eternal joy; no more crying—a hint of the absence of illness and distress; and no more pain—this will eliminate pain and suffering. Side note: This will not be a litigious society! What we see here is the elimination of negatives.

Will all this accent on the positive bring on a climate of boredom in the new heaven? Boredom, a negative emotion, will be entirely unknown. The lack of negatives will not cause a negative reaction, but rather, a *positive one*.

The *key* to what the new heaven is all about is to be found in Revelation 21:23, where John depicts a New Jerusalem without need of the sun. We will read it again, and look for the key:

> The city had no need of the sun or of the moon to shine in it, for the glory of God illuminated it. The Lamb is its light.

The key is found in the phrase "the Lamb is its light." The Lamb, of course, is Jesus. *Strong's Concordance* shows the Greek word for *light* is *luchnos*. Its meaning is *a portable lamp or other illuminator*. This is bothersome if attempting to relate Jesus as another source of light, since we just read in Revelation 21:23 that God's glory illuminated the city!

We read also, in Revelation 21:5: "Then He who sat on the throne said, 'behold, I make all things new.'"

Now we will put the pieces together to find the answer to the question: *what is the new heaven all about?*

With God's glory providing the light source for the city (new heaven), Jesus being its lamp as a source of light seems excessive. So here the key answers the question. Jesus the Illuminator is the dispenser of illumination to residents of this great city—heaven. Jesus, as the Creator of the universe, possesses a vast reservoir of knowledge. Some may question the statement that Jesus created the universe. To resolve this point, we need to read John 1:1–3:

> In the beginning was the Word, and the Word was with God, and the Word was God.
>
> He was in the beginning with God.
>
> All things were made through Him, and without Him nothing was made that was made.

How do we know Jesus is the Word? John answers this question as to Jesus being the Word—the one who spoke the universe into being, and who will speak the demise of the nations into reality at Armageddon using the sword of His mouth (Revelation 19:21). John, in John 1:14 explains:

> And the *Word became flesh and dwelt among us,* and we beheld His glory, the glory as of the only begotten of the Father, full of grace and truth. (Emphasis added.)

So Jesus, the member of the triune Godhead, who spoke the universe into being in six 24-hour days, will be the illuminator of the elect. Jesus, the source of all truth, all power, and all knowledge, the fountainhead of the living water, will give of the living water (Holy Spirit) to all who thirst (John 4:14).

Now, to carry through with this truth, we need to read Isaiah 40:31, which says:

> But those who wait on the LORD shall renew their strength; they shall mount up with wings like eagles, they shall run and not be weary, they shall walk and not faint.

What exactly does the word *wait* mean, as it is used here? Again, in checking *Strong's Exhaustive Concordance of the Bible,* it is found that *wait* in Hebrew is *qavah,* a prime root; meaning to *bind together, collect, to expect—gather, as well as—to tarry or wait for, on or upon.*

So now, with God's elect in the new heaven, waiting on the Lord, we see that they will be *expecting—gathering, and collecting* the essence of what the Lord Jesus Christ will be illuminating them with. They will, in the power of the Holy Spirit, the living water, mount up with wings like eagles; they shall run and not be weary, they shall walk and not faint.

The *new heaven experience* in just worldly terms will be a never-ending, ever-gaining accumulation of proficiency in *truths*, to be received directly from the Source of all things. Though God's elect will be with God, ever-learning, ever-growing in grace, and reveling in the glory of God through Jesus Christ, the elect will not become gods! They will eternally be the sheep of His flock, trusting in Him, looking to Him, and following Him—*for He is the power, and the glory forever and ever!*

We have just looked at the new earth and the new heaven (New Jerusalem)—everlasting ending point for God's elect. We now need to look into the thousand-year millennial kingdom of Jesus Christ on the first earth, which is a sizable Bible subject. It is widely accepted by Christian believers as being just as it has been presented here, the Sabbath Day of God's allotted millennial week, which in effect is an expanded shadow of His creation week. This millennial Sabbath will see Jesus become a reality for many who today do not know Him!

# CHAPTER SIXTY-ONE

# THE MILLENNIAL SABBATH— EARTHLY KINGDOM OF JESUS CHRIST

The prophet Isaiah, hundreds of years in advance, proclaimed by the word, of God both the first and the second advent of the Lord Jesus Christ. Here in Isaiah 9:6 are his words:

> For unto us a Child is born, unto us a Son is given [first advent]; and the government will be upon His shoulder. And His name will be called Wonderful, Counselor, Mighty God, Everlasting Father, Prince of Peace [second advent].

There is considerable said in the prophetic books of the Bible about circumstances of Christ's millennial reign. Some of these statements of prophecy are very clear and easy to understand— some are not. One of the more difficult to comprehend which, in fact, seems quite straightforward, is Amos 9:11–12. These verses, after a closer look, appear to have a double meaning, not entirely uncommon in the prophetic Word. One of these meanings, it turns out, is rather hard to grasp, yet is fully supported by other Bible prophecy.

The subject verses, Amos 9:11–12 deal with the millennial kingdom of Christ and tell us the following:

On that day [millennial Sabbath] I will raise up the tabernacle of David, which has fallen down, and repair its damages; I will raise up its ruins, and rebuild it as in the days of old;

That they [Israel] may possess the remnant of Edom [descendants of Esau], and all the Gentiles who are called by My name," says the LORD who does this thing.

The Gentiles (people here called by the Lord's name) are not the saints, but rather those who will have come to believe in Jesus Christ as the Son of God after His return. These, and all others of all the nations of the earth will be, in a manner of speaking, under the yoke of Israel. This will be true from the standpoint that Israel, being God's chosen people, will establish the benchmark of behavior required by the Lord, and will receive His blessings. Israel then, will be the model for the rest of the world to follow, or else as a consequence, Jesus the King will apply pressure in the form of withholding rain from their soil (Zechariah 14:18–19).

The tabernacle of David is mentioned also in Isaiah 16:5, which gives the following details:

In mercy the throne will be established; and One will sit on it in truth, in the tabernacle of David, judging and seeking justice and hastening righteousness.

Acts 15:16 has Jesus saying the following:

After this I will return and will rebuild the tabernacle of David, which has fallen down; I will rebuild its ruins, and I will set it up.

The Greek word for *tabernacle* in this verse is *skene*, meaning *tent or cloth hut—habitation—tabernacle*. This then is not the stone and mortar temple.

Jesus, as heir to David's throne, is justified through His being descended from David on both His mother Mary's and His earthly father Joseph's side. Jesus is the One who represents the Davidic covenant in its on going relationship with Israel. Jeremiah 33:17 tells of this continuing representation:

> "For thus says the LORD: 'David shall never lack a man to sit on the throne of the House of Israel.

We are now into the middle of the mystery touching the man who will sit on the throne of David, in the tabernacle of David. This is the same man who, in Jeremiah 33:18, will offer burnt offerings before God, and kindle grain offerings, and sacrifice continually. Could this man be Jesus? Jesus, who came to earth to do away with the shedding of animal blood for atonement of sin; Jesus, who came to establish the new covenant in His blood on Calvary! Could it be He who will be the man to sacrifice animals continually to God at His return to rule earth a thousand years?

Before we can answer that question, we need to look at Zechariah. We recall Joshua the high priest, whom we found to be one of the two witnesses. Zechariah 6:9–14 tells about him being given an elaborate crown of silver and gold, that will be a memorial in the millennial temple of the Lord to four particular Israelites who came out of the Babylonian captivity. Verse 11 says this:

> Take the silver and gold, make an elaborate crown, and set it on the head of Joshua the son of Jehozadak, the high priest.

Verses 12 and 13 continue:

> "Then speak to him, saying, 'Thus says the LORD of hosts, saying: "Behold, the Man whose name is the BRANCH! From His place He shall branch out, and He shall build the temple of the LORD;

Yes, He shall build the temple of the LORD. He shall bear the glory, and shall sit and rule on His throne; so He shall be a priest on His throne, and the counsel of peace shall be between them both.'"

Now, to begin putting the pieces together. To do this, we will list some given facts:

1.  The Man whose name is the BRANCH is Jesus Christ.

2.  Joshua the priest (one of the two witnesses) will play a leading part in the operation of the millennial temple, and in ministering to God the Father, whose glory will reside in said temple (Zechariah 6:11-14).

3.  The Man whose name is the BRANCH (Jesus Christ), from His place, the tabernacle of David, will branch out (with authority of His ruling position, and see that the stone and mortar temple is constructed).

4.  The Man, the BRANCH, shall bear the glory, and shall sit and rule on His throne (in the tabernacle of David, not in the temple of God).

5.  The word *bear*, as in *He shall bear the glory* (Zechariah 6:13), according to *Strong's* in the Hebrew language is *nasa*. This word has a number of meanings, two of which are *accept* and *exalt*. It seems then that Jesus shall *accept* glory for who He is, and He will *exalt* God's glory as He *bears the glory*.

6.  He shall be a priest on His throne. This is a highly unusual position for a priest, that is, being on a throne. Only Jesus meets the requirements for this circumstance. He fills the role of high priest in presenting to the Lord God offerings at Sabbaths, feasts, new moons, and at all the appointed seasons of the House of Israel throughout the millennial Kingdom of God (Ezekiel 45:17).

Jesus, in Hebrews 9, is described as a high priest to those who are called (Christians); mediator between God the Father and sinful man. Jesus, whose blood was shed on Calvary for the cleansing of sin in place of the sprinkling of the blood of animals, represents a "greater and more perfect tabernacle not made with hands, that is, not of this creation" (Hebrews 9:11). This compares *saving grace attained through Jesus* with the blood sacrifice of the old covenant. Jesus now provides a better way!

In reference to Jesus "sitting and ruling on His throne" (Zechariah 6:13), He is on the one hand, a priest to His millennial saints, serving as mediator between them and God. He is a priest as well to the millennial remnant Israelites, leading them in worship of God the Father through presentation of offerings and sacrifices in the temple. In contrast, as King, He will sit and rule all nations with a rod of iron from the tabernacle of David in Israel.

7. "And the counsel of peace shall be between them both" (Zechariah 6:13). This refers to Joshua the priest who will minister to God in the millennial temple, and Jesus, who will lead the Israelites in worship of God on Sabbaths, at feasts, new moons, and at all the appointed seasons of the house of Israel (Ezekiel 45:17).

Jesus will not minister to God, as will the temple priests, but rather will represent the remnant people of the House of Israel in worship and presentation of offerings to God the Father on the special days set out above. So the counsel of peace shall be between Joshua and Jesus. They will each attend to their own duties in conducting the business of the temple; the one, in ministering to God, and the other in leading the people in the worship of God.

The important point to remember in attempting to understand the part that Jesus will play in the coming millennial kingdom of

God, is that He is both man and God. He is part of the three-person Trinity; God the Father, God the Son, and God the Holy Spirit. He came to earth, was born through human birth, grew to manhood, and was glorified through resurrection from death at Calvary after three days, to receive a new body, incorruptible; then He returned to the right hand of the Father!

So then, with Jesus being both God and resurrected man with a glorified body, He will fill three roles in the kingdom of God on earth.

In what we can call His first role, Jesus will serve the remnant of the House of Israel as priest, just as noted earlier, leading them in worship of God the Father, whose glory will reside in the newly constructed temple (Ezekiel 43:4). Regarding God's glory, the prophet Isaiah spoke concerning it in the soon-to-come millennial Sabbath. Isaiah 4:2 leads into it concerning Jesus and the bounty of the earth that will bless the remnant at that time. It tells us this:

> In that day the Branch of the LORD shall be beautiful and glorious; and the fruit of the earth shall be excellent and appealing for those of Israel who have escaped.

The prophet now proceeds with how God's glory will extend over all Israel and be covered by a protective canopy over the land in that day (millennial Sabbath). Isaiah 4:5–6 continue:

> then the LORD will create above every dwelling place of Mount Zion, and above her assemblies, a cloud and smoke by day and the shining of a flaming fire by night. For over all the glory there will be a covering.

> And there will be a tabernacle for shade in the daytime from the heat, for a place of refuge, and for a shelter from storm and rain [Jesus Christ].

> But Christ came as High Priest of the good things to come, with the greater and more perfect tabernacle not made with hands, that is, not of this creation (Hebrews 9:11).

So, here we see that God's glory will not be restricted to the temple, but will prevail over all of His land. It will be reminiscent of when He led the Israelites out of Egypt, to the Promised Land. The prophet Jeremiah gave an interesting parallel prophecy on this subject, relating to the return of the latter-day Israelites to their Promised Land. Jeremiah 23:7–8 foretells the details:

"Therefore, behold, the days are coming," says the LORD, "that they shall no longer say, 'As the LORD lives who brought up the children of Israel from the land of Egypt,'

"but, 'as the LORD lives who brought up and led the descendants of the house of Israel from the north country and from all the countries where I had driven them.' And they shall dwell in their own land."

There should be no doubt whatsoever in the minds of those who have read these specific prophecies direct from God, given through the prophets, that the remnant of the House of Israel will retain its land. This is holy land, promised by God to His people, and it will serve the purpose He intended for it. Efforts by Israel's enemies to wrest the land away by military force, coercion, terror, or treaty are, of course, hopeless. God gave it to Israel, and as is obvious in numerous instances of His recorded statements concerning this land, He has His own plans for it. Those intentions place the Jewish remnant, united with God the Father and God the Son, all there together in the land of Israel's inheritance!

The second role of Jesus in His millennial kingdom involving His saints will be closely viewed a bit further on, but for now, we will continue with His first role. At Jesus' return in His incorruptible resurrection body, He is referred to in both Old and New Testaments as a man. Examples follow:

A. Behold, the Man whose name is the BRANCH! (Zechariah 6:12).

B. For thus says the Lord: "David shall never lack a man to sit on the throne of the house of Israel" (Jeremiah 33:17).

C. Jesus, in reference to His second coming, referred to Himself as the Son of Man, meaning that He will return as a man:

> But as the days of Noah were, so also will the coming of the Son of Man be (Matthew 24:37).

So now it can be seen that Jesus will return as a man; yet with all power and glory, and in His imperishable body. Now, to clarify the first meaning of the tabernacle of David as given in Amos 9:11–12. The first meaning, as we have seen, pertains to the reestablishment of the relationship that God had with the House of Israel under the later rule of King David. The situation at that time was one where the Israelites worshipped God whose glory abided in the tabernacle. David had a close relationship with God, and God promised David that he would never lack a man to sit on the throne of the House of Israel (Jeremiah 33:17). God expanded His promise to David in Jeremiah 33:18:

> nor shall the priests, the Levites, lack a man to offer burnt offerings before Me, to kindle grain offerings, and to sacrifice continually. [The cross represents on going sacrifice through current grace until Christ's return.]

There can be no doubt that Jesus is this man. At His return, He will restore the heritage of David with the offering of sacrifice to God, whose glory will occupy the new millennial temple.

Now, for the second meaning of tabernacle of David (Amos 9: 11–12). To gain understanding of it, we need to examine Ezekiel 37:22–27. This is quite revealing in its prophecy of millennial Israel, and the king/prince who shall rule from there. These verses clarify as below:

> and I will make them [children of Israel] one nation in the land, on the mountains of Israel; and one king shall be king over them

all; they shall no longer be two nations, nor shall they ever be divided into two kingdoms again.

They shall not defile themselves anymore with their idols, nor with their detestable things, nor with any of their transgressions; but I will deliver them from all their dwelling places in which they have sinned, and will cleanse them. Then they shall be My people, and I will be their God.

David My servant shall be king over them, and they shall all have one shepherd; they shall also walk in My judgments and observe My statutes, and do them.

Then they shall dwell in the land that I have given to Jacob My servant, where your fathers dwelt; and they shall dwell there, they, their children, and their children's children, forever; and My servant David shall be their prince forever.

Moreover I will make a covenant of peace with them, and it shall be an everlasting covenant with them; I will establish them and multiply them, and I will set My sanctuary in their midst forevermore.

My tabernacle also shall be with them; indeed I will be their God, and they shall be My people.

Here we have seen that Jesus, referred to as David, will be King, and He is also called Prince. With regard to the "tabernacle that also shall be with them": the Hebrew word for *tabernacle* used here is *mishkan*. It can mean *temple*, which is the obvious meaning for it here, since we have just read: "and I will set My sanctuary in their midst forevermore." The sanctuary is an inner area of the temple of God. It can also mean *palace, a holy place, and consecrated thing.*

So when God says in Ezekiel 37:27: "My tabernacle also shall be with them;" this leaves little doubt that this is the millennial temple of Ezekiel 40, 41, 42, and 43.

Now, we need to look at Ezekiel 41:1 to see another Hebrew word with a different meaning for tabernacle. This verse shows measurements of the entryway through an end wall into the sanctuary of the millennial temple:

> Then he [an angel] brought me into the sanctuary and measured the doorposts, six cubits wide on one side and six cubits wide on the other side; the width of the tabernacle.

The Hebrew word for *tabernacle*, as used here, is *ohel*, which means *a tent, covering, dwelling place, or home*. The word temple is not one of these meanings. So here we have a tabernacle within a tabernacle. Or, in other words, a dwelling place within a temple.

Now, if we go a little further on to Ezekiel 41:3, we see that the sanctuary within the temple just referred to as God's dwelling place is divided into two halves. The sanctuary, as first measured in Ezekiel 41:2, is forty cubits long and twenty cubits wide. In verse three, the angel enters into the sanctuary and measures the doorposts, the entrance height, and width of a partition wall, which divides the sanctuary into two equal parts. Ezekiel 41:4 tells about one of the rooms created by the partitioning of the sanctuary. It says this:

> He measured the length, twenty cubits; and the width, twenty cubits, beyond the sanctuary; and he said to me, "This is the Most Holy Place." [The 40x20 cubit sanctuary is now a 20x20 cubit sanctuary and a 20x20 cubit Most Holy Place.]

In Ezekiel 43:4–7, we will see another part of the puzzle.

> And the glory of the LORD came into the temple by way of the gate which faces toward the east.

> The Spirit lifted me up and brought me into the inner court; and behold, the glory of the LORD filled the temple.

Then I heard Him speaking to me from the temple, while a man stood beside me.

And He said to me, "Son of man, this is the place of My throne and the place of the soles of My feet, where I will dwell in the midst of the children of Israel forever.

Now, more pieces of the puzzle are in place, and we can see several important details:

1. God's tabernacle (dwelling place) will be within the temple in the "Holy of Holies." This is also the place of His throne and the soles of His feet. In other words, this is where He will be in the midst of His people.

2. This addresses the first part of the tabernacle of David, that being the presence of the Lord God in the midst of His people, as was the case for a time when David was king of Israel. (1 Chronicles 16:1–2)

3. God will be worshipped, and ministered to in His temple.

What we have attempted to do is separate God the Father from God the Son in the Old Testament prophecies pertaining to the millennial kingdom of God on earth. With this done, we can concentrate on Jesus and His part in Old Testament prophecy.

In Zechariah 6:12–13, we saw where "the Man whose name is the BRANCH" will branch out and build the temple. He shall also bear the glory; "and shall sit and rule on His throne; so He shall be a priest on His throne."

We have already seen how He will bear the glory, and will be a priest on His throne, both to the millennial saints and to the remnant House of Israel. One question that stands out: why is Jesus referred to as the BRANCH? This is an Old Testament prophecy, made hundreds of years before the birth of Jesus. For this reason

Jesus did not, at the time of the prophecy, have a human name. God inspired the prophet to use BRANCH to depict the relationship of the Son to the Father. Jesus the Christ was to be a branch on earth of the heavenly Father, just as He was a branch of the Father in heaven. This relationship continues and will never end.

So now we have to ask: what about Jesus? Where will He rule from? Where will His throne be located? Will it be in the tabernacle of David? In what proximity will it be to the temple and God's throne?

The other meaning for the tabernacle of David, that we are looking for is close at hand. Again, Amos 9:11 reminds us:

On that day [Millennial Sabbath] I will raise up the tabernacle of David, which has fallen down, and repair its damages; I will raise up its ruins, and rebuild it as in the days of old.

Strong tells us that the Hebrew word for *tabernacle* used here is *cukkah*. It can mean *tent, tabernacle, cottage, booth or pavilion*. It is obvious then that it does not mean temple. We can therefore assume that Jesus will rule on His throne in another building. But what other building and where? Does the Bible mention another building in context with the temple? The answer is *yes*! The size and location are given, but that is all. This is, nevertheless, enough to pinpoint Jesus, the King's physical millennial proximity to God the Father.

So now, we need to look at Ezekiel again for reference to this other building in two separate verses. We will look at the second notation of the building first as it locates the mystery building in relation to the temple. Ezekiel 42:1 provides the following information:

Then he [angel] brought me out into the outer court, by the way toward the north; and he brought me into the chamber which was opposite the separating courtyard, and which was opposite the building toward the north.

Key words: "opposite the building toward the north." This tells that there will be another building on the north side of the separating courtyard (inner court) of God's temple, just inside the outer court. The other verse that deals with this structure says something about it other than its location. Ezekiel 41:12 provides the following:

The building that faced the separating courtyard at its western end was seventy cubits wide; the wall of the building was five cubits thick all around, and its length ninety cubits.

Here we learn that besides being located just north of the temple, we see that this building will be seventy by ninety cubits, or 105 feet by 135 feet, to make a footprint of 14,175 square feet. This is not a small building, and should it be more than one story, the square footage can be multiplied by the number of stories. With a wall thickness of seven-and-a-half feet, it would appear that this construction could support multiple stories. But where are we going with this? We have seen God prophesied to be enthroned in the temple while the man, Jesus, is said to have His throne established in the tabernacle of David.

By reading Ezekiel 41:13–15, we verify that the temple is 100 cubits by 100 cubits; so then we can see that without question the building discussed above as being opposite the separating courtyard of the temple and toward the north, is another building altogether. Now the question becomes: why would God mention another building, when He was in the process of describing the future temple in great detail? And then, another glaring question: why would another building be located so close to the temple of God? This question becomes especially relevant when we see in Ezekiel 43:12 the following statement:

This is the law of the temple: The whole area surrounding the mountaintop is most holy. Behold, this is the law of the temple.

The conclusion to be drawn here is that the temple will be on the mountain top, and the whole area surrounding it will be most holy. Since this is the case, we must accept the fact that the other building will be most holy as well!

What is this other building? It appears to be the tabernacle of David, *the location of the throne of Jesus Christ!* Acts 15:16 quotes Jesus as saying: "After this [first advent] I will return and will rebuild the tabernacle of David which has fallen down." The Greek word for *tabernacle* here is *skene. Strong's* listed meanings are: *tent, or cloth hut, habitation — tabernacle, or home.* Since *temple* is not included, it is clear then that Jesus is referring to the place of *His throne, His dwelling place, His home!*

Zechariah 6:12–13 now becomes more easily understood as we review the verses:

"Then speak to him, saying, 'Thus says the LORD of hosts, saying: "Behold, the Man whose name is the BRANCH! From His place [Tabernacle of David] He shall branch out, And He shall build the temple of the LORD;

Yes, He shall build the temple of the LORD. He shall bear the glory, and shall sit and rule on His throne; so He shall be a priest on His throne, and the counsel of peace shall be between them both."'"

Here we see that the mystery building figures prominently in the literal fulfillment of both Amos 9:11–12 and Zechariah 6:12–13. First, we know that Jesus will be a priest to God. It will be He who will lead the Israelites in worshipping God on Sabbaths, feasts, new moons, and at all appointed seasons of the House of Israel (Ezekiel

45:17). We also know that Jesus will be a high priest to His millennial saints, representing them to the Father (Hebrews 9:11).

Then too, we see that Jesus "shall sit and rule on His throne." Who shall He rule? He shall rule the House of Israel; He shall rule His saints; and He shall rule and establish law and order in and among all remaining nations on earth.

One final thought concerning the rebuilding of the tabernacle of David: it could be entirely possible that a replica of the original tabernacle pole/tent structure could be constructed and placed within the larger building. The original tabernacle was quite small, having dimensions of 15 feet by 45 feet, not counting the outer courtyard. The outer courtyard was formed by the use of a portable pole-framed fence structure, that when set up measured about 75 feet by 150 feet. The portable tabernacle was placed within this enclosure so that the privacy of a courtyard was provided all around.

With these measurements in mind, it becomes apparent that a replica of the original tabernacle without the outer courtyard could easily be accommodated within the larger, permanent building. The reality is, however, that we do not know if this will be—we only know that it will be possible.

The fact is, this other permanent building does, just as well meet the requirement of the rebuilt tabernacle of David. This is true since the word for tabernacle here can mean dwelling place and home, as well as tent, cottage, booth or pavilion. This other building then, portends to be the home/headquarters/throne of Jesus Christ when He returns to rule Israel, and with the assistance of His saints, all nations of the world.

Jesus' relationship to God will be as a branch of God, and as a servant to God. We see this relationship in Zechariah 3:8, as we read the verse:

For behold, I am bringing forth My Servant the BRANCH.

With Jesus the Son being the Branch of God the Father, He will not only function as servant to God, He will bear the glory of God in His position as mighty King of His personally chosen planet, in His own self-created universe!

Now to address Christ's second and third roles in the millennial kingdom of God. His second role is His relationship to His saints; while His third role involves His governance of the nations. Regarding Christ's relationship to His saints, Revelation 20:6 reveals much in just a few words. It says:

Blessed and holy is he who has part in the first resurrection [Christ's return]. Over such the second death [lake of fire] has no power, but they [saints] shall be priests of God and of Christ, and shall reign with Him a thousand years.

First Corinthians 6:2 provides a view of another relationship of the saints to Christ.

Do you not know that the saints will judge the world?

This, of course, applies to the millennial rule of Christ.

The Greek word for *judge* is *krino*. It has a number of meanings, three of which are: *judge, determine, and decree.* So here we see that the saints, in their incorruptible bodies, will serve Christ as judges. Although the Bible does not elaborate, it seems obvious that saints will go out in the world to all nations representing Christ. God's Word reveals that their service will be in the categories of judge and priest. This makes perfect sense, since all power will flow from the throne of Christ in Israel. The saints will be conduits connecting Christ to every nook and cranny of His worldwide kingdom. Revelation 2:26 gives Jesus' own words on the subject:

And he who overcomes, and keeps My works until the end, to
him I will give power over the nations;

The saints will serve as priests between God/Jesus and the
people. They will also serve as judges in keeping peace and harmony
in assigned locations, and will issue decrees within a framework
of limited authority from Christ (rod of iron).

In Isaiah 2:2–3, the prophet prophesies of Christ's millennial
reign concerning the nations sending representatives to the mountain of the Lord's House for instructions in His ways, in His law, and
in how to walk in His paths. Then verse four informs us that:

He shall judge between the nations, and rebuke many people;
they shall beat their swords into plowshares, and their spears
into pruning hooks; nation shall not lift up sword against nation,
neither shall they learn war anymore (Isaiah 2:4).

Zechariah 14:16–17 expands upon discipline with the authority
Christ will wield over the nations in exposing them to His power,
requiring them to practice specific behavior. These requirements
will form the foundation of the basic tenet upon which the millennial kingdom of God will be built. The verses reveal this:

And it shall come to pass that everyone who is left of all the
nations which came against Jerusalem shall go up from year to
year to worship the King, the LORD of hosts, and to keep the
Feast of Tabernacles.

And it shall be that whichever of the families of the earth do not
come up to Jerusalem to worship the King, the LORD of hosts,
on them there will be no rain.

Revelation 20:1–2 point out an important aspect of Jesus' millennial reign that will bear directly on it:

Then I saw an angel coming down from heaven, having the key
to the bottomless pit and a great chain in his hand.

He laid hold of the dragon, that serpent of old, who is the Devil and Satan, and bound him for a thousand years.

Satan, being bound and absent from the scene this coming millennial Sabbath, does certainly advance potential for peaceful living, brotherly love, cooperation among people and nations, and the worship of Jehovah God and His Son, Jesus Christ. Since the first inhabitants of this new world order will be the survivors of the wrath of God on mankind, they will carry the traits of their sinful human nature with them into the coming period of freedom from satanic influence. These traits will need to be dealt with by the King, thus the need for the rod of iron. As these people mature in the new environment of honesty and empathy for one's neighbors, not buffeted by the sin-provoking wiles of Satan, they will gradually succumb to and appreciate the pure joy of living according to the twelve commandments. (Yes, there are twelve commandments!)

Coming generations will enter a Satan-free environment, influenced instead by the Ten Commandments plus two additional to the first ten. The additional two will become more in evidence as time passes. Mark 12:30–31 give Jesus' words regarding these two additional commandments: "And you shall love the Lord your God with all your heart, with all your soul, with all your mind, and with all your strength. This is the first commandment."

And the second, like it is this: "You shall love your neighbor as yourself." There is no other commandment greater than these."

Here we see that Jesus has used His great authority to add two more commandments to the original ten. Yes—here again—that special number to God, *twelve* commandments!

With restored Israel poised to be the model for the new world, her position therein becomes a point of some interest.

# CHAPTER SIXTY-TWO

# MILLENNIAL ISRAEL

But you, Bethlehem Ephrathah, through you are little among the thousands of Judah, yet out of you shall come forth to Me the One to be Ruler in Israel, whose goings forth are from of old, from everlasting (Micah 5:2).

Micah 5:4 provides a concise view of the Second Person of the Godhead referred to in the verse just read and His position in the millennial kingdom. It tells us this:

And He shall stand and feed His flock in the strength of the LORD, in the majesty of the name of the LORD His God; and they shall abide, for now He shall be great to the ends of the earth.

So Christ, the Anointed One of God, who came down from God, from old, from everlasting, to be born in a manger in the little town of Bethlehem, Israel, was rejected and killed by His own. The force of death could not hold Him, and He rose after three days and three nights (Matthew 12:40), and after showing Himself to many, He returned to the right hand of the Father. His small band of followers regrouped under the newly acquired power of the Holy Spirit and drew many lost souls to Christ. (Jesus and His church; both born in Daniel's seven weeks—49 years.) His harvesters still work in the fields, which are nearly ripe and ready for reaping the Resurrection. See Revelation 14:15–16.

After this, the first harvest, the grapes of wrath will be gathered and tread in the great winepress outside the city of Jerusalem (Revelation 14:17–20).

After these things: "He shall stand and feed His flock in the strength of the Lord,"—"for now He shall be great to the ends of the earth," (Micah 5:4).

His flock will at first consist of the remnant of Israel; and as His field workers, the saints establish His authority, His flock will grow, extending to cover the planet.

Israel will be the seat of Christ's throne and the site of His activities. It seems safe to say that most of the saints will be distributed about earth in their official roles of representing Jesus in His kingdom. Others of this group will, however, be required to stay with Him in a variety of capacities. These are the ones we shall look at here, along with the remnant of Israel in regard to the division of the land, and location of facilities.

In order to gain a more thorough understanding of the millennial kingdom of God, it is necessary to look more closely at the new Israel since it will be the hub of the worldwide kingdom. To do this, we must enter into a section of the Bible that is avoided to a large extent by many readers due to it being considered to be dry reading, complicated, and of little interest.

The truth of the matter, however, is that these chapters, 40 through 48 of the book of Ezekiel, form the basis of most of what can be known of millennial Israel, and to some extent help to better understand the outlying millennial kingdom.

We have already entered this section of the Bible to find that the temple of God, and the tabernacle of David, Christ's throne, will be opposite one another across a courtyard on a mountain top. We found also, the Most Holy Place; the throne room of the glory of God in the temple, and have learned details of how the King/Prince will lead Israel in worshipping God the Father.

Ezekiel 40–48 provide a view of millennial Israel that incredibly seems completely overlooked today, yet is a gold mine for knowing about that which many will soon be involved.

# CHAPTER SIXTY-THREE

# DETAILS OF MILLENNIAL ISRAEL

(Re: Tables # 2, 3 and 4)

Ezekiel 48:8 shows the entire district that will be set aside for the Lord. It is: "25 thousand cubits in width, and in length the same as adjacent tribal portions, from the east side to the west, with the sanctuary in the center." This strip of land will run from the Mediterranean Sea on the west to a point east of the temple mount in Jerusalem equal in length to the distance from the temple mount west to the Mediterranean Sea. For as the verse says: "with the sanctuary [temple] in the center." This locates the east boundary of the total holy district somewhat east of the eastern shore of the Dead Sea, and equal in length to the adjoining tribal portions to the north and to the south. The tribal portions then extend from the same east and west boundaries.

Now we can divide up the total holy district into three parts. In the exact center from east to west will be what we will call the central holy district. This square area is the hub of the total holy district and represents the mountain top. It will be the spiritual focal point, headquarters, and command center of the Prince of Peace in His rule of God's earthly kingdom. The district's modest proportions are seen in Ezekiel 48:20:

> The entire district shall be twenty-five thousand cubits by twenty-five thousand cubits, foursquare. You shall set apart the holy district with the property of the city.

The city will be located within this central holy district, as we will see later. So then, that leaves a large area on each side of the central holy district, making up the balance of the area of the total holy district. What about these two large sections of land; one on each side of the central holy district? Ezekiel 48:21 answers:

> The rest shall belong to the prince, on one side and on the other of the holy district and of the city's property, next to the twenty-five thousand cubits of the holy district as far as the eastern border, and westward next to the twenty-five thousand as far as the western border, adjacent to the tribal portions; it shall belong to the prince. It shall be the holy district, and the sanctuary of the temple shall be in the center.

So the Prince shall own most of the total holy district; everything on each side of the mountain top central holy district, which is a square section in the center of the holy strip. (See Table #2) Now, if the prince (king) were not Jesus, why would he be given all of this holy land? As we will see in Ezekiel 46:16, the land is His inheritance, here is what it says:

> 'Thus says the Lord GOD: "If the prince gives a gift of some of his inheritance to any of his sons, it shall belong to his sons; it is their possession by inheritance."

The point that needs to be kept in mind is this: Jesus will come back as a man, in His incorruptible body true, but will be seen as a man, not a spirit. Here in Ezekiel we see Him being treated as a man, the BRANCH, the Servant of God. God the Father will reside in the temple as Spirit, the glory of the Lord. Jesus will come back as a man, interacting with humans as will His saints, all having incorruptible bodies, while appearing to be physical and human.

Since Christ will appear as human, and will be interacting with humans in the millennial kingdom, He will live as a human, reside, mingle, teach, and rule as a human. The saints that remain with Him will do likewise, thus the need for land and facilities. The saints being referred to as sons by the Old Testament prophet Ezekiel, is a perfectly biblical relationship reference of the saints to Christ. Luke 20:34–36 gives a crystal clear explanation of why Ezekiel referred to the saints in the millennial kingdom as he did. This explanation is given by Jesus Himself and provides the following insight:

> And Jesus answered and said to them, "The sons of this age marry and are given in marriage.
>
> "But those who are counted worthy to attain that age, and the resurrection from the dead, neither marry nor are given in marriage;
>
> "nor can they die anymore, for they are equal to the angels and are sons of God, being sons of the resurrection."

Since Jesus is a Branch of God, in fact, the second God Person, and since the *saints are equal to angels*, and are called sons of God, they are sons of the Prince as well! With the Prince giving a portion of His land to His saints, those to remain in Israel with Him, then requires their manifestation of physical-appearing bodies for functioning on physical land having physical facilities, with a physical-appearing Prince/King, and with physical human beings. The same circumstances will be in effect in the other nations of the world where saints will manifest human form as well. Since they will be dealing with human populations, they must be able to relate to them as representatives of God and of Jesus Christ on human terms.

To carry on one step further with Christ's land, we will look at Ezekiel 46:17:

But if he [the Prince] gives a gift of some of his inheritance to one of his servants, it shall be his until the year of liberty, after which it shall return to the prince. But his inheritance shall belong to his sons; it shall become theirs.

This verse reveals the fact that the principle of liberty will be in force in Israel, culminating in the Year of Jubilee each fiftieth year. Land that was sold or given away will return to its original owner in a universally celebrated Year of Jubilee. This will be a return to the concept of liberty, as practiced by the children of Israel before their Assyrian/Babylonian captivities. This practice prevents the acquisition of great land wealth.

Jesus Christ is the only one able to satisfy the requirements of the position of prince, as spoken of above. No resurrected saint, not even King David himself can fulfill the requirements set forth for the *Branch*. The most basic reason of all is that the resurrected saints, being like angels, not being given in marriage or marrying, will not be procreating, to produce sons to inherit land. The saints, resurrected and glorified, being called sons of God, relate as sons to God, to the Second Person of the Godhead, Jesus Christ, not to other resurrected and glorified saints, King David included.

We will see that Ezekiel refers to other princes also—*prince* in Hebrew means *one in a leadership position*. This reference by God through Ezekiel relates to division of the land among twelve tribes. (The thirteenth tribe, Levi, being priests and temple workers, will occupy the central holy district.)

In Ezekiel 45:7 we saw that the Prince will receive the portion of land on each side of the central holy district—that twenty-five thousand cubit, foursquare mountain top section at the center of the total holy district. (See Table #2) Now, for a view of the other princes, we shall read Ezekiel 45:8–9:

The land shall be his [Prince's] possession in Israel; and My princes shall no more oppress My people, but they shall give the rest of the land to the house of Israel, according to their tribes.

'Thus says the Lord GOD: "Enough, O princes of Israel! Remove violence and plundering, execute justice and righteousness, and stop dispossessing My people," says the Lord GOD.

In verse seven we saw that the context of the verse separated the Prince (Jesus), from the author of the verse (God the Father), in providing the Prince with a certain land allotment within the total holy district of millennial Israel.

In verse eight, God says: "My princes shall no more oppress My people." These princes (meaning leaders) then are of His people; leaders of remnant Israel, carrying with them into the kingdom of God their intact sinful nature at this early stage of the new beginning.

Then again, in verse nine, we see God speaking:

'Thus says the Lord GOD: "Enough, O princes [leaders] of Israel!" God verifies that these are, indeed, princes of Israel; human leaders of the Jewish remnant, having human emotions and the sinful human nature still functioning as they embark upon a new way of life; not as yet completely understood!

So God, in His endless wisdom, knowing the beginning from the end, is telling us through Ezekiel of human relations problems that will develop between some of the Jewish remnant and their human leaders. The difficulty will arise due to disputes over ownership of the land, as spoken of in Ezekiel 48:1-7, and detailed in Ezekiel 45:8-9. The disputes also seem to involve the plundering of the value of produce derived from the land, resulting in dispossession of the people's right to fair measurements, as seen in verses 10–12. These verses deal with fair measurements for agricultural products, apparently to be administered by these Jewish leaders.

The division of the land among the tribes of Israel is spoken of in Ezekiel 45:8, where we read again:

> The land shall be his possession in Israel; and My princes shall no more oppress My people, but they shall give the rest of the land to the house of Israel, according to their tribes. (See Table #2)

The tribes in early Israel, during and after the Exodus, each had a tribal leader who exercised a degree of control over the tribe. It seems that this system will again be used in the establishment of millennial Israel as well. And as was the case in early Israel in seeing that God's directions as to tribal boundaries were adhered to, so it will be again, that tribal leaders will be involved in following God's directions as to boundary locations. Just what the actual title of these leaders will be becomes quite clear when we look at the meanings of the Hebrew word for prince and princes, as rendered by *Strong's Concordance*. The Hebrew word for *prince* and *princes*, as used by Ezekiel in these verses is *nasiy*. This word has no less than eleven meanings: *exalted one, king, sheik, rising mist, captain, chief, cloud, governor, prince, ruler, and vapor.*

So, we quickly see that of the eleven possibilities, *governor* fits the princes of Israel and *king* applies to the Prince, Jesus Christ. We can see as well that the Hebrew word *nasiy* has several meanings for the *glory of God*, which are *rising mist, cloud, and vapor*. These are the mediums through which God chooses to show Himself to His people separate from His Branch, Jesus Christ.

Viewing millennial Israel could not be complete without a look at millennial Jerusalem. One thing that we shall notice is that the rebuilt city will be considerably smaller than the Jerusalem of today. How do we know this? Ezekiel gives the new measurements and tells us its new name.

# CHAPTER SIXTY-FOUR

# MILLENNIAL JERUSALEM— RENAMED "THE LORD IS THERE"!

The city will be within the twenty-five thousand cubit square mountain top central holy district. It, along with its eastern and western adjacent cropland, will account for the entire southern portion of the central holy district. This strip of land will be five thousand cubits wide by twenty-five thousand cubits long. (See Tables #3 and #4)

Ezekiel 45:6 provides for the entire strip of city property, both for the city and its adjacent cropland in the following statement:

> You shall appoint as the property of the city an area five thousand cubits wide and twenty-five thousand long, adjacent to the district of the holy portion [property of the priests, Levites]; it shall belong to the whole house of Israel.

Ezekiel 48:15 describes the city property in somewhat more detail, as we see here:

> The five thousand cubits in width that remain, along the edge of the twenty-five thousand [property of the priests, Levites], shall be for general use by the city, for dwellings and common-land; and the city shall be in the center.

Verses 16 and 17 deal with the city proper being four thousand five hundred cubits square, with a common area two hundred fifty cubits wide all around it. This makes the city proper with its common area all around, five thousand cubits square, or equivalent to just over two square miles in area.

Verse 18 explains the two strips of cropland; five thousand cubits wide by ten thousand cubits long, one on each side of the city:

> The rest of the length, alongside the district of the holy section, shall be ten thousand cubits to the east and ten thousand to the west. It shall be adjacent to the district of the holy section [property of the Levites], and its produce shall be food for the workers of the city.

Verse 19 continues:

> The workers of the city, from all the tribes of Israel, shall cultivate it.

God gave Ezekiel this vision of millennial Israel for him to carefully comprehend; then pass on the details to the remnant survivors: "Son of Man, look with your eyes and hear with your ears, and fix your mind on everything I show you; for you were brought here so that I might show them to you. Declare to the House of Israel everything you see" (Ezekiel 40:4).

It is here that we see written instructions to the House of Israel, directly from God, providing minute details and instructions on how to lay out the tribal land, the holy portions for the priests, the Levites, the Prince, and the city. We see also the precise measurements given for the temple, with basic dimensions for the other building across the courtyard from the temple, which we have come to see as being the tabernacle of David, the throne/home of Jesus Christ. (All located on the level mountain top that shortly before had been the city of Jerusalem).

Another statement of interest concerning the city is found in Ezekiel 40:2, which informs us:

> In the visions of God He took me into the land of Israel and set me on a very high mountain; on it toward the south was something like the structure of a city.

This city then, being on the south side of the mountain top will be most holy.

Now, about the mountain itself; it is not there now. So, how will it get there? Revelation 16:18–19 provide a big clue! As we read these verses we see the answer forming before us:

> And there were noises and thunderings and lightnings; and there was a great earthquake, such a mighty and great earthquake as had not occurred since men were on the earth.

> Now the great city [Jerusalem] was divided into three parts [A part for each the Priests, Levites, and the city], and the cities of the nations fell. [Fourth fragment at fifth trumpet!]

This, then, will be the largest magnitude earthquake to ever strike earth. Besides the city of Jerusalem being divided, Zechariah 14:10 tells of an occurrence that is coincidental with the earthquake, and focuses on a section of the Priest's part, which will be one of the raised up three parts that Jerusalem will later be divided into. It provides this insight:

> All the land shall be turned into a plain from Geba [north] to Rimmon south of Jerusalem. Jerusalem shall be raised up and inhabited in her place from Benjamin's Gate to the place of the First Gate and the Corner Gate, and from the Tower of Hananeel to the king's winepresses.

These boundaries represent the restricted area of the current temple mount. This locates the millennial temple to the north of the new city, which shall be situated on the south of the new mountain top that shortly before will have been the current city of Jerusalem, raised up to become the mountain of the Lord's house! (See Table #4)

So, prophets of the Bible, living in greatly different time periods, and under varying circumstances, have brought us God's truth. They confronted God's people with His Word for them, which after having been recorded in the Scriptures, now serves as road signs to this last generation, giving ample evidence that not only is God's plan for His first phase in its last stages, but that the end of the road is just ahead!

The Bible, graciously provided by a loving heavenly Father, yet so denigrated, maligned, and ignored by so many, is a treasure-trove of answers to difficult questions. It, in fact, holds the solutions to mankind's most urgent challenges in facing the reality of an uncertain future. A big difference between Christians and those who do not follow Christ is that Christians know what the future holds; that is, the ultimate future, and look forward to it. Non-believers, however, fear the future and unfortunately, as we have so vividly seen, their fears are justified and entirely well founded.

Israel will be the center of the millennial world. This is fact, because God's presence will be there; God's King, Jesus Christ, will rule from there; and God's chosen nation, Israel, will practice a way of life established in detail by God Himself that will set the standard for the entire world!

The Israelites failed God in their first tenure of the land, which He had promised their fathers. This time they shall not fail. Satan will be removed from the scene, and Christ's saints, His ambassadors, will be established worldwide in leadership positions. They will convey Christ's love, His law, and His power to a newly open-minded world. All on earth will have seen God's power, and will have a healthy respect for it. Peace and goodwill will rise to the surface, and the majesty of the Prince of Peace shall be evident throughout His worldwide kingdom.

If you would like to be included in this peace corps of princes to be charged with establishing a new paradigm on earth, conceived and ordained in heaven, and to be spiritually empowered to meet and exceed demands of the job, begin building your resume now! Since you will be involved in furthering the King's government within established guidelines, but with great latitude for freedom to work within set parameters of the job description, it is recommended that applicants begin to prepare early. There are no limits on who can apply, or how many; as there are openings for all until the vacancy counter is closed; however, serious dangers are prevalent, as already discussed, in waiting until the last minute.

Please do not become complacent about this free gift of grace, so agonizingly purchased by Jesus Christ that allows this window of opportunity to exist. Many have been preparing for most of their lives for their part in this select group; however, late comers receive the same consideration for their efforts as do the early starters! Only one criterion is required for acceptance into an entry level position; that being: loyalty to the King. You are strongly encouraged to begin putting into practice, this important attribute now (which equates with worship), as only those who exhibit this quality will qualify to be chosen for placement.

One admonition: Just being a good person does not meet the qualifications—loyalty, meaning faithful, true to, and allegiance to the King, as previously discussed are what count!

Do not be misled by a cunning, modern deception that teaches that there is no good and evil (evil meaning sin), but only right and wrong. The flawed logic of this illusion provides the practitioner cart blanch authority to establish his own standards for what is right and what is wrong. This places man at odds with the King, a hopeless plight to be avoided at all costs!

There is an open position waiting for each one of us in the very soon to come kingdom of God on earth. It is the King's desire to say to you upon your entry into His earthly kingdom—*well done good and faithful servant!*

Isaiah, by God's Holy Spirit, was given a glimpse of the millennial Sabbath, whereby he was caused to prophesy long before the fact, the underlying principle of this soon-to-be kingdom of God. Isaiah 11:6–9 provides examples of brotherhood, that whether actual or symbolic, we have yet to learn. He tells us this:

> The wolf also shall dwell with the lamb, the leopard shall lie down with the young goat, the calf and the young lion and the fatling together; and a little child shall lead them.

> The cow and the bear shall graze; their young ones shall lie down together; and the lion shall eat straw like the ox.

> The nursing child shall play by the cobra's hole, and the weaned child shall put his hand in the viper's den.

> They shall not hurt nor destroy in all My holy mountain, for the earth shall be full of the knowledge of the LORD as the waters cover the sea.

Undeniably, another prophecy foretelling the new trends of brotherly love, forbearance, kindness, and cooperation that will mark the millennial Kingdom of God. A time devoid of satanic influence, and as full of the knowledge of the Lord as the waters fill the sea.

Israel is God's lightning rod for prophecy fulfillment. Almost all Bible end time prophecy touches Israel in one way or another. Israel then, for those interested in future world events, is a barometer by which to read the various pressures that are in the process of building worldwide. Pressures that include conflicting national political attitudes, social and economic disparity, the growing world energy crisis, ecological constraints, the growing water crisis, the growing nuclear proliferation crisis, the growing communicable disease crisis, and, of course, the accelerating religious/terrorist crisis!

All these pressures and others now have, or will have a short-term impact upon tiny Israel. At present, the main pressures to impact the nation are political, religious/terror, and economic disparity between Israel and Palestinians. Clouding the near future, we can add a serious water shortage, and the ominous proliferation of nuclear technology into and out of Iran, which is said to have delivery systems in an advanced stage of development. At this writing, Iraq has been neutralized by America with assistance from Britain, backed by a coalition of supporting nations; some unnamed. The United Nations is presently rendered irrelevant by unrestrained factionalism; its humiliating Iraq failure and the oil for food problem will serve to point up this fact and the need for strong leadership. A new leader awaits over the near horizon.

While on this subject, a recent news report (9/6/04) is being mentioned here, which may qualify as a high-water mark in last days Bible prophecy fulfillment. Seemingly, the world has no knowledge of its potential importance in serving to establish this time in which we live as that time which the Bible so unerringly points to.

The underlying prophecy for this current possible milestone event is found in Revelation 13:2–3. It pertains to one we call Antichrist, and says this:

> "Now the beast which I saw [with seven heads] was like a leopard, his feet were like the feet of a bear, and his mouth was like the mouth of a lion. And the dragon gave him his power, his throne, and great authority.

> I saw one of his heads as if it had been mortally wounded, and his deadly wound was healed. And all the world marveled and followed the beast."

As we know, the fifth head of this beast represents the Seleucid dynasty of the ancient divided (leopard) Greek empire and one of its kings, (Antiochus IV Epiphanes). The Bible says that Antiochus, in his second life as Antichrist, will wield worldly power. We understand the meaning of the beast's mouth being like a lion, (Babylonian empire), and its feet like feet of a bear (Medo-Persian empire); the lion conquered by the bear, and the bear conquered by the leopard, with both empire's heredity traits passing on to the leopard.

Revelation 13:3 says that one of the beast's heads would be mortally wounded and then healed, and all the world marveled and followed the beast. There is no question that the mortally wounded head is the primary fifth head, that of the leopard representing the ancient Greek empire and its notorious king, who in his second life is no less than he who is known as the antichrist! The verse does not imply a head wound as some believe, but rather that the man himself, who is represented by the head to receive the wound, was to be wounded unto death.

Question: How would he be wounded? For the answer, we must look at the Greek word for wounded. Strong renders this word as "sphazo", a primary verb with several meanings. One (to butcher), another (to slaughter); (to maim violently), (kill, slay), (wound).

So now to the point: On September 6, 2004 news coverage was all about one of America's previous presidents having had quadruple, bypass heart surgery. This charismatic, prior United States president died on the operating table, and was physically dead for one hour while his bodily functions were kept going by modern medical technology! But you probably already knew this as it was widely reported.

Now back to the word wounded, as in mortally wounded. Since medical surgery was not in the common vocabulary 2,000 years ago, it is not surprising that the Greek word meaning to butcher, would have been used to describe the incident leading to the death of the person represented by the beast. Anyone who knows anything about open-heart surgery, can readily relate it to a butcher cutting into flesh and bone. This necessary procedure to expose the blocked arteries in the vicinity of the heart, in today's modern medicine, is a strict procedural science with no tolerance for error; and those who practice it are highly qualified surgeons with impeccable credentials. They are in fact, fully prepared with life support in case it becomes needed.

This is all true of modern scientific medicine, and of course Jesus knew all of this when He inspired the apostle John to write it down for future generations.

Now, about the world marveling and following the beast after this latest triumph over adversity (an hour long period of death) as pointed to in Revelation 13:3: The marveling has been a fact for some time, however, with this latest event, hardly considered a miracle by today's standards; two thousand years ago—it would be one! The world likes this person and marvels at his ability to persevere and triumph over calamitous circumstances. So it would seem that he should yet have an active and important part in coming world affairs, as it becomes more and more apparent that the world judges qualifications by superficial values.

It has become well known that this man had been actively seeking the currently lackluster, but potentially highly prestigious office of Secretary General of the United Nations. Will he be successful? As we know, a serious obstacle has been thrown up in his path (another appointed to the post). Will he become beneficiary of it, or go on to an entirely different means of achieving the goal of world power? We will know soon enough.

It is suggested that you read all of Revelation 13, as it will apprise you of certain near term details of the end time that are rapidly coming our way! Now, back to modern Israel.

Israel and Jerusalem presently are flash points for world opinion, world political posturing, and Middle East religious strife. The UN may have an expanding role in overseeing a new government in Iraq. This would serve to advance its standing in assisting to settle the Israel/Palestinian problem. The final solution will include partial or total Palestinian control of East Jerusalem, and their shared oversight with Israel of the temple mount. These are Bible terms to be included later in the already begun peace accord between Israel and her enemies. With Jerusalem again divided, and East Jerusalem subject to Palestinian control and UN oversight, this will lead to fulfillment of Revelation 11:2, which states: "And they [Gentiles] will tread the holy city underfoot for forty-two months." This three-and-one-half years, we will recall, shall be instituted well after the already commenced peace agreement with likely forced termination of Palestinian control sometime before the end of Antichrist's 1,290 days in the temple of God. This UN treachery would not go unnoticed nor unpunished at the first opportunity.

Now we will look one more time at how God Almighty feels about Israel, and His final words on the subject. Ezekiel 34:26 provides this view:

> I will make them [millennial Israel] and the places all around My hill a blessing; and I will cause showers to come down in their season; there shall be showers of blessing.

And Ezekiel 34:23–24 says:

> I will establish one shepherd over them, and he shall feed them; My servant David. He shall feed them and be their shepherd.

> And I, the LORD, will be their God, and My servant David a prince among them; I, the LORD, have spoken.

Here in this writing we have seen the words of God displayed in various future settings, and have seen how they will influence the near term as well as the eternal future of this planet. We have seen also that the Bible's prophecy writers were unlike historians of today who, having a window of history to peer through, still sometimes don't get it right.

As we have observed, there are common threads running through groups of Bible prophecies given by various prophets. These common threads, or similar subject matter, bind the prophecies one to the other by means of one adding support to another. Instead of just one prophet giving prophetic enlightenment on a subject, for example: The "dark and cloudy Day of the Lord," we find a number of various prophets in vastly different time periods, both in the Old and New Testaments, providing their own versions of the same Holy Spirit inspired insight of this awesome near future occurrence.

The Holy Bible was not written by a group of men all cooperating to produce a slick, easy-to-follow format of coming world events for the casual reader to pick up, give a cursory look, and thereby know God's plan for mankind. Quite clearly, the opposite is true.

It is not surprising that there is so much misinformation being put forward today in the realm of Bible prophecy. Jesus knew this would happen. He said it would in Matthew 24:11:

"Then [end time] many false prophets will rise up and deceive many. [Prophecy fulfilled in our time!]

Bible prophecy springs directly from the complex mind of God by way of His Holy Spirit interacting with the prophets. In many instances, these prophets had no idea of what the strange communications meant. The Bible and its projections were not intended to be an easy read. Jesus' earthly ministry is a good example of it, though: "seeing they do not see, and hearing they do not hear" (Matthew 13:13). Jesus hid much from the people, while explaining it in detail to His disciples. He did this for two reasons. First, to prepare the disciples to start His church with authority. Second, the primary principle underlying the New Covenant to be written in His blood was not yet accomplished. After His glorification, this fundamental truth, a new kind of *grace* provided by God to the new believer, subsequent to repentance, was greatly dependent upon *faith*. Believers in Jesus as the Son of God and the Author of the New Covenant must believe by *Faith. No faith, no grace!* This was then proclaimed to all who would listen by His disciples.

Jesus was about to turn the religious life of new followers up-side-down with—after repentance, salvation by God's Grace only through faith. Jesus' sacrifice and glorification *had to be a fact,* which would and did galvanize His disciples to teach and followers to believe by *faith*!

In order for faith to function effectively, it must transcend doubt; or the process is not the working of faith at all, but rather, a processing of inputs that result in the formation of knowledge. Limited inputs will result in an output of limited knowledge. Incorrect, or untrue, inputs always a threat, result in compromised understanding. It is so true, that where some believe in their carefully processed knowledge, they are actually believing a lie. Evolution is too good an example not to use here, but; the fact is, what starts out incorrect ends up that way. God is the author of truth; man, the collector of knowledge. God is *perfect*: man is *not*. Faith is never lost on God; so trust in God's Word, not man's compromised knowledge!

Jesus gave His disciples a lesson in faith found in the book of John. Jesus, after His resurrection, showed Himself to some of His disciples. Thomas was not among them. They later told him, and Thomas responded that he would not believe unless he could put his finger in the nail holes, and his hand into the hole in Christ's side. Later, Jesus appeared to them again. This time, Thomas was there. Jesus told Thomas to put his finger into a nail wound, and his hand into the hole in His side. John 20:28 gives Thomas' reply: "And Thomas answered and said to Him, 'My Lord and my God!'"

Verse 29 gives Christ's response: "Thomas, because you have seen Me, you believed. Blessed are those who have not seen and yet have believed."

Thomas believed because he had seen—seeing is believing, as the saying goes. As Jesus said: "Blessed are those who have not seen and yet have believed." Blessed by God's *grace* because of their faith—to escape the eternal, punishing penalty of sin—by Jesus' selfless sacrifice on the cross!

Bible prophecy being, at times, difficult to comprehend, must have its truth searched out; then believed by faith!

# CHAPTER SIXTY-FIVE

# THE END OF ONE GRACE, AND BEGINNING OF ANOTHER

Here we observe a transition from nearly two thousand years of God's grace for Christians being terminated at closing of the sixth day, then replaced by a different kind of grace for the survivors entering the Sabbath rest. God's law will be reinstated and not only encouraged, but made a requirement the world over!

Regarding grace: there are several meanings for the Hebrew word for *grace*: *chen*, one being *favor*, another is *kindness*. With this in mind, we will look at Zechariah 12:10, which tells of another act of grace or favor. The context is the second coming of Jesus Christ, when the Jews will see their true Messiah coming on the clouds of heaven with power and great glory (Matthew 24:30). Zechariah 12:10 provides the details:

> And I will pour on the house of David and on the inhabitants of Jerusalem the Spirit of grace and supplication; then they will look on Me whom they have pierced. Yes, they will mourn for Him as one mourns for his only son, and grieve for Him as one grieves for a firstborn.

Knowing that the Hebrew word for grace can mean kindness and favor, we now must look closely at the Hebrew word for supplication.

Strong shows the word as being *tachanuwn*. It means *entreaty, and earnest prayer*. Now we can see that what Zechariah 12:10 is saying is this: when Christ returns, He will show kindness and favor to His people by instilling in them a spirit of supplication, that is, they will entreat or call on God through earnest prayer. Though unstated in the verse, it is obvious that the supplication will be for Jesus/God to forgive them and take them to be His own. This is, of course, what He will do. He will by Michael, see that the remnant of one-third is brought miraculously through the tragedy of Armageddon; then back into their own land. (Zechariah 13:8–9.)

This is borne out in Zechariah 13:1, which says:

> In that day a fountain shall be opened for the house of David and for the inhabitants of Jerusalem, for sin and for uncleanness.

The above references God's law, which will be in force in the millennial kingdom. Our period of *grace* as we now know it will be over; and Satan will not be a factor until the end of the thousand years. Those entering the kingdom, however, will bring with them their sinful nature, thus the need for a means of atonement for unintentional sin. Since our finite period of grace will have ended, the need for a regimented form of worshipping God the Father will have become necessary.

God has details for the solution to this need well established and in writing. They can be found in Ezekiel 44 and 46. They provide a picture of a king, called prince, who will lead the people in worshipping God the Father at all feasts and other special times. Details covering duties of the temple priests, and the division of the tribe of Levi into two groups, based on heredity, are included as well. Levites descended from the priest Zadok will minister directly to God. The other Levites will serve as temple ministers. These will have routine duties, but will not minister to God.

While Ezekiel 44 deals generally with duties of the temple priests, verses 23 and 24 tell of the relationship that the priests will have with the people:

And they shall teach My people the difference between the holy and the unholy, and cause them to discern between the unclean and the clean.

In controversy they shall stand as judges, and judge it according to My judgments. They shall keep My laws and My statutes in all My appointed meetings, and they shall hallow My Sabbaths.

It is quite clear that the grace to be shown to inhabitants of the millennial kingdom will be kindness tempered with firmness in requiring adherence to God's law. This is an entirely different grace than that which we now enjoy, which was procured by Jesus on the cross and will soon expire!

Zechariah 2:10–11 tell us this:

"Sing and rejoice, O daughter of Zion! For behold, I am coming and I will dwell in your midst," says the LORD.

"Many nations shall be joined to the LORD in that day, and they shall become My people. And I will dwell in your midst. Then you will know that the LORD of hosts has sent Me to you."

This is the God person Jesus speaking, and His saints shall minister to the nations; those nations said to be "joined to the Lord in that day." These shall be joined by way of the saints. Recall that Jesus will rule with a rod of iron. His law will go out to the nations by the saints, and Israel will be the seat of power and shall set the example for the world.

# CHAPTER SIXTY-SIX

# GOD'S RECLAMATION PROJECT

Jesus' return will result in cleaning up of circumstances we refer to as the human condition, a running sore, festering badly. This, in effect, will be a reclamation project; the restoration of humanity to its original intent. The Bible tells of a geographical reclamation project to be undertaken by God in the millennial kingdom that, in a way, can be looked at as a parallel on a tiny scale to the cleaning up of mankind by Jesus Christ, in store for our rapidly approaching, soon-to-arrive, biblically projected future!

This parallel reclamation project is alluded to by the prophet Joel in chapter 3, verse 18, where he says:

> And it will come to pass in that day that the mountains shall drip with new wine, the hills shall flow with milk, and all the brooks of Judah shall be flooded with water; a fountain shall flow from the house of the LORD and water the Valley of Acacias.

Now, with that beginning, Ezekiel 47 will provide all the details. Verse 1 tells where the water of the fountain comes from:

Then he [angel] brought me back to the door of the temple; and there was water, flowing from under the threshold of the temple toward the east, for the front of the temple faced east; the water was flowing from under the right side of the temple, south of the altar. [From the Holy of Holies, Ezekiel 47:12.]

Verse 3 expands further on the water of this fountain:

And when the man went out to the east with the line in his hand, he measured one thousand cubits, and he brought me through the waters; the water came up to my ankles (Ezekiel 47:3).

Verses 4 and 5 carry on with the water capacity of the flow, by giving the following details:

Again he measured one thousand and brought me through the waters; the water came up to my knees. Again he measured one thousand and brought me through; the water came up to my waist.

Again he measured one thousand, and it was a river that I could not cross; for the water was too deep, water in which one must swim, a river that could not be crossed (Ezekiel 47:4–5).

Verses 6, 7, and 8 begin the reclamation project:

He said to me, "Son of man, have you seen this?" Then he brought me and returned me to the bank of the river.

When I returned, there, along the bank of the river, were very many trees on one side and the other.

Then he said to me: "This water flows toward the eastern region, goes down into the valley, and enters the sea. When it reaches the sea, its waters are healed (Ezekiel 47:6–8).

Now here we see that the fountain that will originate from under the right side of the temple south of the altar will become a deep river, flow through a valley and enter the Dead Sea. Upon the river entering the sea, the sea's bitter, high salt content will decline to support fish of moderate salt tolerance, similar to those found in the Mediterranean Sea, being no longer poisonous to fish and plant life. This cleanup of the Dead Sea will not result just because a fresh water river flows into it. As we know, the Jordan River, which is fresh water, flows into the Dead Sea with the result that the sea's water remains extremely salty due to it having no outlet. It is evaporation that maintains the water level of the sea within its banks; not an outflow.

Ezekiel 47:9–12 continues with the plan for restoration of this parched and salt deadened locale:

> And it shall be that every living thing that moves, wherever the rivers go, will live. There will be a very great multitude of fish, because these waters go there; for they will be healed, and everything will live wherever the river goes.

> It shall be that fishermen will stand by it from En Gedi to En Eglaim; they will be places for spreading their nets. Their fish will be of the same kinds as the fish of the Great Sea, exceedingly many.

> But its swamps and marshes will not be healed; they will be given over to salt.

> Along the bank of the river, on this side and that, will grow all kinds of trees used for food; their leaves will not wither, and their fruit will not fail. They will bear fruit every month, because their water flows from the sanctuary. Their fruit will be for food, and their leaves for medicine.

Here we have an excellent example of God in action when the source of sin is removed from the earth. Verse nine refers to wherever the rivers go, indicating that the river branches out into several rivers, possibly forming a large multi-river delta at its entry to the Dead Sea. One strong indication that this may be true is that verse ten says "It shall be that fishermen will stand by it [river] from En Gedi to En Eglaim." En Gedi is about halfway down the west shore of the Dead Sea, and En Eglaim is at the extreme southeast end of the sea. This is a distance of approximately thirty miles from one point to the other.

We see, too, in verse eleven that the sea's swamps and marches will not be healed: "They will be given over to salt." It seems that there could be two reasons for this. First, one of the few good things about the Dead Sea as it presently exists is that it is an excellent source of salt. Leaving the marshes and swamps bathed in salt would provide a local source of this important mineral in Israel. Second, it could be God's intention that this area remain a contrast, a visual sign to Israel and the world of God's cleansing presence while retaining a symbolic wormhole in its midst. Though the worm will be gone, evidence of its damaging earlier presence will linger!

The balance of Ezekiel 47 and most of chapter 48 deal with the division of the land among the tribes of Israel and that which is to be set aside for the holy portion. See Tables 2, 3 and 4 for details. By studying Table #2, it becomes immediately apparent that millennial Israel will be considerably larger than Israel is today. It will contain some land east of the Jordan River and the Dead Sea that it had controlled in the kingdom years under King David and later under his son Solomon.

We will close this study with two reminders, which, if understood, will clarify Christ's intent for the coming millennial kingdom years. First, in Matthew 5:17–18, He said:

Do not think that I came to destroy the Law or the Prophets. I did not come to destroy but to fulfill.

For assuredly, I say to you, till heaven and earth pass away, one jot or one tittle will by no means pass from the law till all is fulfilled.

This seemingly paradoxical statement largely explains Jesus' mission right from the beginning on through to the onset of eternity, details of which are outlined here:

1. Jesus fulfilled the prophets (prophecies of the Messiah). From His prophesied birth in Bethlehem (Micah 5:2), and His being given as a covenant to the people (Israel) and as a light to the Gentiles (Isaiah 42:6), to His destiny with death, to suffer and die in fulfillment of His earthly mission (Isaiah 53), that is, to be: "cut off" (Daniel 9:26).

2. Jesus' new covenant did not destroy the Law of Moses (Ten Commandments), but rather replaced certain statutes and judgments (Deuteronomy 4:13–14) that had been added to the first covenant (Ten Commandments, Law). According to the words of Jesus Christ Himself (Matthew 5:18), not one jot or tittle (smallest stroke of a Hebrew letter) would pass from the Law (Ten Commandments) until heaven and earth passed away. We have seen that when the heaven and earth, as we know them, shall pass away, the New Jerusalem will be in place, and eternity will be underway. This will end the Law and begin the enhancement of the relationship with Christ for residents of the new heaven that only Christians now, in a limited way, enjoy. This will be an ongoing, never-ending relationship of development, of purpose, and of achievement!

Christ did not destroy the Law, but rather, temporarily nullified certain extraneous statutes and judgments that were attached to, but were not part of the first covenant (Law). How was this selective adjustment to the Law accomplished? For the answer, we must read Hebrews 9:13–15:

For if the blood of bulls and goats and the ashes of a heifer, sprinkling the unclean, sanctifies for the purifying of the flesh, how much more shall the blood of Christ, who through the eternal Spirit offered Himself without spot to God, cleanse your conscience from dead works to serve the living God?

And for this reason He is the Mediator of the new covenant, by means of death, for the redemption of the transgressions under the first [old] covenant, that those who are called may receive the promise of the eternal inheritance.

Here, we see that Jesus Christ replaced certain statutes and judgments that were attached to the law and that were loosely called Law. They were, in fact, appendages to the Law, *and were being used for redemption from sin!* Jesus replaced these requirements by shedding His own blood, thus nullifying them. As Mediator of the new covenant, He accomplished this so that those who are called (hear the gospel) may be chosen. The chosen have repented of their sins and accept Jesus as Lord and Savior! They, then receive the promise of the eternal inheritance, eternal life with Christ.

The fact is, God considers all people dead in their sins. This sad reality was begun with Adam's fall and carries on down through history, with its ultimate conclusion scheduled for the Great White Throne Judgment at the end of the millennial Sabbath (Revelation 20:11–15). Sacrificing for atonement of sin, in effect, started with Adam and Eve. Before Adam and Eve's sin in the Garden of Eden, they were naked and were not ashamed (Genesis 2:25). After their sin, they sewed fig leaves together for coverings Genesis 3:7). God, however, in Genesis 3:21, made tunics for them from skins to cover their shame. The shedding of the blood of an acceptable animal was agreeable with God as a substitute for the death of the sinful human, providing that repentance on the part of he or she who sacrificed was an integral part of the act of sacrificing.

Jesus Christ, Son of God, Second Person of the Godhead, provided a better way. Hebrews 4:15–16 explains:

For we do not have a High Priest who cannot sympathize with our weaknesses, but was in all points tempted as we are, yet without sin.

Let us therefore come boldly to the throne of grace that we may
obtain mercy and find grace to help in time of need.

The *grace* of God's forgiveness is what Jesus has provided for
those who will accept it. Some do not because they believe that
the Old Covenant Law precludes the substitutional New Covenant.
They draw this conclusion based not on fact, but rather, on delusion. (See Isaiah 66:4.) They do not accept the author of the New
Covenant for who He is; their long-awaited Messiah. In spite of
this, as we have seen repeatedly in this work, there are those in this
group whom God will bring into the millennial kingdom alive and
will change their hearts, make His abode in their midst, be their
God, and they shall follow the Old Covenant of their fathers under
the direction of Jesus Christ their Messiah and King (Daniel 12:1;
Ezekiel 45:16–17). There are, though, some of the above who hear,
do believe, and join the saints!

All today have the opportunity to come to Christ and accept
His saving grace, a grace accomplished on the cross, and made
available to all who will reach out and accept it. This, however, is
a limited time offer as Jesus said in Matthew 24:14:

And this gospel of the kingdom will be preached in all the world
as a witness to all the nations, and then the end will come.

The preaching is still underway, but when all have heard, the
end will come! A sidelight on this spreading of the gospel: communications technology is highly refined today, with many satellites
circling the earth. Also, many missionary outreaches are hard at
work training indigenous pastors, preaching, teaching, and caring
for the physical and spiritual needs of the lost. All will soon have
heard!

Our second reminder then, of Christ's intent for the coming
millennial kingdom of God, rests in the reality of the Law (Ten
Commandments) and its companion statutes and judgments. With
the Law in force throughout the millennial kingdom's entire one

thousand year existence, the House of Israel and the Gentile nations will clearly see the difference between the Old and the New Covenants. The saints will be a constant and vivid reminder of the superiority of the New Covenant, *which shall supremely reign throughout the eternal kingdom!*

With all having heard, then those entering into the millennial Sabbath will have rejected Jesus' gospel, the good news of God's grace, attainable only by belief in Jesus Christ. They will have demonstrated that Christ's sacrificial death on the cross had no meaning for them. With Jesus having said Himself that He did not come to destroy the Law, the Ten Commandments, and we have seen that He did not, then it becomes apparent that they are still intact. *They are still functional; they are still God's law; and they now await all those who will enter into the new age of God's millennial kingdom!*

Now, God being a just God, requires that we expect no less than that life in His Sabbath rest will be governed by His Law, the Ten Commandments, administrably modified by a group of statutes and judgments, that Jesus once replaced as a sacrificial gift to mankind. Since unintentional sin will be a fact of life, some might call it poetic justice that Jesus Christ, with assistance from His saints, will administer God's Law in full measure and with supreme authority!

The removal of satanic/demonic force from the scene of human existence will allow Christ's two additional commandments to surface unhindered, and so to flourish without any necessity of enforcement. Love God and Love Your Neighbor will become passwords to live by and the passport to *eternal glory!*

# CHAPTER SIXTY-SEVEN

# THE FINAL DAYS OF GOD'S MILLENNIAL KINGDOM

God's millennial kingdom, as we know, will end after one thousand years. The prophesied circumstances of this ending sound somewhat familiar, because they will be caused by the same catalyst that is responsible for the fateful ending that our present time faces. This destructible force is Satan, and he will be given a brief time with mankind at the end of the millennial kingdom to have his way with the unwary.

Revelation 20:7–9 tells what to expect at that time:

Now when the thousand years have expired, Satan will be released from his prison

and will go out to deceive the nations which are in the four corners of the earth, Gog and Magog, to gather them together to battle, whose number is as the sand of the sea.

They went up on the breadth of the earth and surrounded the camp of the saints and the beloved city. And fire came down from God out of heaven and devoured them.

History will repeat itself with different characters, but the same underlying objective; to screen out those ungrounded in Jesus Christ, preparatory to entering the New Jerusalem. The reference to Gog and Magog is simply a means in few words, of showing that similar circumstances leading to trouble will again be in play as they were a thousand years earlier. So the seventh millennial day will end much as it will have begun; with destruction of the rebellious pawns of a vindictive Satan.

"Jesus in explaining the mysteries of the kingdom of heaven to His disciples spoke in parables. Matthew 13 records these, with verse 30 providing a picture of a harvest at the end of the one thousand years and a clear depiction of God's harvesting method. Jesus said in reference to weeds called tares growing in among the wheat:

> Let both grow together until the harvest, and at the time of harvest I will say to the reapers, "First gather together the tares and bind them in bundles to burn them, but gather the wheat into my barn."

A new heaven and a new earth shall succeed the first, which will pass away. Then the New Jerusalem will descend out of heaven from God, prepared as a bride adorned for her husband [Showcasing the saved within it], See Revelation 21:1–2.

God's word has proven to be:

Too accurate to be ignored!

Too dependable to be disregarded!

Too promising to be rejected!

A final thought: Modern day culture in some ways, may be compared with having defective vision. In this case, as with healthy vision, the image is reflected by light through the cornea; on through the lens and then focused upside-down on the retina. The image is then carried by the optic nerve to the visual center of the brain where nerve impulses are interpreted to form shape and color, and then perceived by the viewer with healthy vision as being in the upright position.[27] In the case of unhealthy vision, a defect in this intricate system might prevent the image from being perceived right side up, and so produce an opposite view from reality.

There are powerful forces aligned and unleashed against each man, woman, and child inhabitant of this earth. The apparent intent is to so cloud the perception of reality that truth is seen as a lie and lies are seen as truth. Some powerful interests engaged in entertainment, information distribution, communication, and advertising it seems, have been coopted by this mindset, and are freely injecting their perverted values called mainstream thought into the absorptive mental processes of citizens of the world. Left alone and to their own devices, those being programmed are becoming more and more in danger of being corporatively owned-mind, body, and soul!

Truth is still truth; neverthless, and two plus two still equals four. So add it all up; the answer is obvious! This spacecraft is headed for a hard landing; *but Jesus Christ can be your golden parachute!*

# ENDNOTES

[1] Commentary on Pharaohs Tutankhamen, Ay, and Horemheb other than reigning dates, taken from The World Book Encyclopedia, 2001 Edition, Vol. 19, p. 525.

[2] Date, 2012 taken from "Maya Civilization" by T. Patrick Culbert, 1993 Edition, p 37, St. Remy Press.

[3] Mayan religious practices and 365 day calendar commentary taken from Encyclopedia Americana, Edition 2000, Vol. 18, p 544.

[4] Commentary on the National Security Act of July 26, 1947 is taken from "History of the National Security Council," 1947–1997, page 1, by Condoleezza Rice, 2/12/00.

[5] Commentary on Tyre's destruction in the year 332 B.C., taken from The World Book Encyclopedia, 2002 Edition, Vol. 19, p 542.

[6] Commentary on Seleucid Dynasty taken from Encyclopedia Americana, 2000 Edition, Vol. 24, pp 531–532.

[7] Commentary on naming of Antiochus IV Epiphanes taken from Illustrated Dictionary Of The Bible, By: Herbert Lockyer Sr., Editor, Thomas Nelson Publishers, 1986, p 169.

[8] Commentary on Jewish Festival of Lights known as Hanukkah, taken from Illustrated Dictionary Of The Bible, By:

Herbert Lockyer, Sr., Editor, Thomas Nelson Publisher, 1986, p 665.

[9] Commentary on Armageddon taken from Illustrated Dictionary Of The Bible, By: Herbert Lockyer, Sr., Editor, Thomas Nelson Publisher, 1986, p 693.

[10] Commentary on polystrate fossils taken from "Are You Being Brainwashed?", by: Dr. Kent Hovind, p 11. Published by Creation Science Evangelism, 29 Cummings Rd., Pensacola, Florida 32503, ph (850) 479-3466, Fax-(850) 479-8562, www.drdino.com, email *dino@drdino.com*
Commentary on evolution—Macro Evolution, the origin of major kinds, taken from same publication, p 6.

[11] Commentary on misidentification of fragmentary fossils and resulting creative evolution artistry, taken from "Evidence for Creation" by Tom DeRosa, 2003, pp 62, 63, published by Carol Ridge Ministries, P.O. Box 40, Fort lauderdale, Florida 33302, www.coralridge.org, letters@coralridge.org.
Commentary on index fossils and layering of fossils, taken from same publication, p. 38.

[12] References to the following entities, taken from Illustrated Dictionary Of The Bible, By: Herbert Lockyer, Sr., Editor, Thomas Nelson Publisher, 1986. (Gog p 436), (Magog pp. 669 and 959), (Rosh p 929), (Meshech p 699), Tubal p 1,076), (Gomer p 437), (Togarmah p 1,059).

[13] Reference to the following entities, taken from Illustrated Dictionary Of The Bible, By: Herbert Lockyer, Sr., Editor, 1986, Thomas Nelson Publisher. (Sheba p 974), (Dedan p 292), (Merchants of Tarshish p 1,030).

[14] Commentary on "Chub" taken from Smith's Bible Dictionary, by William Smith LL.D., 1975, p 108, Pyramid Publications, for Fleming H. Revell Co.

[15] Commentary on location of ancient Migdol and Syene taken from Illustrated Dictionary Of The Bible, by: Herbert Lockyer, Sr., Editor, 1986, Thomas Nelson Publishers, (Migdol p 707), (Syene, p 1,018).

[16] Commentary on "Azal" taken from Smith's Bible Dictionary, by: William Smith LL.D., p 63, 1975, Pyramid Publications, for Fleming H. Revell Co., Old Tappan, New Jersey 07675.

[17] Locations of Kedar and Hazor taken from Illustrated Dictionary Of The Bible, 1986, by: Herbert Lockyer, Sr., Editor, Thomas Nelson Publishers, (Kedar p 612), (Hazor p 465).

[18] Commentary on Mayan long cycle, taken from 1993 Edition of "Maya Civilization", by: T. Patrick Culbert, p 37, St. Remy Press, Montreal.

[19] Commentary on the reigns of Herod the Great and Herod Archelaus, taken from Illustrated Dictionary of the Bible, by Herbert Lockyer, Sr., Editor, 1986, pp 476, 477 Thomas Nelson Publishers.

[20] Commentary on coin taken from article by Dr. J. Randall Price, titled "The Proof of Christmas Past" in Midnight Call magazine, December 2004, p 19.

[21] Commentary on comet composition, orbit, structure, and size, taken from The World Book Encyclopedia, 2002 Edition, Vol. 4, pp 867, 868.

[22] Encyclopedic commentary on fragmented comet, Shoemaker-Levy 9 crashing into Jupiter, taken from the World Book Encyclopedia, 2001 Edition, Vol. 11, pp 200, 201.

[23] Commentary on an unknown asteroid, or comet striking earth with only a few seconds warning, taken from an article titled "Let's Take it Seriously," written by David H. Levy, page 14, Parade Magazine (Science On Parade) section, May 10, 1998.

[24] Commentary on Chemtrails, taken from an article by James Lloyd, titled "Contrails" in Fall, 1999 issue of Christian Media publication, Vol. VI #3, PO Box 448, Jacksonville, OR 97530, ph (541)899-8888.

[25] Commentary on adopting, ratifying, and putting the Constitution into force, from Reader's Digest Great Encyclopedic Dictionary p 290

[26] Commentary on Revolutionary War and birth of the Federal Government of the United States, taken from The World Book Encyclopedia, 1962 Edition, Vol. 15, p 260 and Vol. 18, pp 94–96.

[27] Commentary on the working of the eye, taken from Reader's Digest Family Health Guide and Medical Encyclopedia, pp 66, 67. Based on medical writings of Benjamin E. Miller, M.D., 1976 Edition.

Speculation on possible result of unhealthy vision effect upon perception of image is entirely this writer's.

Table No.1 - Daniel's Seventieth Week - Last "7" Years of current 6,000

Top labels:
- Six Months of Wrath
- Six Days (not to scale)
- 1st through 3rd Trumpets
- 4th Trumpet - Jesus' Return
- 5th Trumpet - Great Earthquake
- 6th and 7th Trumpet and all Bowls
- 45 days Jewish remnant saved through Armageddon - WWIII
- 4th Seal
- 3rd, 6th, and 7th Seals
- Jesus' Return 6 days into the wrath of God

Year columns: 1st year | 2nd year | 3rd year | 4th year | 5th year | 6th year | 7th year

Dates: 1/1/07, 1/1/06, 6/19/05

- A new UN Secretary General
- Treaty confirmed (strengthened) with many by Antichrist and Temple of God built within this period
- Antichrist breaks Treaty
- Palestinians gain control of East Jerusalem for 1,260 days- most likely beginning within this period
- 1,260 days - (Jewish remnant) - kept from Antichrist
- 1,290 days Antichrist in Temple
- Saints in Antichrist's hand - 3 1/2 years
- 1,277 1/2 days
- 1,260 days two witnesses ministry + 3 1/2 days dead in street
- 2 1/2 days
- 3 1/2 days
- 182 1/2 days
- 176 1/2 days
- 5th Seal - Saints will see persecution
- 6 days into wrath = '1/3' loophole
- 1st and 2nd Seals

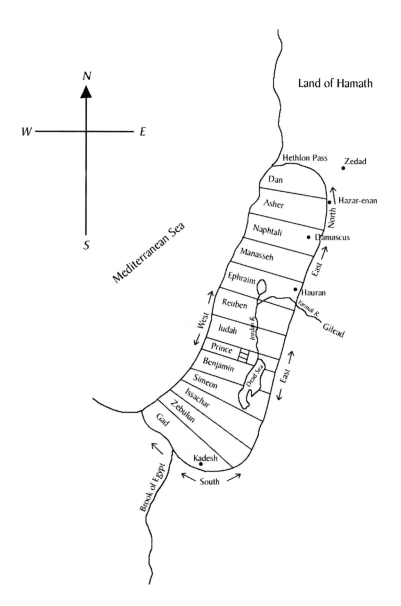

Israel in the Millennial Kingdom

Table No.2

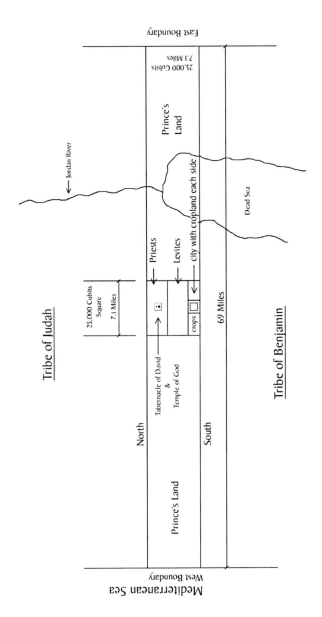

The Mountain of the Lord's House

Table No.3    The Lord's District - 25,000 cubits square with Prince's Land on each side

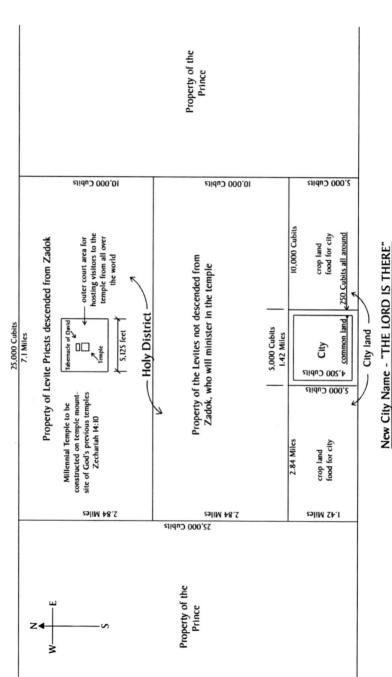

New City Name - "THE LORD IS THERE"

Table No.4    New City constructed on site of modern Jerusalem

Zechariah 12:6

ETERNITY →

Creation of Adam

Exodus - crossing the Red Sea
Pharaoh Horemheb's death

Actual End of BC years

Actual Birth of Christ
Actual Beginning of AD years

Return of Jesus - 2nd Advent
End of 6,000 Free Will years

Millennial Kingdom Under Jesus Christ

2,669 years | 1,319 years | 2,012 years

Israelites Leave Egypt

12 BC | 11 BC | 2012 AD

| Sunday 1,000 years | Monday 1,000 years | Tuesday 1,000 years | Wednesday 1,000 years | Thursday 1,000 years | Friday 1,000 years | Saturday 1,000 years | Millennial Sabbath |

6,000 Free Will Years for Mankind

God's Seven Millennial Day Week

Table No.5     Six – 1,000 year Free Will Days for Mankind Followed by Sabbath

# 6,000 Years For Man Scale

Reckoning of Years From Adam To The
End of Free Will Years For Mankind!

- Adam to The Exodus ( Pharaoh Horemheb's Death )          2,6 6 9   Years

- The Exodus to The Common Era ( A.D. 1 ) ( calendar error seen here )          1,3 1 9   Years

- Total Years From Adam to The Common Era ( A.D. 1 )          3,9 8 8   Years

- Subtract Years of Jesus' Life Prior To A.D. 1 ( Born 11 B.C. )          ( 1 1 ) Years

- Total Years From Adam to Jesus          3,9 7 7   Years

- Total Free Will Years For Mankind          6,0 0 0   Years

- Subtract The Years From Adam to Jesus          ( 3,9 7 7 ) Years

- Total Years From Jesus' Birth to The End of Free Will Years For Mankind          2,0 2 3   Years

- Subtract The Years From Jesus' Birth ( 11 B.C. )  Beginning of The Common Era ( A.D. 1 )          ( 1 1 ) Years

- The Year A.D. In Which The Free Will Years For Mankind Shall End          A.D. 2 0 1 2

Table No.6 - Adam to the Earthly Kingdom of Jesus Christ

Sky becomes black as sackcloth of hair

Locusts come upon the earth.

Rising from          the Ashes

Dec. 19, 2011 Two Witnesses' death sentence read - Comet strikes Earth's atmosphere

1st Trumpet - Fragment
2nd Trumpet - Fragment
3rd Trumpet - Fragment
4th Trumpet -- 1/3 Darkness
5th Trumpet - Fragment

6 days

Oil must be had -
So then: A stampede
into the oil fields!

The Kingdom of God on Earth
begins- The mess must be
cleaned up. Nuclear fallout
must be avoided- Still a deadly,
chaotic and difficult time
for mankind.

The Mayan tradition seems
correct. Infertility, drought,
famine, and great hardship
will be hallmarks of this
new beginning-until things
are up and running again.
Dec. 23rd 2012 may turn out
to be a milestone date in seeing
this happen!

Death sentence carried out

Resurrection at Christ's return
(Dec. 25, 2011) Christmas Day

Jan. 1, 2012

June 19 2012 - End of WWIII and the 6,000 years - Jesus Christ Reigns

Dec. 22, 2012 End of current Mayan Long Cycle
Dec. 23, 2012 Beginning of New Mayan Long Cycle

2 1/2 days

3 1/2 days

6 months-(182 1/2)     Days of Wrath   Israel buries          dead 7 months

Theoretical Estimation - Possible Dating of God's Wrath, Christ's Return, and

Aftermath of the Destruction up to the Beginning of the New Mayan Long Cycle

Table No.2                                    Not to Scale

Printed in the United States
101785LV00003B/4-9/A

9 781414 101361